OP 759

APARTHEID, IMPERIALISM
—— AND ——
AFRICAN FREEDOM

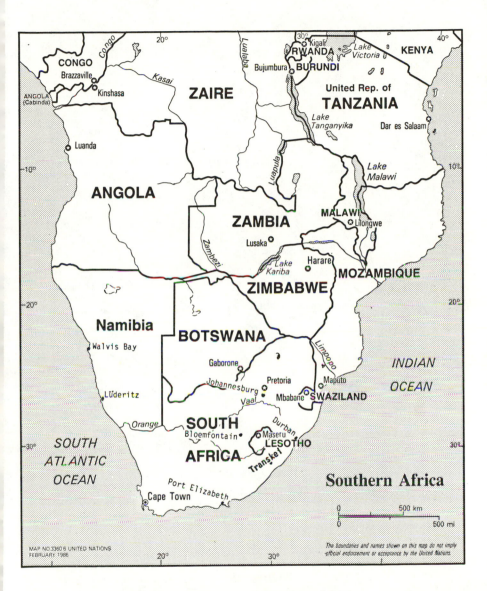

UN Map 3360.6, February 1986
Adapted with permission

iii

APARTHEID, IMPERIALISM
—AND—
AFRICAN FREEDOM

WILLIAM J. POMEROY

INTERNATIONAL PUBLISHERS

New York

© 1986 by International Publishers Co., Inc., New York
All rights reserved
First edition, 1986
Manufactured in the United States of America

Library of Congress Cataloging-in-Publication Data

Pomeroy, William J., 1916–
   Apartheid, imperialism, and African freedom.

  Bibliography: p.
  Includes index.
  1. United States—Foreign relations—South Africa.
2. South Africa—Foreign relations—United States.
3. United States—Foreign relations—Namibia.
4. Namibia—Foreign relations—United States.
5. Apartheid—South Africa. 6. Apartheid—Namibia.
I. Title.
E183.8.S6P65 1986   305.8'00968   86-10488
ISBN 0-7178-0640-5
ISBN 0-7178-0632-4 (pbk.)

CONTENTS

*Illustrations are from the journal
"Sechaba" and used with permission*

*To all those South Africans
who have given their lives
in the struggle to end apartheid
and to bring about complete national liberation
in South Africa*

APARTHEID, IMPERIALISM

AND

AFRICAN FREEDOM

INTRODUCTION

In the modern era, certain episodes in the struggles of nations to achieve liberation, to resist an aggressor, or to bring about a democratic betterment of a way of life have become great focal points of struggle for all peoples who believe in freedom, in democracy, and in equality.

One such episode occurred in the 1930s when the determination of Spanish people to defend their democratic republic against a fascist onslaught aroused the passionate support of concerned democrats everywhere. That struggle of the Spanish people, and of the famous International Brigades that came across numerous frontiers to their aid, was a microcosm of the world war that followed in which an alliance of democratic peoples fought and defeated the fascist aggressor. Those who stood up for the Spanish republic in 1937-39 were called "premature anti-fascists" but they were premature only in the sense that they recognized before most others the significance of the struggle that was taking place, its meaning for all people. That significance lay not only in the need for virtually the whole world to be drawn finally into a struggle to defeat fascism, in the war of 1939-45, but in the fact that such a victory resulted in the release of enormous liberation impulses, in Europe, Asia, Africa and elsewhere.

Another episode that profoundly stirred the consciences and the active support of people internationally was the more recent struggle of the Vietnamese people, for over 30 years, for national liberation and for the defense of their independent republic. The Vietnam War, as it became known, epitomized, as no other such struggle had done, the powerful anti-colonial, anti-imperialist movement of oppressed nations for freedom, which is one of the outstanding features of the modern age. More than that, it brought into being in many countries powerful protest movements of opposition to the U.S. war of intervention, especially in the United States itself. The tremendous movement of U.S. citizens against the war embodied both identification with the rightful aims of the Vietnamese and rejection of the aggressive aims of the U.S. military-industrial establishment. In the heroism of the just war of resistance of the small Vietnamese nation, an era of liberation was summed up and given universal significance. One region and the determination of its people to be free became the focal point and the progenitor of progressive humanity as a whole.

At the present time, in another part of the world, a contemporary fight for liberation has awakened the indignation, the protest and the active democratic support of countless people around the globe. It is the great anti-apartheid national liberation struggle of the oppressed Black majority in South Africa. Resistance to apartheid, which is the ruthless domination and exploitation of the Black and other non-white people in that country by a white minority of owners and rulers, has been occurring in one form or another for decades, but it has now attained the stage where growing masses of the people are being brought into the struggle in a revolutionary manner. In the course of time that struggle has won international sympathy and support. Today the Black majority in South Africa are no longer willing to live under a system that oppresses them, while the international movement in unity with their anti-apartheid wishes is intensifying its campaigns of support, determined in unison to end the most brutal racist system ever devised.

The question of apartheid and of the struggle against it is not an issue that concerns merely the behavior of a racist white minority in South Africa. Powerful business interests, military establishments, and governments in the leading western capitalist countries find it profitable and useful to themselves to invest in the apartheid economy and to have forms of alliance with the apartheid state. They comprise a defensive bulwark for apartheid which must be resisted, with those involved persuaded to abandon what amounts to an alignment on the side of racism. It is an alliance that tends to help perpetuate racism in western society in general. The anti-apartheid movement, therefore, has inevitably become a movement against racial oppression everywhere, in all its manifestations. As in other instances that have challenged the conscience and the moral sensibilities of humankind, the anti-apartheid issue extends far beyond the forces and circumstances of a single country where the issue is being fought out, and has become the focal point of one of the great historical struggles for the advancement of the human race.

I APARTHEID: WHAT IT IS AND HOW IT CAME ABOUT

In simple terms, South African apartheid is racism carried to an extreme. As a long-standing, persistent phenomenon, racism is present in the societies of all the leading western countries, where it is usually a case of Black or other nonwhite minorities suffering discrimination or persecution at the hands of white groups who are the majority of the population. In South Africa, Blacks who are in the overwhelming majority are the victims of cruel oppression and deprivation by a white minority of rulers.

Today in South Africa there are roughly 21.5 million Black people. Other nonwhites denied equality make up an additional sector of the population: 2.5 million Colored people of mixed race, and about 1 million Asians, chiefly Indians. Ruling over all is a white master minority of 4.5 million.

Most developed western powers had a long experience of owning and ruling colonies of colored peoples, in Africa, Asia, the Caribbean and elsewhere. Some of those colonies were huge, with very large populations, like India and Nigeria, but small numbers of white settlers, businessmen and administrators were able to control and dominate them, maintaining a racially superior attitude. This was managed through military force, a police-backed system of colonial law, control of the economy, and the purchased loyalty through corruption of local headmen. In this way the United States ruled its Philippine and other colonies for half a century. No "subject people" ever escaped the effects of racial discrimination.

This is precisely the way in which the apartheid system has been maintained in South Africa. It is a vast structure of oppressive laws which establish and implement the absolute power and privilege, economically and politically, of the white minority, backed up by military and police force. In effect, it is an internal colonial system of the most ruthless kind.

The Background of Racist Power

In fact, the South African situation derived from a long colonial past. It began with the establishment of a way station by Dutch commercial interests, the Dutch East India Company, in 1652, in what is now the Cape region. The outpost developed into a farming community that cut itself away from the Company, evolving an independent or autonomous way of life, fiercely inward-looking, resisting Company dictates while imposing its own domination over the native Black people whose lands it spread upon and took into possession.

Apartheid apologists have put forward the "theory" that the Dutch arrived in South Africa before, or at the same time, as did the Blacks. This has been exploded by archaeological findings in recent years. The largest Iron Age village ever found in Africa was unearthed near Pretoria in 1972, and in 1980 artifacts were discovered showing the presence of a Bantu civilization 1200 years before the arrival of the Europeans.

Members of the early white community became known as the Boers, a Dutch word meaning "farmers," to distinguish them from the Company traders. Today those of Dutch origin make up about three million of the 4.5 million whites in South Africa, and they call themselves Afrikaaners, speaking a variant of the Dutch language called Afrikaans. The type of society they evolved from the 17th century, drawing on an extreme fundamentalist Calvinist interpretation of the Bible, was featured by a rigid master-slave relationship with the Black people whose land and cattle they seized. That racist attitude became institutionalized in Boer-Afrikaaner society.

The narrow world of the Boers was disrupted in 1795 when the Cape region was annexed by Britain as a consequence of the Napoleonic Wars. Subsequently, British possession was extended east and north along the coast to include the present-day Natal area. The Boers preferred to move inland rather than submit to or cooperate with British rule. In 1830 this was carried out in what they called the "Great Trek." During the course of it they developed the "laager" system of drawing their wagons in a protective ring when encamping, staying "within the laager" in a way similar to that of the early American pioneers with their covered wagons.

Occupation of the new lands could be done only through dispossession of the Black people who lived on them, and through a brutal crushing of their resistance. One of the Afrikaaner holidays to the present time celebrates their victory at Blood River. The Boers set up two inland states, Orange Free State and Transvaal (the latter called by them the "Republic of South Africa").

During the 19th century these states and the two British-ruled colonies of Cape Province and Natal developed separately. In the 1860s British sugar plantation owners in Natal began importing Indian workers as indentured labor, laying the basis for the Asian sector of the population, which is still chiefly concentrated in that province and its largest city, Durban. The sizable racially mixed population group, known as Coloreds, tended to gravitate to the Cape Province cities, particularly Cape Town. One of the resentments of the Boers was against the slightly more liberal British racial policies, which gave a few minimum concessions to Blacks in order to incorporate them into a capitalist-run colonial system. As a British Native Administrator in Natal—Shepstone—said, it was needed to transform Zulu warriors "into laborers working for wages."

Conflict between the British and the Boers arose in the latter part of the 19th century. Essentially it was provoked by the British desire to get control of rich mineral resources that had been discovered in the Boer states in 1870: diamonds at Kimberley in the Orange Free State, and gold at Johannesburg in the Transvaal. Leading the British drive was the imperialist empire-builder, Cecil Rhodes, who wanted to seize all of southern Africa up through what is now Zambia as a British colonial preserve.

The Boers, independent and isolation-minded, tried to fight off British encroachments but were forced into the imperialist Boer War of 1899-1902. Although they resisted strongly, inflicting heavy British losses, they finally had to capitulate on Britain's terms, including British rule over their once independent states. Some international sympathy at the time went to the Boers because they were victims of a colonial war of aggression in which ruthless methods were used, including concentration camps and the starving of Boer civilians, but the war had nothing to do with freedom for the African people, who suffered oppression at the hands of both Boer and British.

British Rule Reinforces Afrikaaners

After the war, Britain set about consolidating its colony. In 1910 the Union of South Africa was proclaimed, with the original states converted into four provinces of the new domain. The defeated Boers, however, remained a strong force; their nationalist and racially intolerant outlook was neither subjugated nor altered. In fact, the Boers-Afrikaaners were the majority in the white population of the colony, and British rule became a history of compromise and concession to them as their racist nationalism became more pronounced rather than modified.

British colonial rule itself, it must be stressed, reinforced the oppression of the Black majority, treating them as cheap labor on which colonial fortunes were made. It was Black labor, in appalling conditions, which dug out the gold and diamonds in the world's deepest pits. The British colonial policies included nonextension of political rights to Africans, pass laws, job reservation for whites, and other discriminatory acts. Lord Milner, the British colonial administrator and shaper of policy, said in 1911: "The ultimate end [of British policy] is a self-governing white community, supported by well treated and justly governed Black labor, from Cape Town to the Zambezi."[1]

In 1913 the British rulers agreed to the Afrikaaner-devised Native Lands Act which, by law, set aside 87% of land in South Africa, including all the most fertile and mineral-rich land, for the white minority, while only 13% of land area was designated for the Black majority. This meant that impoverished Black South Africans, unable to eke out a living on limited marginal land, would be compelled to seek work as cheap labor in the white-owned mines, farms, and urban industries.

During the first four decades of the century, two key trends occurred in South Africa: the Afrikaaner nationalists, with their chief base among the landowning, rural, most-bigoted whites, maneuvered to win political dominance, while the British, source of most foreign capital, were predominant in industry, mining, finance and trade. In 1914 the political party of racist Afrikaaner nationalism, the Nationalist Party, was founded by one of the most diehard of the former Boer leaders who had fought the British, General J.B.M. Hertzog. It defined its position toward the Black people as "the dominance of the European population in a spirit of Christian trusteeship, with the strictest avoidance of any attempt at race mixture."[2]

This outlook of racial separation, with the white minority dominating, was developed over the next three decades in the colonial politics of South Africa. By 1924 the Nationalist Party had become the majority party in the colonial government and held that position until 1938. In that time, it pushed through legislative acts to cancel out limited rights for Blacks, including the imposition of color-bar job reservation in the mines, railways and other fields of employment, the abolition of the common roll vote in Cape Province where Black voters had for a time been able to participate in elections (although only in voting for white candidates), and numerous other restrictions in political, economic and social areas.

In pressing its racist program, the Nationalist Party had a guiding instrument in an elite secret society that operated behind the scenes, the Broederbond (Association of Brothers). Created in 1918, it never had more than a few thousand members (little more than 13,000 even today), but its power and influence became great. Broederbond policy was to insert its members, who are committed to an extreme form of white supremacy, in every possible key position in government, the economy, the police, and the army, the education system, and other sectors of society. Every head of the racist state that finally came into being when the Nationalist Party won full power (Malan, Strijdom, Verwoerd, Vorster and Botha) have been members of the Broederbond.

The ideology of this right-wing grouping among the Afrikaaner nationalists has been little different from that of the Nazi party of Germany. Just prior to the outbreak of World War II, the Broederbond set up an organization patterned after the Nazis—the Ossewa Brandweg (Ox-Wagon Brigade). During the war it supported Hitler and his fascist military conquests in Europe and its special force, the Stormjaers (Stormtroopers), carried out armed acts of sabotage to disrupt South Africa's participation in the anti-fascist war on the side of Britain. Among the Ossewa Brandweg leaders arrested and confined in an internment camp during the war was B.J. Vorster, later to be a Nationalist Party prime minister.

Significant changes occurred in South Africa during the war. As elsewhere in the British empire, the position of British capital was weakened and Afrikaaner capital, organized by the Broederbond, was able to begin to move into finance and manufacturing. During the war years the colony was governed by a coalition of parties representing the English-speaking Europeans and the section of the Afrikaaners that saw its interests hinging on victory for Britain and its allies. However, during the war period the Nationalist Party was able to strengthen its following among those Afrikaaners who were gaining broader economic holdings. In the first postwar election of 1948, it made a major bid for overall power.

In that election the Nationalists put forward for the first time the slogan of "apartheid." In Afrikaaner terminology it means "separateness, segregated, separate existence and development," and it was projected in a pledge to intensify racial discrimination against Blacks and to reinforce the system of white control. The greater influx of

Black workers into wartime-expanded industry was used to arouse racist feeling among white voters. Said a Nationalist program pamphlet:

> The policy of our country should encourage total apartheid as the ultimate goal of a natural process of separate development.
> It is the primary task of the State to seek the welfare of South Africa, and to promote the happiness and well-being of its citizens, non-white as well as white. Realizing that such a task can best be accomplished by preserving and safeguarding the white race, the Nationalist Party professes this as the fundamental guiding principle of its policy.[3]

The pamphlet said further that "the Bantu in the urban areas should be regarded as migratory citizens not entitled to political or social rights equal to those of whites."[4] This was elaborated by the head of the Nationalist Party in the Transvaal, J.G. Strijdom: "The only alternative is the policy of the Nationalist Party of separation and apartheid in the sense that the natives must stay in their own territories and should come to the cities only temporarily as workers." Declared Strijdom: "Our view is that in every sphere the Europeans must retain the right to rule the country and to keep it a white man's country."[5]

In the election of 1948 the Nationalist Party had 140,000 votes less than the combined vote of its opponents but won the biggest number of seats in the parliament; 70 out of 153. However, the Nationalists were able to form a coalition with the small Afrikaaner Party which had 9 seats. This alliance formed a Nationalist-Afrikaaner government with a 79 to 74 majority over the combined opposition that included the English-speaking groups.

This was still not a sufficient margin to put through the kind of apartheid program the racists had in mind. One of the first acts of the new government, therefore, was to enact a measure giving representation to the white minority in South West Africa (Namibia), although this was not even part of South Africa, properly speaking. Furthermore, the 24,000 whites then in that territory were apportioned 6 seats, one for each 4,000 people, although in South Africa itself the proportion was one for 9,000 to 12,000 people. Next, the Nationalist Party absorbed the Afrikaaner Party. Then it eliminated or drastically restricted the franchise for nonwhites, which culminated in ending the three (white) Native Representation seats in parliament. On top of these moves, a law was adopted for enlarging the Senate, from 48 to 89 seats, on a basis greatly favoring the Nationalists, who promptly were able to win 77 of the seats.

By means of these steps and others that served to fragment and reduce the opposition, the new regime of apartheid put itself in a position to impose the most relentless racist system that has even been devised.

Economic Power for the Racists

The central aim of the Afrikaaner whites in gaining political power was to increase greatly their share in all sectors of the South African economy, i.e., to attain economic power. In 1948 Afrikaaner interests were still practically excluded from the sphere of monopoly capital in the country, which was chiefly in British or other foreign hands. A majority of Afrikaaners still lived in the countryside, where accumulation of capital was derived from nearly slave-like Black labor but was relatively slow in growth.

To give itself a free hand, the Nationalist government declared South Africa a republic in 1960, making itself independent of the British crown. This was made complete on May 31, 1961, with a proclamation of South African withdrawal from the Commonwealth. British colonial mechanisms of control were shaken off in this way.

An extended state capital sector was utilized as an Afrikaaner base. Long before, in 1922, a state monopoly corporation, ISCOR, had been established in the iron and steel industry. Under Nationalist administration, ISCOR came to control 75% of steel by the mid-1970s. State monopolies proliferated, embracing the railways, ports, civil airlines, and electric power stations; extending into the manufacture of synthetic fuels and fertilizers, and into engineering and light industry.

These state monopolies were employed to establish Afrikaaner control over capital accumulation through state channels. A more significant role in the process was played by the Broederbond which set about organizing and directly accumulating capital for the financing of Afrikaaner industry and a share in mining. The first step in this had been taken by the Broderbond in 1934, when it was instrumental in setting up an Afrikaaner bank, the Volkskas. The Rupert (Rembrandt) interests were among those repeatedly and heavily backed by capital raised by the Broederbond.

By the early 1970s there had occurred a three-fold increase of Afrikaaner capital in manufacturing, banking and trade, and a ten-fold increase in mining. By the early 1980s at least 60% of overall investment capital in the country was reported to be in the hands of the Afrikaaner-controlled state.

An incredibly swift and rapacious process of monopolization took place in the 1970s and early 1980s, marking the rapid accumulation of Afrikaaner capital. Between 1972 and 1982 the assets of the 100 largest industrial corporations increased by 600%. Total assets of 4.9 billion rands in 1972 had soared to 31.65 billion rands in 1982.[6]

In 1984, among the three giant monopolies controlling nearly all the shares (85%) on the Johannesburg stock exchange, the wholly Afrikaaner SANLAM was the second largest, while Afrikaaner capital had a sizeable presence in the other two, Anglo-American Corporation and Barlow Rand. SANLAM, beginning as a life insurance company, now has 38 conglomerate companies, 4 banks and several mining finance houses. Of the three biggest banks in the country, one is the Afrikaaner-owned Volkskas; the other two, Barclays and Standard, are British. The Afrikaaner Rembrandt interests, moving from tobacco into printing, wool and weaving industries, had capital of 900 million rands in 1973 and was realizing 100 million rands profit a year. In the Afrikaaner-controlled state sector, South African Transport Services (SATS) had assets of 11.8 billion rands, the electricity supply corporation (ESCOM) had assets of 11.6 billion rands, and the Post Office, which was moving into the key electronic equipment fields, represented investments of 8.5 billion rands.

Today Afrikaaner share capital is interlocked with British capital, and with U.S., West German and other capital, in virtually all areas of the economy. The average Afrikaaner has long ceased to be a "Boer" and is associated with industry and finance. He has moved out of the country-side, into the modern cities. Whereas 46% of Afrikaaners lived in the countryside prior to World War II, by 1973 80% were living in cities, and the trend has continued.

This comparatively rapid advance of the Afrikaaner to industrial and financial power has been due chiefly to an accumulation of capital extracted literally from the cheap forced labor of Black workers. It has been the product of apartheid.

Building the Apartheid System

The Nationalist Party, representing the most racist sector of the white minority, has achieved this ascendency over the past four decades. It has gained its ends through the erection of a vast system of laws and policies to implement apartheid and to prevent or suppress opposition to it.

A full-fledged concept of apartheid and of how to organize and administer it had not really been worked out in 1948 when its advocates came to power, beyond the employment of slogans and generalized projections. Hence a virtual thicket of laws and amended laws has sprung up, added to continuously, piecemeal.

The basic thesis of apartheid, "separate development," has driven an enormous color bar through South African society, with the ultimate aim of literally excluding the Black 70% of the population from South African citizenship. As worked out by the successive governments of Malan, Strijdom, Verwoerd, Vorster and Botha, South Africa is presumed to be a "white republic" occupying 87% of the land area, with the remaining 13% divided into 10 crazy-quilt areas called the "Bantu homelands" or "Bantustans." These are conceived as the allegedly ancestral tribal homes of the supposedly ethnically divided Black people.

As devised by the Afrikaaner ideologues, there are 10 Bantustans: Transkei, Kwazulu, Ciskei, Bophuthatswana, Lebowa, Qwa Qwa, Venda, Gazankulu, KwaNdebele, and KaNgwane. Blacks are supposed to have their citizenship in the Bantustan to which they theoretically belong. In the blueprint of "separate development," each Bantustan is an "independent" state. In other words, on the present territory of South Africa there exist, in the apartheid ruler mind, one white nation and 10 Black nations.

So far, four Bantustans have been granted "independence": Transkei (1976), Bophuthatswana (1977), Venda (1979) and Ciskei (1981). In each, defense and foreign affairs are kept in the hands of the South African white regime, which is the only government in the world to recognize them as states. When the first Bantustan, Transkei, became "independent" in 1976, the then-Minister of the Interior Connie Mulder explained the step in this way: "I would prefer to live in a paddock next to a fenced bull than walk around with a black mamba in my bosom.":[7]

An assessment of the Transkei after "independence" appeared in a leading South African newspaper in 1979:

The Transkei is simply not viable economically and is dependent on South Africa for its survival as a politically independent state. The bulk of its people are quasi-peasants who are forced to subsidize meager produce which they raise on their allotments by selling their labor as contract workers in SA. As far back as the mid-1950s, the need to reduce the number of peasants on the land was recognized, but little if anything has been done to fulfill that requirement. Transkei, a theoretical "breadbasket" for South Africa, has to import most of its food. The post-independence period has brought no tangible relief to peasant-migrant workers. It has brought new and heavier taxes. It has imposed a growing and palpably ambitious class of civil servants on them, without reducing the pressure on the land.

In the last year the Transkei Development Corporation (TDC) has created less than 850 new industrial jobs, Mr. Roy Gammie, TDC managing director says. In the same period the labor force grew by 30,000, which means more pressure on the land and longer queues for contract work in SA. Transkei remains heavily dependent on SA financially.[8]

None of the Bantustans, with their unproductive marginal land and their almost complete lack of industries, is economically viable. By 1980 there were 11 million Blacks living in these "homelands." According to figures of the South African Bureau of Economic Research, 5.2 million out of the 6.2 million in the "non-independent" Bantustans had "no measurable income in 1980," while only 1 million of the 4.6 million in the "independent" Bantustans could be called "economically active." In the six "non-independent" Bantustans the growth in per capita GrossDomestic Product from 1975 to 1980 was almost nonexistent, from 44 rands to 47 rands. Although there had been an increase of 7 million people in these areas since 1960—mainly as a result of forcible removals for Blacks from white areas—a mere 75,000 jobs had been created in all the Bantustans.[9]

In Bophuthatswana the chief investment venture is not in industry but in the operation of casinos, combined gambling and entertainment clubs, which are forbidden in the straitlaced Afrikaaner society. These provide illicit pleasure for white South Africans who drive in from their own areas, and for tourists. Sun City, the main location of the casinos, was built by the Southern Sun Hotels chain (12th largest in the world in profits) as a joint venture with the Bophuthatswana Development Corporation. Huge fees are paid to U.S. and other western entertainers who can be thus bribed to defy an international anti-apartheid cultural boycott.

The madness of the "independent" Bantustan concept was perhaps best shown when KwaNdebele "homeland" made a formal request for independence in 1982, a request seriously considered by the South African regime. Mrs. Ina Perlman of the Institute of Race Relations said: "If it were not so tragic, KwaNdebele's decision for independence would be hilarious, pure music hall comedy." She pointed out its complete lack of development, no capital city, only one town besides 12 "settlement" camps, not a single industry, less than 200,000 in population—most brought in in trucks by the government and dumped in the camps on the bare veldt as removals from other areas—only 2,640 employed in the homeland itself and another 35,500 working in nearby white areas, no hospitals, a perpetual serious water shortage: "what people worry about is to have a roof over their heads and where the next meal is coming from."[10]

In the "self-governing" Bantustans only a minority of members of parliament are elected, from officially approved parties. In Transkei, for example, of the 109 assembly members, 64 are chiefs with auto-matic appointed membership and just 45 are elected. In Kwazulu, headed by Chief Gatsha Buthelezi, there are 66 appointed members of parliament and 55 elected. In Ciskei, only 20 are elected out of 50. (The Ciskei security chief, Colonal Charles Sebe, a brother of the president, Lennox Sebe, was a member of BOSS, the South African Bureau of State Security, until the Ciskei Intelligence Service was set up.) Trade unions are banned in the Bantustans, as well as anti-apartheid organi-zations and democratic political parties; the policies in general are even more repressive than in white-ruled South Africa.[11]

The South African government sustains the Bantustans after a fashion with subsidies, but these in total correspond almost exactly to the salaries of those in administrative or other posts, including the overall 800 members of parliament. While the per capita income is barely 100 rands in the better-off Bantustans, the salaries of their leaders are enormous. President Patrick Mphephu of Venda is paid 48,700 rands a year. Ciskei's President Lennox Sebe receives 29,808 rands plus 12,000 rands personal nontaxable allowance. Chief Kaizer Matanzima of Transkei gets 27,700 rands plus an allowance of 8,300 rands. In Bophuthatswana Chief Lucas Mangope receives 34,212 rands a year besides an undisclosed allowance. The salaries come from the South African subsidies, assuring the paid loyalty of collaborators.[12]

Despite the favorable situation for investors to go into the areas of cheap labor themselves, by the 1980s only a few South African and foreign employers had taken advantage of it to set up industries in the Bantustans, and then only on a small scale. Conditions of industrial labor in Qwa Qwa, the smallest of the Bantustans, came to light in mid-1985. In factories, workers were being paid as little as $4 a week, and the average was $6.50. Trade unions are not allowed in Qwa Qwa nor are strikes, and the laws governing industrial relations in South Africa, where Black workers in recent years have wrested concessions from employers and apartheid rulers, do not apply.[13]

For the most part, however, outside investment and industry have not flowed to the Bantustans, which have been kept as large pools of very cheap labor, hired to serve as contract, migratory labor in the white industrial centers of South Africa. In actuality, the Bantustans have their origin in the old "native reserves" system, as the British colonial administrators called the 13% of the land allocated to Blacks. From the time of the 1913 Native Land Act, the impoverished Black people in these overcrowded areas had been recruited as contract labor for the farms, mines and factories of the South African colony. To a far more intensified extent, this is precisely the way the apartheid system works, except that Black migrants today are considered aliens when outside their "homelands" and are subject to deportation at the whim of employers or apartheid officials.

The physical, geographical separation of Black and white through the Bantustans is but one phase of the vast segregation carried out under apartheid. Color barriers extend through every aspect of life. One of the first acts of the Nationalist government was the adoption in 1949 of a ban on mixed marriages. Segregation was applied to bathing beaches, parks, train compartments, benches, hotels, toilets, restaurants. Black travelers from segregated localities into the center of cities for any purpose have told of not drinking anything for the entire day because there are almost no toilet facilities for them, and they are forbidden to use the "whites only" toilets. An apartheid policy that immediately had international repercussions has been the segregation of sports. A government policy statement in 1976 decreed "that the Sportsmen and Sportswomen of the white, Coloreds, Indian and black people belong to their own clubs and must control, arrange and manage their own sports matters." The Prevention of Political Interference Act of 1968 prohibited blacks and whites from belonging to the same political party, or from attending together non-social political meetings.

In 1950 the Nationalist government adopted the Group Areas Act which gave it the power to denote any area in South Africa as an ethnic area in which specific groups could be placed. This was intended particularly to carry out the removal of nonwhites from the centers and residential districts of all South African cities and towns, and their resettlement in locations either in the "homelands" or on the peripheries of the urban areas. Resettlement Boards were set up first in Johannesburg in the mid-1950s and subsequently in the rest of the white areas. The result was the creation of racial ghettos on a huge scale within the "white" state.

Called townships, some of these locations are enormous. Soweto, outside Johannesburg, a name abbreviated from South West Township, has an estimated million or more Black inhabitants, made up chiefly of workers who commute by train or bus to factories, commercial shops, offices or domestic employment in Johannesburg and surrounding towns. There are townships comprised of Colored people and others with a large proportion of Asians (Indians). All told, there were 299 townships of this kind in South Africa in 1983.

Under the Group Areas Act and the host of amendments and subsidiary laws which buttress it, Blacks without legally defined employment are denied residence in such areas and are "endorsed out" for resettlement in the Bantustans. The consequence of this has been one of the worst examples of population displacement in the world. Between 1968 and 1983 an estimated 3.5 million black South Africans were forcibly removed to the Bantustans. Some could return only if hired on a short-term contract basis as migratory labor.

Between 1-1/2 to 2 million migrant workers from the Bantustans exist in the "group areas" at any one time. Contracted for periods of 6 to 18 months, they must return to their "homelands" for rehiring when their work periods terminate. South African employers, especially the mine owners, also hire labor on the same terms in neighboring countries like Mozambique, Malawi, Lesotho and Botswana: in 1979 these foreign workers totalled 367,000. In addition, large numbers of "illegal migrants" have made their way to the townships from the Bantustans, where employers have taken advantage of their "illegality" to pay them lower than usual wages. In 1981 a new, tighter law was adopted to stop the entry of "illegal migrants." It imposed stiff fines of up to 500 rands on any employer hiring a worker without the required documents.

Migrant workers are frequently packed into hostels with the barest of facilities. They are forbidden to bring their families with them, and are thus forced to live separately from their wives (and children) for excessively long periods. This deprivation of normal family life is a prime cause of destroyed family relationships and personal demoralization. Said a report in the South African press in 1980:

> *Financial Mail* investigations have revealed that a number of Cape employers are responsible for housing their African contract labor employees in dormitories described as 'pigsties' by one inhabitant of a rodent-ridden shed. A senior official of the Peninsula Administration Board said that they "are unfit for human habitation."
>
> The housing can be described as minimal. Large overcrowded draughty sheds, concrete floors with occasional meager or patchy covering offer scant comfort during the Cape winter, though occasionally a coal heater is supplied. Only one dormitory was seen to have an interior ceiling and often the asbestos roofs leak. In the summer they are hot, stuffy and smelly. Three bare bulbs, or three fluorescent lights, are the sole standard

lighting provided, serving to illuminate two dingy rows of 20-25 metal double bunks. The bunks and foam mattresses are generally the only furniture supplied by employers along with narrow wire lockers which serve as storage space for personal possessions. There is no privacy. The absence of interior ceilings often results in condensation and moisture dripping on those who sleep in the upper bunks. A corridor formed by the arrangement of the bunks down either side of the walls is the only recreational space. The kitchen unit has no fully separated kitchen space. One outside tap is shared by the occupants of two sheds. Ablution and toilet facilities are sordid.[14]

This was a report on migrant labor conditions in the township of Langa, near Cape Town. At that time there were 18,479 "single men" in Langa, out of a total population of 26,000.

Some of the townships where workers with more permanent residence permission live are no better off, and are squalid in the extreme. A reporter of the *Johannesburg Star* visited such a "rotting slum" only 20 miles from the city, a place known as "Zombies Hell." About 5,000 people, a large number of them children, lived there in "appalling conditions." He saw "clusters of hovels surrounded by mounds of filth" where "thirty people use one latrine bucket overflowing where children played."[15]

"We see migratory labor," has said the anti-apartheid African National Congress, "as one of the major methods that successive racist regimes in our country have developed for the purpose of exploiting the African people not only of South Africa but of the southern African region, *while simultaneously immobilizing them socially and politically*. In other words, to make sure that the African worker loses his humanity, his self-respect, and therefore his urge to resist exploitation and injustice, his family life is disrupted and so also his working life. He is always on the move."

One of the grim worries of the migratory worker is over what is happening to his children left with virtually no support in the Bantustan. The South African Catholic Bishops' Conference reported in 1981 that the Black infant mortality rate in the "homelands" was thirteen times higher than the white in the one- to four-year age group.[16] John Rees, director of the South African Institute of Race Relations, said in 1980 that 50% of all children two to three years old in Ciskei were malnourished, while overall eight out of ten children in the rural Bantustans were malnourished.[17] Care for the children and the sick can be measured by doctor-patient ratio in the Bantustans of 1 to 50,000 (in South Africa as a whole, white areas included, the ratio is 1 to 1900). It was estimated in 1982 that 60,000 Black doctors are needed to serve the Black population with any degree of adequacy, but only 300 had been produced in the previous 25 years.[18]

Those who live in the townships on a more or less permanent basis, as permanent as the uncertainties of employment and official attitude permit, experience other aspects of the apartheid system that are equally demeaning. Said an interviewed Black woman domestic worker in Natal:

> In my long life as a domestic worker I felt as if I were a sub-human from a sub-world. Although I did not work for many employers, I had many interviews in my time, and that is where the feeling always started. Each time I was interviewed on the doorstep—never once was I asked to come in. This made me feel I was not human enough to put my foot inside an employer's kitchen until I was employed. At the interview I was always told the exact time for starting work but not for finishing off—that depended entirely on what time my employers decided to have supper. Sometimes I worked until late into the night while entertaining went on, and I was expected to start work at the usual time next morning. I found that employers could not care about my physical welfare so long as I was able to do the work. They did not worry about the long hours, the lack of freedom or the poor wages . . . I do not want to think about the many single domestic workers who have four or five school-going children. I believe that it is the opinion of some employers that domestic workers cannot appreciate comfort and that therefore they must all have plain fare and have rooms like dungeons to eat in and retire to.
>
> "After all, what is the point of spending money making life easier and comfortable for a lot of ungrateful people who could not care less what you did for them"—I once overheard these words from one of my ex-employers, where I had only a bed for furniture, a bare concrete floor and three nails behind the door for a wardrobe.[19]

Black servants retained to work in white homes must be kept in quarters wholly separate from the house. The law forbids any connecting passage or door; white families are fined $500 for any violation of this.

From its inception the Group Areas Act did not recognize rights of residence or property rights for Blacks in the townships. Without a permit, no Black person can stay in an urban area for more than 72 hours. He or she may thereafter be subject to arrest and penalties. By law, all Blacks must carry pass books with photograph, and with information on tribal origin, homeland in which "citizenship" is held, law infractions, and a full employment record including present employer. Periodically, there are swoops by the police on the townships, places of employment and transport, to check passes. Annually, 200,000 to 300,000 Blacks are arrested and prosecuted for pass law violations, crowding the jails with offenders against apartheid. In a typical year, 1983, a Black man or woman was prosecuted under the pass laws every 2-1/2 minutes.

In April 1986 the Botha government announced that the pass laws would be scrapped. It was directed that certain categories of those Africans currently in prison for pass law violations would be released. However, a new identity document to be issued to all South Africans requires identification by race, and any failure to identify one's self satisfactorily to an "authorized officer" can still result in a six-month prison sentence or 500 rands fine. In connection with this change in the influx control system, legislation was to be introduced in the apartheid parliament in 1986 amending 34 laws and regulations. Movement to or residence in townships would be made conditional not on whether an African had a job but on whether he or she had "approved accommodation" in an "approved area." The basic residence segregation law, the Group Areas Act, has remained in force. Essentially, the pass law change is due to the demands of South African and foreign big business for less restricted labor mobility.

Apartheid Exploitation

The main purpose of the wholesale relegation of the Black population to a "separate" existence is, of course, to put them in a position of being paid on a separate basis, to keep them as cheap labor, considered deserving of but a fraction of the wages paid to whites. Out of such super-exploitation the great profits and wealth of the white ruling groups, South African and foreign, have been and are being made.

In 1973 the wage gap between Black and white workers was extreme. Black miners were paid the tiny sum of 27 rands a month, the average white miner receiving 405 rands. Black workers in manufacturing industry had somewhat better wages, 67 rands a month compared with the 376 rands for whites.

An official Poverty Datum Line, worked out in the 1970s, set a minimum requirement of $104 a month for a Black family of six. It was estimated that in 1976 over 74% of Black wage workers did not earn that much. During the 1970s, inflation running at 15% annually further worsened Black living standards, contributing to successive waves of strikes that, howsoever illegal, forced wage increases out of white employers. The wage gap, however, was only partially narrowed because white workers received increases to match.

Thus in 1983, Black miners had attained 272 rands a month, but for whites wages had risen to 1,500 rands. Overall in that year, the wage gap showed Black workers getting an average of 290 rands a month while whites on average had 1,100 rands. (Among other nonwhites the following averages prevailed in 1983: Colored 385 rands, Indian 540 rands.) In the economy as a whole, Blacks are presently paid roughly one-fifth the wages of whites.

The huge racial wage gap is aggravated by the notorious job reservation policy which allocates virtually all skilled jobs to whites in every field of industry. For Black workers, this has been particularly onerous in mining in which they do the hardest and most dangerous below-ground work. Between 1936 and 1975 a total of 22,306 miners, mostly Black, were killed. Mine deaths in 1978 were 877; injuries in 1974 were 355,000.

Racism in the Classroom

"Separate development" has been applied with special savagery to education for Africans. One of the early apartheid legislative acts was the Bantu Education Act of 1953 that separated the education of the Black majority from the national and provincial departments of education and transferred it to the Department of Bantu Affairs. When this was being presented to the Nationalist-controlled parliament, Hendrick Verwoerd, who became prime minister in 1958, said:

> I just want to remind Hon. Members that if the Native in South Africa today in any kind of school in existence is being taught to expect that he will live his adult life under a policy of equal rights, he is making a big mistake . . . There is no place for him in the European community above the level of certain forms of labor. For that reason it is of no avail for him to receive a training which has as its aim absorption in the European community . . . What is the use of teaching a Bantu child mathematics when it cannot use it in practice? . . . It is therefore necessary that native education be controlled in such a way that it should be in accordance with the policy of the state.[20]

The apartheid education policy was extended with the adoption of the Colored Persons Education Act in 1963 and the Indian Education Act of 1964, which shifted education for Colored and Indian children from provincial departments to the Departments of Colored and of Indian Affairs.

Separation in the education system has meant gross inequality in every aspect of education. On average about 2.5% of South Africa's Gross Domestic Product has been spent on education, but only 0.5% has been for Blacks who comprise 70% of the population. The per capita expenditure for white schoolchildren in 1979 was 551 rands; for Black schoolchildren it was 45.9 rands in primary schools and 93.42 rands in high schools. In that year the total state budget for education of all categories was 1,832 million rands, of which only 315 million rands was for the Black 70%.

Salaries of African teachers correspond to the wage gap in other fields. Male African teachers in the 1970s received one-half of the payments of white male teachers, while Black women teachers were paid one-third. From 1953 the number of Black teacher trainees steadily declined while the number of Black pupils in the growing population greatly rose. In 1979 there was one teacher for every 20 white schoolchildren, and one Black teacher for every 48 Black pupils.

School facilities reflect the contrasting expenditure. White schools are modern and equipped in a manner matching those in leading western countries. Black pupils, however, must attend classes in poor shacks or sheds in most cases, many totally lacking in toilets or other facilities; it is not unusual for a school building to be nonexistent and for classes to be held in the open air.

Because of the shortage of Black teachers and the meager salaries paid to them by the state, the tendency has been for Black parents to sacrifice to try to pay privately for teachers and even to pay for building and maintaining of schools. By 1969 the Minister of Bantu Education admitted that Black parents were spending two million rands for private teachers and 535,000 rands for erecting schools that the state did not provide. On top of this, Black parents have had to pay by state requirement for school fees, textbooks, uniforms and other needs. Not surprisingly, the dropout rate for Black pupils has been enormous. In the 1970s it was estimated that nearly 95 out of every 100 Black pupils dropped out before reaching secondary school and that out of 2.5 million Africans in school in a given year, only 750,000 had received more than four years schooling. Even those wanting to go to secondary school, however, were frustrated by the lack of secondary schools. In Soweto there were 54 higher primary schools but only 8 secondary schools to absorb the pupils from them.[21]

When the large-scale anti-apartheid unrest and upheavals began in the mid-1970s, it began in the deprived, segregated Black schools.

Suppression: An Apartheid Fundamental

The apartheid system, with its thoroughgoing racial discrimination and exploitation that pervades all aspects of life in South Africa, could only be imposed and maintained by equally thorough repressive laws and agencies of force. Blacks did not submissively accept their own enslavement; they showed resistance during the colonial period of British rule, and they displayed massive resistance as the apartheid plan began to unfold under Nationalist rule.

One of the first steps of the Afrikaaner Nationalist government was the passage in 1950 of the Suppression of Communism Act, which has been the cornerstone of an edifice of laws for banning and penalizing opposition to apartheid. In this Act, which outlawed the South African Communist Party, the definition of Communism, its principles and aims is intentionally so broad and vague as to be applicable to virtually any opposition or criticism directed at the government or its measures. According to that definition, "the doctrine of Marxian socialism" is one "which aims at the establishment of a despotic system of government" and "which aims at bringing about any political, industrial, social, or economic change within the Union by the promotion of disturbance or disorder, by unlawful acts or omissions or by the threat of such acts or omissions or by means which include the promotion of disturbance or disorder, or such acts or omissions or threats." Besides outlawing the Communist Party, the Act authorized the outlawing of "any other organization . . . which engaged in activities calculated to further the achievement of any of the objects of Communism."

It is an Act that can be and has been applied to virtually all forms of anti-apartheid organization and activity, justified in the government propaganda that has sought to depict anti-apartheid movements as "Communist-inspired." The propaganda has extended also to the international movements and campaigns against apartheid, which are portrayed as creations and instruments of the Soviet Union.

Outlawing of the Communist Party was but the starting point for the elimination of opposition to apartheid. A Criminal Law Amendment Act in 1953 proscribed heavy fines and up to three years imprisonment and ten lashes for going against a law in order to protest or for campaigning against any law. In 1956 a Riotous Assemblies Act effectively did away with the freedom of assembly, banned most forms of picketing with the threat of fines and imprisonment, forbade boycotts, and penalized the "intimidation" of others to stay away from work (i.e., to strike) or to join a trade union, and made unlawful such picketing features as "jeering at people."

Adoption of these laws did not stop protest movements and campaigns against apartheid, its pass laws and segregation decrees. The

African National Congress led a broad movement of resistance to the whole program of apartheid in the 1950s, including the holding of a Congress of the People in 1955, at which an alternative program for a free and democratic society, the Freedom Charter, was adopted. This large and growing mass movement was met by the savage repressive act known as the Sharpeville Massacre, when white police opened fire on peaceful demonstrators against pass laws at Sharpeville, a township near Johannesburg, on March 20, 1960, killing 69 men, women and children (mostly shot in the back) and wounding over 200 others. The incident was seized upon by the government to claim an insurrectionary threat and to rush through an Unlawful Organizations Act which banned the African National Congress and its split-away off-shoot, the Pan-Africanist Congress.

The banning of organizations that forthrightly sought to campaign against apartheid in an open, legalistic and peaceful manner inevitably led to underground resistance. With all peaceful means of protest prohibited, the African National Congress in 1961 formed an armed wing, Umkhonto we Sizwe (Spear of the Nation), to carry on armed struggle for liberation from apartheid. The government then resorted to a series of General Law Amendment Acts to deal with activities and attitudes that were considered illegal.

Most sweeping and severe of these was the 1962 General Law Amendment Act known as the "Sabotage Act." Actually this lists 22 declared offenses, only one of which concerns sabotage as such, that are punishable by penalties of from five years imprisonment to the death sentence. Included in acts considered sabotage is simple trespass upon any land or building. If found guilty of simple trespass, an accused may be subjected to the entire range of penalties unless he or she can *prove* that there was no *intent* to promote general dislocation or disorder, to cripple any industry, to injure or endanger or cause loss to a person or the state, to further a political aim, to cause feelings of hostility between different sections of the population, or to cause resistance to or embarrassment of the government. Under the Act, people may be subjected to house arrest or banning for indefinite periods; in the latter case, having to report daily to the police and being forbidden to make statements for publication. When this Act was presented to the South African parliament, the International Commission of Jurists commented that it curtailed a citizen's liberty to a greater extent than did the most extreme dictatorship.

Further Law Amendment Acts followed in 1963 and 1964. These provided for the detention of persons without trial, and for continued confinement without the process of trial of persons after the completion of a sentence. A notorious Act, the "90-day detention" law, was passed in 1963; it permitted detention, without trial, for the purpose of interrogation, for a period of 90 days, at the end of which rearrest could immediately occur for an additional 90-day detention. In 1965 the detention period that could be repeated was increased to 180 days. A law in 1964 specified that anyone refusing to give evidence, even if self-incriminatory, could be confined in prison for twelve months.

Another law as sweeping as the Sabotage Act came in 1967—the Terrorism Act. This was designed for penalizing acts "endangering law and order" and the *intention* to commit such acts. The penalties ranged from a five-year minimum prison sentence to the death penalty. Included in the Act was a provision enabling indefinite detention in solitary confinement of anyone *suspected* of "terrorism" and of anyone *suspected of having information about "terrorism."*

In 1982 the government of Prime Minister P.W. Botha adopted a new Internal Security Act that combined all previous laws on security for apartheid. The bill presenting it contained 99 pages of provisions and a definition of Communism even broader than that devised earlier. Under these laws, and others penalizing violations of apartheid measures, the South African prisons have been the most crowded of any in the world. In 1981 the average daily prison population was 102,000, crammed into prisons (many 90 to 100 years old) built to hold a maximum of 70,000 inmates. Chiefly through the ruthless application of apartheid and security laws, South Africa's prison population is, proportionately, nearly double that in U.S. federal and state prisons. Isolated Robben Island, off the coast near Cape Town, has held 800 political prisoners at a time, mostly leaders of the African National Congress, South West African Peoples Organization and other liberation movements. Between 1960 and 1981 a total of 1,426 people were placed under banning; 164 others were banished, which means being transported hundreds of miles and dumped in barren lands without means of livelihood.

This Is the Apartheid System in South Africa

By the end of the second decade of Nationalist rule, that system had been organized as tightly as its racist and police-minded architects could make it, with an all-pervading network of security agencies, police and armed forces to enforce it. The most powerful of the repressive instruments, created in 1968, was the Bureau of State Security or BOSS. In 1981 it was restructured as the National Intelligence Service, with military intelligence and police security branches kept separate. The system as such has been intensified rather than moderated. A virtually untouchable agency, BOSS and its successors have had vast powers of investigation, arrest and detention. Their activities extend beyond the borders of South Africa into operations that have a CIA-like character (with CIA links). These agencies are surrounded by an enormous cloak of secrecy: anyone who mentions or communicates to anyone else any reference to them or the matters with which they deal may be charged with committing an offense, a stipulation that applies in particular to the press or other media. Nothing relating to BOSS, the NIS or their findings or methods may be submitted as evidence in a court and no witness, whether in his own defense or not, may disclose information that may be considered within the scope of BOSS/NIS (embracing all matters of information "prejudicial to the security of the state").

Despite the massive police state that is embodied in the apartheid system and its security apparatus, the history of South Africa for the past four decades has been one of constant conflict and instability, of virtual warfare between the oppressed majority and the racist minority that has manufactured the divisions. During the last two decades that conflict has reached proportions that make the apartheid state increasingly untenable.

The nature of the conflict was sharply described in 1984 by the president of the anti-apartheid African National Congress, Oliver Tambo:

The South African constitution excludes the blacks. They are outside the constitution. There is nothing they can do about the decisions, the policies of the South African regime. They don't belong. They are fighting from outside this white state. This is not a civil rights struggle at all. If we were part of the constitution, if we were citizens like any other, then of course there would be rights to fight for, as there are rights to fight for in the United States. But in South Africa the position is different. Our struggle is basically, essentially, fundamentally, a national liberation struggle.[22]

II THE IMPERIALIST-APARTHEID ALLIANCE

The erection of the apartheid system in South Africa coincided with, and ran counter to, two major developments that were strides forward for the peoples of the world. First of these was the founding in 1945 of the United Nations which provided a means for major steps toward the elimination of colonialism and racism. In the following decade came the second great advancement: the beginning, with the attainment of independence by Ghana in 1958, of the liberation of colonial Africa.

Both of these developments embodied rejections by the overwhelming majority of the states and peoples of the world of the concept and of the motive forces of racial oppression and discrimination. It has been a majority that has kept increasing as country after country in Africa, Asia, Latin America and other regions has won independence and aligned itself with those opposing overt racism. Condemnation of South African apartheid and concerted steps to terminate it have been a central feature of the United Nations agenda. Resolutions condemning apartheid, calling for its abolition, endorsing international embargoes and sanctions for isolating South Africa and compelling it to heed worldwide demands for an end to apartheid have been introduced repeatedly.

If adopted and carried out determinedly by all United Nations members, these actions would long ago have made it impossible for the racist system in South Africa to survive in a hostile world. That this has not been the case has been due to the fact that the South African rulers have had powerful allies and supporters. These, the few countries commonly known as the imperialist powers, have vetoed, blocked and made unworkable most United Nations' resolutions on apartheid, and have provided South Africa with the economic and military means not only to survive but to become a country wielding power—with a dominant role in its part of the world.

The liberation of colonially enslaved Africa, which began with the freedom of Ghana from British rule in 1958, has been a phenomenon wholly different from the separation of South Africa from the British crown by the Afrikaaner Nationalist government in 1960. In throwing off rule by white imperialists, the newly independent African countries released black populations from enforced subservient positions. In many cases a neocolonial condition replaced the old colonialism, but even in such countries it was a stratum of Blacks in power who, for class reasons, collaborated with imperialist interests and made this possible. The strongest trend in liberated Africa, which brought about the 51-nation Organization of African Unity, was for the freedom and self-determination of Black Africans on the entire continent of Africa. In the development of the United Nations' anti-apartheid policy and in the shaping of other forms of an international anti-apartheid movement, the OAU has played a prominent part.

Apartheid South Africa has been not just an odd-man-out in the mainstream of African liberation. It has comprised a reactionary bulwark against liberation for Blacks, not only within South Africa but in Africa as a whole. More important, it has served as a base and an instrument for imperialist forces wishing to reverse or to control the independence won by African countries so as to place them in neocolonial subordination to western corporations, banks and military bases all over again.

In sum, apartheid is more than a system employed to keep a South African white minority in power and prosperity. It is also a system giving great profit to imperialist interests while acting as an imerialist ally against African liberation and against the forces of progress in the world in general.

The Foreign Investment Stake

When the Nationalist Party, the party of apartheid, came to power in South Africa in 1948 the total foreign investment in the country, direct and indirect, was little more than $2 billion. The bulk of this, exceeding 70%, was British.

In the first years of tightening apartheid, the rise of the foreign investment stake was gradual, reaching $3.7 billion by 1960. Although the Sharpeville massacre occurred in that year, drawing international condemnation and causing a temporary outflow of capital, this was soon checked and transformed into renewed investment as suppression of Black resistance seemed effective. In the short space of eight years after Sharpeville—by 1968—foreign investment had nearly doubled, to $6.4 billion.

From that point, in spite of the mounting campaign in the United Nations and outside that world body for demanding an end to the racist system, an actual acceleration occurred of foreign investment and loan capital to South Africa. British direct investments of around $2.5 billion in the early 1960s have risen to nearly $12 billion at the present time. West German direct investments, amounting to about $280 million in 1956, stood at nearly $1.9 billion in 1974. As for the United States, its direct investments increased at the fastest rate of all, jumping from $288 million in 1956 to $692 million in 1968 to more than $2.6 billion in the latter part of 1984.

Total foreign direct and equity capital in South Africa in 1984 was estimated at approximately $25 billion. In other words, from the time apartheid was installed and during the years of its condemnation internationally, the stake of foreign companies and banks in the system increased by at least 12 times.

The main reason for this has been simple: the very cheap Black labor in a system in which Black wages range from one-fifth to one-seventh of those paid to white workers. As a consequence, the rate of profit for foreign companies in South Africa has ranged between 20% to 25%, compared with 12% to 14% in most developing countries. This has made South Africa the choicest investment area in the world for approximately 2,000 companies from the leading capitalist countries.

Among these countries are many of the biggest transnational firms that exert a powerful influence on the foreign policy of their country of origin. In 1984, 65 of the major transnationals —22 from the United States, 19 British, 11 West German, 3 French, 3 Japanese, and the rest from Netherlands, Belgium and others—had large holdings in South Africa.[1]

All told, by the latter 1970s foreign companies employed one-fourth of all economically active workers, Black and white, in South Africa. Between 2 and 3 million workers depended, directly or indirectly, on the foreign investment sectors of the economy. Of private industrial production, nearly 80% was accounted for by foreign companies, and about 74% of all manufacturing firms were dependent on foreign sources for technology.

The large state sector in the economy has relied equally on foreign capital which has come in the form of bank loans. There were 30 major international banks with subsidiaries or offices in South Africa in 1984, while 328 foreign banks were involved in loans in just the

1972-1978 period. In 1974-1975 alone U.S. banks provided nearly $2.5 billion, and loans raised by British banks amounted to $1,854 million in 1970-1976. From the beginning of 1979 to the early 1980s western banks and financial agencies contributed $2,756 million, and in 1982, mainly through U.S. intercession, the International Monetary Fund extended a $1.2 billion loan to South Africa. This readiness of western financial institutions to make loan capital available to the apartheid economy led by 1985 to a South African foreign debt variously estimated at $17 to $21 billion.

Western Ties With South Africa

Without this huge influx of foreign capital, which at certain times of crisis was actually stepped up to save the economy from collapse, apartheid South Africa could not have survived. In particular it could not have expanded from the mainly mining and agricultural base that predominated in 1948 to the diversified manufacturing sectors that began to grow in the latter 1950s and reached near boom proportions in the 1960s (for whites, that is). From the 1960s onward between 40% to 50% of foreign investment was in manufacturing.

The highly profitable returns from investing in the apartheid economy account for the ease with which British interests adjusted themselves to the Afrikaaner ascendency after the Nationalist victory in 1948. At the same time, the ambitious Afrikaaner interests, which had resented their exclusion from monopoly economic power in the past, found it both necessary and convenient to encourage foreign investment and loans, so long as their government controlled the huge and expanding state sector of the economy. What took place essentially was a joint venture partnership between British and Afrikaaner capital, particularly in mining, manufacturing and finance. Despite the Nationalist break with the crown and with the Commonwealth, British governments, although sometimes voicing moral condemnation of apartheid to appease public opinion, protected their corporations and South Africa from anti-apartheid measures.

Cecil Parkinson, Minister of State for Trade in the Tory government of Prime Minister Margaret Thatcher elected in 1979, declared in arguing against proposed anti-apartheid sanctions: "We cannot allow our trade with a country like South Africa to be reduced without endangering our own economic health. Our bilateral trade with South Africa is not something that is peripheral to our economy, it is of central importance." Parkinson then put to the British House of Commons the standard western justification for ties with apartheid: "We believe the question of sanctions is, and should remain, hypothetical. South Africa needs more foreign investment to promote its economic growth—economic growth brings the best hope of peaceful change in South Africa. We must maintain trade and investment links."[2] In 1984 Mrs. Thatcher, still defying widespread protest against the British involvement with apartheid, went to the extent of inviting South African Prime Minister P.W. Botha to a state visit to Britain.

Despite international anti-apartheid campaigns that compelled the European Economic Community to draw up a "Code of Conduct" in 1977 for companies of EEC countries with subsidiaries in South Africa, as late as mid-1980, 33 British companies were charged with paying starvation wages to their black African workers. An estimated 20,000 Black workers were reported to be paid less than 20 rands a week by the companies concerned, among them Burmah Oil which has on its board of directors Denis Thatcher, the husband of the British prime minister. The lame excuse for this situation given by the British companies was that the directors of their subsidiaries were South African nationals.[3]

The conclusion is inescapable that the foreign capital poured into South Africa, far from merely taking advantage of favorable investment opportunities, has helped to create those opportunities for greater profit by being the main financing factor in the development and implementation of apartheid.

As the imperialist investment stake in South Africa grew, the imperialist defense of the apartheid regime and its system became more determined, and became more devious to evade international demands for an end to apartheid and for isolation of South Africa. Numerous arguments were advanced to justify ties with the apartheid regime.

It has been argued, geopolitically, that "the west" could not exist without South Africa and without a government there that would guarantee access to its natural resources. The mineral resources of South Africa, which are indeed vast and diverse, include a reported 86% of the world's platinum, 83% of chrome, 64% of vanadium, 49% of gold, 48% of manganese ore, and a large share of the world's uranium, tritium, lithium and other scarce ores. Some of these have their importance as components in special metallurgy in the manufacture of nuclear missiles and other weaponry. A distinct corollary has been observed between the heightening of the arms race and the stubbornness of the western powers in supporting South Africa. The argument has been pushed to the point of contending that South

Africa, with its valuable resources, is part of the "free world" supposedly under threat from "Soviet-inspired attack".

A part of this theme is the contention that the Cape sea route—that is, the sea route around the Cape of Good Hope from Asia and the Middle East to Europe, the U.S. and Latin America—is vital to the security of the west. From the latter 1960s, proposals and moves came from the councils of the North Atlantic Treaty Organization (NATO) for the extension of NATO to the South Atlantic, to be linked with a South Atlantic Treaty Organization that would include South Africa. In April 1982 the *Johannesburg Times* published a story that asserted the existence of a secret 13-year old pact allegedly linked with NATO, tying together South Africa, Argentina, Brazil, Paraguay, Uruguay, Israel and Taiwan.[4]

Even without formal treaty arrangements, South Africa is known to be monitoring all maritime traffic around the Cape, in the adjoining areas of the Atlantic, and in the southern Indian Ocean, and to be passing the information on to NATO intelligence agencies. The movements of Soviet and other socialist-country shipping are the main surveillance targets. Apologists for apartheid in the west go to the extent of arguing that in exchange for this "vital" service (which space satellites are capable of rendering), the NATO powers should have a military alliance with South Africa and assist in defending its regime against anti-apartheid forces.

The West Defends and Arms South Africa

In February 1960 the British prime minister, Harold MacMillan, delivered a significant speech in Cape Town in which he pointed to "the winds of change" that were blowing through Africa and to the need for the imperialist powers to trim their sails to veer with them. MacMillan was referring to the sweeping movements for national liberation and independence that were then occurring in all of central and northern Africa and that had already detached Ghana, Guinea, Egypt, Cameroun and other countries from the colonial system. The British prime minister, known for his pragmatism, was one of those looking for the neocolonial adjustments that would have to be made in order to preserve imperialist holdings if a full-scale revolutionary upheaval were to occur. His speech, in one respect, could be seen as a veiled warning to the regime in South Africa, where strong movements against apartheid laws were underway.

However, in southern Africa the colonial and racist rulers had other designs. The Portuguese had no intention of surrendering an inch to the African peoples of Angola, Mozambique and Guinea Bissau. The sizeable white settler community in Rhodesia, numbering a quarter of a million, refused to consider the prospect of a multiracial or a substantially Black-governed state. In South Africa the apartheid regime had its closed mind set on a continual tightening of white minority rule.

Each of these countries had enormous mineral wealth desired by the western powers. Above all, the winds of change needed to be diverted from this key region of imperialist interest and control. In the month following the MacMillan speech, on March 21, 1960, the South African police massacred Black anti-apartheid demonstrators at Sharpeville, beginning the implementation of increasingly tougher repressive measures that included the outlawing of the African National Congress.

The newly independent Republic of the Congo, proclaimed in June 1960, was drowned in the blood of murdered national liberation leaders, of whom the most outstanding was Patrice Lumumba, slain in January 1961. By 1964, after white mercenary troops were hired to crush an armed liberation struggle (led by the South African "Colonel" Mike Hoare) and after repeated intervention by the U.S., Belgium and other western powers, the big foreign mining companies obtained the subservient regime they wanted, first under Moise Tshombe and then under General Mobutu, in what was renamed Zaire.

In the Portuguese colonies the colonial authorities refused to permit any form of nationalist political activity. The result was the beginning of armed struggle for liberation by the People's Movement for the Liberation of Angola (MPLA), in 1961, by the Independence Party of Guinea and Cape Verde (PAIGC) in 1963, and by the Mozambique Liberation Front (FRELIMO) in 1964. These developed into full-scale wars of national liberation, in which Portugal with the aid of its NATO allies used a colonial army for brutal repression.

The white settlers of Rhodesia, led by Ian Smith and his Rhodesia Front party, declared a "unilateral declaration of independence" in 1965, severing themselves from a Britain that had had the outlook of negotiating a neocolonial independence with Black participation. Smith set up a dictatorial government that brutally sought to suppress Black resistance.

In South West Africa (Namibia), which had been under South African rule since 1915, by League of Nations mandate from 1920, a

United Nations resolution in 1966 terminated the mandate on grounds that South Africa had failed to ensure the welfare and well-being of the Namibian people: this, and a subsequent U.N. call in 1969 for South Africa to withdraw were spurned by South Africa. An armed guerrilla struggle for independence was met by ruthless South African military measures.

By the mid-1960s the imperialist powers and their local allies had literally drawn a line marking off southern Africa as a region where the winds of change should not blow. Within this region another line of "defense" was clearly designated: it set off South Africa as the prime area to be preserved for western interests. The strategy that took shape was one that viewed South Africa as the main bastion of foreign investments, loans and trade, with the Portuguese colonies, Rhodesia and Namibia serving as outer works or buffers safeguarding the chief prize. As the rest of Africa became free and independent, apartheid South Africa emerged with increasing clarity as an ally of imperialism in a strategy of halting the march of liberation.

In the opinion of western policymakers this was a wholly feasible strategy. One of the clearest statements to that effect was a confidential memorandum commissioned in 1969 for the U.S. National Security Council by Henry Kissinger, then a leading adviser to President Richard Nixon. A review and projection of U.S. policy in southern Africa, the memo (NSSM 39), even had a racially derogatory nickname, the "Tar Baby report." Its estimates read:

> The whites are in Africa and plan to stay there. Constructive changes can only take place with their assistance. The blacks have no chance of winning the political rights they want by force. Violence would only lead to chaos and more possibilities for Communist interference. After making our attitude toward the white regimes more flexible on some issues, we could secure some change in the colonial and racial policies. By extending more substantial economic aid to independent African nations we could foster a union of white and black states and influence them . . . Underlying our contacts in this region of the globe are our considerable interests, and we can safeguard them only by paying an acceptable price.

In other words, the U.S. at this stage was confident that southern Africa could be held, that the situation could be stabilized, and that independent black Africa, after a little juggling of "change," could be made to accept a "union" with the white-ruled South, all under U.S. "influence." The core of the "Tar Baby report" was an estimate that African liberation movements were not "realistic or supportable," and that "the depth and permanence of black resolve" was questionable. In conclusion, the report "ruled out a black victory at any stage."[5]

In the light of this report, the Nixon administration proceeded to lift the U.N.-decided U.S. embargo on importing Rhodesian chrome ore, which was sent out through South Africa, thus helping to bolster the Ian Smith white settler regime; poured $500 million to Portugal in aid of its colonial wars in Angola, Mozambique and Guinea Bissau; and gave emphasis to vetoing U.N. resolutions for sanctions against South Africa.

Pursuing NSSM-39 estimates, the U.S. and its western allies, in particular Britain, West Germany, France and Japan, stepped up investments and aid for southern Africa in this period. The Nixon administration encouraged a rapid growth of U.S. investments in South Africa, which rose from $864 million in 1970 to $1.4 billion by the end of 1973. Between 1968 and 1973 the amount of U.S. direct investment in South African mining doubled, but the amount in other fields, particularly manufacturing, went up at an even faster rate. West German direct investments had their fastest rise in those years, going into steel, chemical and other heavy industries of a long-range nature. Japan moved into the picture, its exports to South Africa increasing by 74% in 1968-1974, while its imports of South African raw materials soared by 2,426% in the same years, with Japanese firms contracting for the infrastructure construction enabling heightened exports of iron ore, manganese and other minerals.

Confidence in the durability of the South African bastion, expressed in the investment trend, was reinforced by a vast buildup of the military potential of the apartheid regime. In disregard of a U.N. resolution of 1963 that called on member states to observe a voluntary arms embargo of South Africa, the U.S., West Germany, France and Israel in particular supplied the apartheid state with masses of arms, military equipment, and licenses for arms manufacture. After that date, and especially after the "Tar Baby report," U.S. planes, British naval vessels, planes and communication equipment, French missiles, submarines, armored cars and helicopters, and every variety of small and medium arms and equipment were supplied. A Stockholm research body estimated that South Africa was provided in this way with at least $1.1 billion of military means between 1963 and 1975. When a mandatory arms embargo resolution was finally adopted by the U.N. in 1977, the supplying countries all abstained on the motion. France alone at that time had between $800 million and $1.8 billion in arms contracts outstanding, and made it plain that these would be fulfilled.

The U.N. arms embargoes, which made it increasingly difficult for South Africa's western partners to engage in direct military assistance, were evaded by the simple process of enabling South Africa to create its own arms industry. In 1960 its military expenditure was only 44 million rands but this jumped to 707 million rands by 1974. By 1969 South Africa, almost wholly through the use of western licenses, was already self-sufficient in rifles, mortars, ammunition, grenades, bombs, mines and napalm, and was manufacturing a surface-to-air missile (the Crotate or Cactus, with a French license) and a jet aircraft (the Impala, with an Italian license).

In this arming of a racist state the most ominous feature was supplying South Africa with the know-how and the means for manufacturing nuclear weapons.

A South African Atomic Energy Board was set up in 1957, and the U.S. proceeded to sign an agreement to provide technical information for a period of 10 years, up to 1967, at the end of which the agreement was extended for another 10 years. A U.S. company, Allis Chalmers, built South Africa's first nuclear reactor, Safari-1, in 1960-1965, following it with a second reactor, Safari-2, in 1968. Between 1965 and 1977 the U.S. sold South Africa 136 kilograms of enriched uranium.

West Germany entered the picture in 1959, establishing links between its Karlsruhe Society of Nuclear Research and the president of the South African Atomic Energy Board, A. Roux. West German training was given to numerous South African nuclear specialists and engineers, including the head of the Pelendaba nuclear center, Prof. F. Selshop. The West German company, Strag, built a secret uranium enrichment plant in South Africa. In 1970 Prime Minister Vorster claimed that a "South African method" for enriching uranium had been developed, but this was an attempt to screen the West German role.

As a result of this nuclear collaboration, the vice-chairman of the Atomic Energy Board, Louw Alberts, was able to boast on July 12, 1974 that South Africa was capable of producing its own atomic bombs. In May 1976 Prime Minister Vorster announced that South African defenses included nuclear capability.[6] The Pelendaba plant was then producing 25 kilograms of plutonium a year, enough for three 20-kiloton bombs.[7]

In 1977 a report that a nuclear test was about to be held in the Kalahari Desert in the western Cape region caused international protest that forced its postponement. Having refused to sign the Nuclear Non-Proliferation Treaty, South Africa pressed ahead with its nuclear program until, in 1979, evidence that a nuclear weapon test had been held multiplied the menace of the armed apartheid rulers.

Colonial Alliance in Southern Africa

The western economic and military support that was poured into South Africa in the latter 1960s and early 1970s underpinned the country that was to serve as the core of the racist bulwark in southern-Africa. Within the imperialist-apartheid alliance, South Africa played its own part in building up the bulwark. Steps were taken to knit the Portuguese colonies of Angola and Mozambique to the South African economy.

A series of economic agreements were signed between Portugal and South Africa from 1964 onwards, leading to the extensive entry of South African capital into Angola. The Anglo-American Corporation was most active in this; its subsidiary, De Beers, becoming a major shareholder in Diamang, the monopoly corporation that mined and exported Angola's chief money-earning product, diamonds. The General Mining and Finance Corporation and the South African Consolidated Investment Group were other companies exploiting Angolan resources. South African trade with Angola that was an insignificant 2 million rands in 1964 had risen to 44 million rands by 1974. Of greater importance in the developing arrangement was the big Kunene River hydroelectric project in southern Angola near the border with Namibia, in which the largest shareholder was South Africa; it was intended to provide power for the South African power system.[8]

Electric power also linked South Africa with Mozambique, where a huge $360 million hydroelectric project was under construction in this period at Cabora Bassa on the Zambezi River in Tete province. The consortium constructing this, ZAMCO, was headed by South Africa's Anglo-American Corporation and had West German, French, Canadian and Portuguese participation, but two-thirds of the total financing came from South Africa. The U.S. Export-Import Bank was involved in supplying much of the remainder, and the U.S. General Electric Company provided the transformer equipment.[9]

The consolidating of southern Africa as an anti-liberation bastion around the South African core was facilitated by the pattern of colonial infrastructure in the whole region, mainly built by the British. Rail lines and road systems radiated from South Africa, particularly into the landlocked countries of Rhodesia, Botswana, Malawi and Zambia. These countries depended largely on South African ports for exporting their products and importing their needs. The port of Laurenco Marques in southern Mozambique was heavily reliant on South African exports.

Independent African countries like Zambia and Malawi, within the zone of southern Africa, were made virtual captives of the racist bloc. Zambian copper had to be exported chiefly by rail through Rhodesia and South Africa or westward through Portuguese Angola on the Benguela railroad. Most significant in the southern African situation, however, was the case of Rhodesia.

United Nations sanctions, particularly on oil shipments to Rhodesia, were adopted on December 16, 1966, three months after the white settler minority announced a "unilateral declaration of independence." The main flow of oil had been previously through a pipeline from the Mozambique port of Beira, but this was shut off by a closing of the pipeline, owned by Lonrho, a British company that was obliged to comply with the sanctions. Sanctions also required U.N. member states to "prevent the import into their territories of asbestos, iron ore, chrome, pig iron, sugar, tobacco, copper, meat and meat products, and hides, leather and skins originating in Rhodesia."

At no time, from 1966 to the end of "u.d.i." in 1980, did these sanctions succeed in strangling the Rhodesian white dictatorship. They failed solely because apartheid South Africa served as the export-import channel for Rhodesia. Oil not only came through South African ports and over South African road and rail links to Rhodesia, it was supplied through devious illegal means by British-Dutch Shell, U.S. Mobil and Caltex, and French Total oil companies. Furthermore, Rhodesia not only kept up its exports by the same route but actually increased them in several categories, often through the device of affixing South African labels to conceal origin. For imperialism, the case of Rhodesia, as long as it lasted, was a successful working out of the southern Africa bastion concept.

South Africa had a military as well as an economic role in maintaining the bastion. Troops of the South African armed forces, under a secret alliance with the Portuguese fascist regime, first of Salazar and then of Caetano, were engaged in anti-guerrilla operations in both Angola and Mozambique. In 1968 a large South African air base was set up in the Moxico district of southern Angola, giving support to Portuguese colonial forces. In the same year a South African air base was established at Katimo Mulilo in the Caprivi Strip, the long finger of northwestern Namibia that runs across to the Zambian border, from which aerial reconnaissance was carried out over eastern Angola. Active aid to Portuguese troops in Mozambique became stepped up in 1969, with South African units operating against FRELIMO guerrillas all the way up to the Cabora Bassa dam site. The most open intervention by apartheid troops, however, came in

Rhodesia, by agreement with the Ian Smith regime: in 1967 a South African force of 1,700 troops, with planes, was stationed in southern Rhodesia. By 1970 these had been increased to 4,000 and were participating with the Rhodesian army in suppression campaigns as far north as the Zambezi valley on the Zambian border, using armored cars and helicopters.

At the same time the South African army was engaged in Namibia in a war against the armed wing of the South West Africa People's Organization (SWAPO), which had launched an armed struggle for independence in 1966. Across the whole of southern Africa the army of apartheid was engaged directly in trying to stamp out the bush fires of liberation war.

Collapse of the Colonial Fortress

The dream nurtured by the western powers and South Africa of keeping all of southern Africa in colonial control indefinitely came to an abrupt end in April 1974 when a popular revolution overthrew the fascist regime in Portugal, bringing about the collapse of the Portuguese colonial empire. The process by which this occurred was an interreaction of the liberation movements and their struggle in the colonies and the anti-fascist movement in Portugal, with the economic drain on Portugal of fighting colonial wars weakening the fascist power. In January 1975, transitional governments of independence were established in Angola and Mozambique, formed out of the liberation movements that imperialism and its apartheid ally had worked hard to eliminate.

One of the outcomes of this development was the acceleration of the guerrilla liberation struggle in Rhodesia, where the Patriotic Front forces of the Zimbabwe African National Union and the Zimbabwe African People's Union could now rely on a secure base area and on logistical support lines in Mozambique. By 1980 the white settler dictatorship of Ian Smith had been brought down, with the British colonial administration restored only long enough to negotiate the terms of independence for the new free state of Zimbabwe.

Victory for the liberation movements in these three important countries of southern Africa, containing enormous natural resources which the imperialist powers had hoped to control indefinitely, stripped apartheid South Africa of its buffer zone where other white settler armies could be depended upon to keep the spread of African liberation far from its borders. On those borders now were not merely independent countries but countries with left-leaning governments proposing to build socialist economies and societies, governments that were forthrightly anti-apartheid in outlook and supportive of the anti-apartheid forces in South Africa.

The new situation sharply altered the relations of forces and the perspectives in the region. For imperialism and its corporations, access to the resources and investment fields of South Africa and Namibia became a greater obsession, and the safeguarding of South Africa from sanctions and anti-apartheid isolation was more essential. To guarantee South African security, the apartheid state itself was developed to a far greater extent as a military power, not just for a defensive posture but as an aggressive strike force.

In the new strategy worked out politically and militarily between South Africa and its western partners (particularly the U.S., Britain, France and West Germany), South Africa should not succumb to a laager-like, hemmed-in isolation but should strike out to establish dominance over an expanding area around it.

The first major move in the new strategy occurred in October 1975. An armored column of up to 4,000 South African troops drove into Angola from bases in Namibia, with the aim of storming all the way across the 600 miles or more to Luanda, the Angolan capital, by November 11.

In Angola, three separate disparate movements had contested for leadership of the independence government—the Marxist influenced MPLA headed by Agostinho Neto, the National Front for the Liberation of Angola (FNLA) headed by Holden Roberto, and the National Union for the Total Independence of Angola (UNITA) headed by Jonas Savimbi. Of these, the latter two were right-wing groups that had been in collaboration with Portuguese and other western interests even during the liberation struggle. After the capitulation of Portuguese colonialism, imperialist interests feared most the emergence of the MPLA as the leading independence force. In January 1975 the U.S. National Security Council approved the grant of $300,000 each to Roberto and Savimbi, to encourage them to attack the MPLA. Such attacks began the following month. In June 1975 the U.S. stepped up its intervention, donating $10 million each to Roberto and Savimbi, plus $50 million in arms and other military equipment. The CIA channeled this to the FNLA and UNITA and provided advisers to both.[10] Roberto and Savimbi had both had links with South Africa and these were now extensively enlarged. By September 1975 large numbers of South Africans were training, advising and supplying arms to UNITA and the FNLA. UNITA, operating from southeast

Angola, was developed as the main South African ally. When South African troops invaded Angola in October 1975 it was in coordination with UNITA forces serving under South African command.[11]

Shortly after the South African invasion, the U.S. magazine, *Newsweek,* interviewed South Africa's Prime Minister Hendrik Vorster on the circumstances of his armed forces' action:

> Q. Would it be accurate to say that the U.S. solicited South Africa's help to turn the tide against the Russians and Cubans in Angola last fall?
> A. I do not want to comment on that. The U.S. government can speak for itself. I am sure you will appreciate that I cannot violate the confidentiality of government-to-government communications. But if you are making the statement, I won't call you a liar.
> Q. Would it also be accurate to say you received a green light from Kissinger for a military operation in Angola?
> A. If you say that of your own accord, I will not call you a liar.[12]

Invasion of Angola and the general effort to overthrow the MPLA government were a joint operation of the apartheid army and the CIA. In one of the decisive episodes of African liberation, it failed, due to the combination of fraternal support by Cuban troops, aid from other socialist countries, and the determined resistance by the MPLA. The South African spearhead was smashed before it could reach Luanda, and the South African forces, along with their UNITA-FNLA and other mercenary hirelings, were compelled to retreat from Angola.

This initial act of aggression by South Africa ended in a relatively humiliating setback but it did not cause a change in the strategy that had been designed. This was merely perfected and intensified. Tactics of direct and indirect armed intervention, combined with subversion and terrorism, became the order of the day in southern Africa, aimed at the destabilization of independent neighboring states and their subordination to South African control.

A Covert Western Military Alliance

The role of South Africa as a strike force against independent neighboring states was being developed, however, while other major military burdens were mounting for the apartheid regime. In Namibia the armed liberation struggle conducted by SWAPO was proving to be unsuppressible. As a territory outside South Africa proper, Namibia required what amounted to an expeditionary army to wage war on SWAPO, and the cost was great. As the border wars and aggressions grew, the pent-up apartheid system inside

South Africa began to explode. Within a few months after the defeat in Angola, the Black population of the huge Soweto township near Johannesburg revolted, in June 1976, with echoes of upheaval in other parts of the country.

As a consequence, the buildup of South Africa as a military power, both for outward aggression and internal suppression, went on at a rapid rate from that time onwards. The South African arms budget that stood at 650 million rands in 1975 was tripled in the next four years to reach 2,189 million rands in 1979. This was but the beginning of this militarization of apartheid: the military budget rose to nearly 4,000 million rands by 1984, and 5,123 for 1986-87.

The regular strength of the South African Defense Forces (SADF) which was 59,000 in 1974 increased to 72,000 in 1979, while the total of army, reserve forces and police in the same period jumped from 250,000 to 456,000. The total regulars and reserves—the mobilization strength—topped 500,000 in 1982. In the SADF there were 250 commando units by 1980, with 150,000 commandoes trained in counter-insurgency warfare and special operations, designed as strike forces.

Expansion of the SADF occurred mainly after the 1977 United Nations arms embargo resolution, to which virtually all U.N. members, including the U.S. and other NATO countries, were supposedly bound. Nevertheless, the London-based International Institute for Strategic Studies revealed in its "Military Balance for 1980-81," published in 1980, that South Africa had acquired large numbers of new heavy weapons in the preceding two years:

> 100 new Centurion tanks (a late British model), bringing the tank total up to 250, plus 40 Sherman tanks (U.S.) not listed in previous years:
> 25 new Augusta-Bell 205 multi-purpose helicopters, an Italian-licensed and built model of the U.S. air force's Bell UH-1D and UH-1H used in Vietnam;
> 200 new 120 mm. heavy mortars, a category unnoticed two years earlier;
> 40 new 155 mm. towed and self-propelled M-109A1 howitzers and 15 M-7 105 mm. self-propelled guns (no national origin given, but the only 155 mm. howitzer with the designation M-109A1 is in service in the U.S. Army);
> 6 new FAC(Ms) multi-missile gunboats with another 6 on order, whereas two years previous South Africa had only 3 older Minister class gunboats.[13]

These were all imported items, not manufactured in South Africa. Importation of military equipment is concealed in South African trade figures, under the heading "unclassified imports" or sometimes "strategic imports." From the first to the second quarter of 1980 alone this sector of South African imports soared by 70%, and amounted to 2,845 million rands in the first eight months of the year. In part, this figure included oil purchases (also an embargoed item) but the bulk went for arms.

The period and the equipment are cited as an example. A surreptitious supply of arms to South Africa on a large scale has gone on steadily before that time and after. The sources have been western and pro-western countries.

West German arms, including antitank missiles, have been channeled to South Africa by way of Paraguay. Portugal, after 1977, sent arms by an indirect route, using manifests with destinations in Gabon and Thailand for military items that never arrived in those countries. A Danish shipping line was used to transport 12,600 unarmed grenades from Montreal to Durban.

A more open military collaboration has existed since the early 1970s between South Africa and Israel. It is underpinned by substantial South African investments in and financing of Israel's arms industry: 11 million rands in 1975, 20 million rands in 1976, 32 million rands in 1977, steadily rising as the arms embargo closed in on South Africa.[14] Arms supplied have included Gabriel sea-to-sea missiles, Shaffir air-to-air missiles, Sa'ar and Reshet class missile-carrying gunboats, planes (in 1983 negotiations were occurring for Kfir II fighter-interceptors), ammunition, and light weapons. A report in 1983 claimed that a secret agreement existed between the U.S., Israel and South Africa for the deployment of U.S. Tomahawk cruise missiles in Cape Province.[15]

The U.N. Commission on Africa said in 1981 that the growing collaboration of South Africa and Israel "has provided each country with an additional source of arms, spies and technical know-how, as well as classified information on strategy and tactics."[16]

Most ominous of the South African–Israel military links was the report that a nuclear explosion detected over the South Atlantic on September 22, 1979, was the testing of a tactical nuclear warhead jointly by South Africa, Israel and possibly Taiwan.

In 1980 an arms smuggling ring was uncovered in Britain, but only due to a tip-off to Customs by a disgruntled employee of the company involved. The ring was operated by a team of South African agents headed by a Colonel Hendrick Botha and the managing director of a large British engineering firm, Derek Salt. British, U.S. and West German companies were involved in the deals carried out, which supplied South Africa with parts for guided missiles, gunsights, machine tools for making detonators, ammunition dies, aircraft parts for planes invading Angola, and unspecified "high tech" items from the U.S.

Also in 1980, two U.S. officials of the Space Research Corporation, George Bell and Rodger Gregory, were charged with arms embargo violations. Using fake shipping papers in an elaborate scheme, they had routed to South Africa via Antigua in the Caribbean two 155 mm. cannon, 36,000 howitzer shells, and a radar tracking system. The weapons turned up in South Africa in 1978. It is believed that such a cannon (howitzer), mounted on a ship, was employed to fire the nuclear weapon in the test that occurred in the South Atlantic in 1979.

Smuggling activities that have come to light (usually after the event) are obviously but the tip of the concealed iceberg of the illegal arms trade with apartheid South Africa. The extent to which the South African Defense Force has been armed and equipped, as the largest and best equipped armed force in Africa, points to large-scale military shipments arriving in South Africa. It is hardly possible for this to occur without the knowledge of the ubiquitous western intelligence agencies.

An adjunct of the military support for the apartheid regime has been the supplying of oil, without which both the South African economy and its military machine would be immobilized. An oil embargo of apartheid has been one of the demands of the international anti-apartheid movement. Following the overthrow of the Shah in Iran, which had been the main source of oil for South Africa, not only were Iranian shipments halted but the Organization of Petroleum Exporting Countries (OPEC) declared a boycott of oil sales to the racist state. South Africa's ties with Israel influenced this step. However, the western oil companies and their chartered tankers and "spot traders" have been guaranteeing through mostly surreptitious means that not just South Africa's daily needs are met but a flow sufficient to build huge stockpiles be maintained. An estimated 300,000 barrels a day have arrived in South African ports, while oil-from-coal extraction plants are producing up to 100,000 barrels a day (in 1985). A surplus of 50,000 or more barrels a day has been accumulated over a considerable period. In September 1985 international oil analysts estimated that even in the event of a strict embargo, South Africa had enough stockpiled oil to last three years at normal use and six years if rationed.[17]

The struggle for Southern Africa

That the extensive buildup of South African military power had far more than defensive aims was indicated by the public launching by the Botha government in March 1979 of the concept of "a constellation of states of southern Africa." It was to be a constellation revolving around South Africa, to include the so-called independent homelands and the neighboring independent African states. As a leading South African newspaper explained, the aim was "to draw into South Africa's orbit all Southern African states up to and including Zaire."[18]

In furtherance of the "constellation" scheme, Botha appointed one of the leading South African economic experts, Dr. Gerhard de Kock, as chairman of a "special constellation committee" to work out a program for monetary arrangements having to do with a "rand monetary area": a multilateral development bank, related fiscal and financial arrangements, a regional development plan for both industry and agriculture (especially food production), and a customs union agreement. Along with this, a drive was undertaken to boost South Africa's trade with the rest of Africa. (This was already not inconsiderable, passing one billion rands in 1980.)

Having failed to maintain a colonial fortress in southern Africa, western powers hoped that South Africa could extend itself as the dominant power in the region and accomplish economically what could not be done militarily. At a symposium in South Africa in mid-1980 the concept of a power grid stretching from the Congo River to the Cape was put forward. In five years, "political considerations aside," the link lines and substations could be built, it was said, converting the whole of southern Africa into one vast international power grid. South Africa, it was boasted, had "engineers in sufficient quantity and expertise to undertake the technical leadership of Africa."[19]

The answer of the neighboring "frontline states" came immediately. In the same month of March 1979 when the "constellation" scheme was projected, Angola, Mozambique, Zambia, Tanzania and Botswana leaders met in Arusha, Tanzania and decided to set up a regional transportation and communication committee as a first step toward reducing dependence on South Africa. In the communique announcing this, South Africa was condemned as "racist and fascist."

This initial step of reaction to the South African move for dominance was followed up by the holding in April 1980 in Lusaka, Zambia of a major Southern Africa Development Coordination Conference

(SADCC). Nine states were brought together on this occasion: Zambia, Angola, Mozambique, Tanzania, Zimbabwe (newly independent), Botswana, Lesotho, Swaziland and Malawi. Agreed to was a document entitled "Southern Africa Towards Economic Liberation." Its preamble said;

> In the interests of the people of our countries it is necessary to liberate our economies from their dependence on the Republic of South Africa, to overcome the imposed economic fragmentation, and to coordinate our efforts toward regional and national economic development. This will be as great for Namibia as it is for all the independent states of the region.

Included in the stated aims were: the reduction of dependence particularly on the Republic of South Africa, the forging of links to create genuine and equitable regional integration, the mobilizing of resources to promote national, interstate and regional policies, and concerted action to secure international cooperation "within the framework of our strategy for economic liberation." A permanent supervisory machinery was set up and a regional development bank launched.

The nature of the dependence from which the SADCC has sought to free its participating states may be seen in these facts: nearly 100% of the electricity supply of Lesotho and Swaziland comes from South Africa, 52% of that of Botswana, and 60% of the capital city of Maputo in Mozambique: on average, 45% of the combined imports and exports of Zambia, Zimbabwe and Malawi are transported through South Africa, and virtually 100% of those of Botswana, Lesotho and Swaziland.[20]

In November 1980 a second SADCC conference took place in Maputo, Mozambique. Set forth were the priority areas: transport and communication (including a rail and road network to run west to east in place of the existing colonial-built north-south network that tied the frontline states to South Africa), agricultural development to achieve food self-sufficiency in place of present reliance on South African exports of maize and other food staples, industrial development and coordination, and the establishment of a development fund, manpower development and training, and energy conservation.

To the Maputo meeting were invited representatives from 30 non-African states and 18 international development agencies. The major western countries were urged to participate in funding SADCC programs. A total of $650 million in aid was tentatively committed, spread over a period of five years.[21]

The SADCC step was referred to in South Africa as "counter-constellation." It enraged the Botha regime and the architects of the policy for South African expansion and control in the region.

"Constellation" plans receded from public discussion, and an aggressive campaign for the destabilization of the frontline states, the disruption of SADCC plans, and the elimination of the independent countries' progressive governments was put into effect.

One feature of that campaign was a series of terror attacks on the various frontline states, using the excuse that South African and Namibian liberation movements were based there and were launching raids into South Africa and Namibia from such bases. Repeated invasions of Angola that subsequently took place were allegedly for removing SWAPO bases that were said to be there, but it was plain that the real aim was the ravaging and destabilizing of Angola and the MPLA government.

On November 11, 1982, the Angolan President Jose Eduardo dos Santos declared that the cost of South African depradations, in property destroyed alone, amounted to over $10 billion, a huge drain on the country's economy, seriously retarding development programs, including those of the SADCC. South African sabotage raids on Angola were often ascribed to, and claimed by, UNITA, but have invariably been carried out by South African white soldiers or intelligence agents. In a raid that blew up part of the oil refinery at Luanda in 1982, two white South African soldiers were killed. A similar glaring episode in the South African destabilization assault on Angola was revealed in 1985 when a sabotage team of South Africans was trapped and killed or captured in Angola's oil-rich Cabinda territory; a captured South African soldier admitted that the operation target was not a SWAPO base but the blowing up of oil installations in order to damage Angola's economy.

In Mozambique, armed subversion by counterrevolutionary bands organized and supplied by South Africa was accompanied by direct aggression by South African regular forces. A South African army commando force crossed the Mozambican border on January 30, 1981, and attacked homes in the Matola district of Maputo. Among the 12 people killed, mostly refugee supporters of the African National Congress, were Mozambique citizens. It could hardly be said that the residential houses in Matola were an "ANC base." The purpose of the attack was clearly to terrorize and disrupt life in the Mozambican capital. This aim was more glaringly displayed on May 25, 1983 when seven South African Impala jet aircraft strafed and rocketed the Matola district again, killing 6 and wounding 40 people. The Botha government announced that it had destroyed an "ANC main base," but even the British ambassador who toured the attacked site immediately afterward stated that there was no conceivable sign of ANC presence and that the destroyed homes had contained merely ordinary Mozambican citizens.[22]

On September 14, 1981, South African troops in four armored cars crossed into southern Zambia at Sesheke Boma with air cover from four South African planes and attacked both military and civilian targets.[23]

Lesotho, which is in the disadvantageous geographic position of being entirely landlocked by South Africa, has been a frequent target of apartheid subversion and attack. The Lesotho president, Dr. Leabua Jonathan, had maintained friendly relations with the ANC and led his country into the SADCC grouping. South Africa, in retaliation, has assisted an opposition organization, the Lesotho Liberation Army, to establish a base on nearby South African territory and to make armed raids into Lesotho.

In January 1986 the South African government imposed a blockade of Lesotho, threatened its inhabitants with hunger, and forced the ouster of President Jonathan and his government. The blockade was then continued until the new military government of General Justin Lekhanya was made to compel the departure from Lesotho of ANC members and refugees.

On December 9, 1982, South African commando troops invaded Lesotho and attacked part of the capital city of Maseru with mortars, missiles and machine guns, killing 41 people, both refugees from South Africa and Lesotho citizens.

Zimbabwe, from soon after its independence in 1980, became the target of constant infiltration attacks. Prime Minister Robert Mugabe asserted that South Africa had trained 5,000 men, largely drawn from counterinsurgency Black hirelings of the old Ian Smith regime who had fled from retribution to South Africa, and was sending them into Zimbabwe to cause disorder and instability by raiding farms in the Matabeleland area. They were pretending to be supporters of Joshua Nkomo and his Zimbabwe African People's Union, intending to foment conflict between ZAPU and Mugabe's ZANU.[24]

On June 14, 1985, the capital of Botswana, Gaborone, was raided by South African commandoes, who blasted a section of the city, resulting in the death of 16 people.

Stategically speaking, Mozambique and Angola, which have received the heaviest South African attacks, provide the port terminals for the contemplated east-west rail and highway network of the SADCC program. Disruption of that program had been effected only in part, however, by the South African attacks and destabilization campaign. The other half of a bad coin has been the failure of significant western assistance to materialize as promised to the SADCC. To all intents and purposes, the main coordination in southern Africa has been tacitly between South Africa and western imperialism.

Apartheid Aggression

A pertinent aspect of the expansion of the South African Defense Force was the addition to its ranks of trained members of the armies that had fought against the liberation movements in Rhodesia, Angola and Mozambique. Virtually the entire Rhodesian Light Infantry Regiment, white officers and men, went over the border to South Africa when Zimbabwe's independence came in 1980. South Africa, in fact, actively recruited white members of the Rhodesian security forces, offering $2,200 as a signing-on bonus. Other units that joined the apartheid army were the Selous Scouts and the Special Air Services, the most ruthless and hated in Zimbabwe of the counterinsurgency forces. Among the Selous Scouts elements who were accepted were Black auxiliaries; they were used along with white officers to train Black collaborator units in Natal and the Transvaal Phalabora camp area, units suspected by neighboring countries as being prepared for infiltrating-sabotage activities.[25]

Portuguese hirelings who had fought against the MPLA in Angola and against FRELIMO in Mozambique also fled to South Africa and were incorporated either in the SADF or in counterrevolutionary mercenary units that were equipped and sent back into those countries for destabilizing purposes.

A large unit of this type, comprising 1,100 men, known variously as 32 Battalion and the Buffalo Regiment, was organized and sent into Angola from the SADF base at Rukunku in northern Nambia. Of those in its ranks, 80% were reportedly Portuguese-speaking black mercenaries from the FNLA of Holden Roberto, CIA-financed and advised. The remainder were South African, West German, Portuguese, British and others. One, a former U.S. officer, Captain Christopher Clay, had fought in Vietnam, had later joined Ian Smith's Rhodesian army and participated in its brutal anti-guerrilla operations for four years. He had moved on to South Africa's war in Angola because he saw it as "a continuation of the same thing." In West Germany recruits were obtained through advertisements in two publications for mercenaries to fight for South Africa, advertisements that offered to pay 2,000 rands for the death of each SWAPO member.[26]

A British mercenary in 32 Battalion, Trevor John Edwards, deserted early in 1981 while on leave in England. In an interview given to the British press, Edwards said that South Africa's excuse for invading Angola repeatedly, allegedly to eliminate SWAPO bases, was to cover the true purpose, to make attacks on Angolan targets. According to Edwards, all of 32 Battalion's operations were of this type—attacks on Angolan villages, roads, bridges, and military camps. Angolan civilians, he said, were indiscriminately killed, their livestock slaughtered, their homes burned. Members of the Battalion wore unmarked, camouflaged uniforms, had no documents of any kind on their persons, and carried East European weapons. The British mercenary said: "I've had just about enough of it. I just thought people ought to know what we have been doing there."[27]

The Edwards story was confirmed by a captured black Angolan mercenary, Captain Joe Belmundo, who told an international panel of lawyers in Luanda of his two years in 32 Battalion. Belmundo said that the Battalion was under instructions to destroy schools, hospitals and houses, and to kill civilians and cattle.[28]

Operations of this kind, consisting of both commando-style raids and prolonged South African invasions and occupations to a depth of several hundred miles, occurred repeatedly in 1976, 1977, 1978, 1979, 1981 and 1984, the latter operation continuing well into 1985 with no complete withdrawal. Horrific massacres have marked these attacks: at Cassinga on May 4, 1978, a camp housing 4,000 to 5,000 refugees from Namibia was heavily bombed by South African planes which then dropped paratroopers who slaughtered the old men, women and children who made up the inhabitants of the camp; the bodies of nearly 1,000 women, children and elderly men were found in huge pits after the South African withdrawal, and over 1,000 others were wounded.

It was reported that in 1981 alone there were nearly 2,000 South African attacks, operations and incursions in Angola: 50 aerial strafings, 13 troop landings by helicopter, 4 para-drops, 26 ground force reconnaissances, 54 ground attacks, 7 ground bombardments, 9 mine-laying operations, and numerous sabotage raids, plus 1,617 aerial violations.[29]

Attacks by South African armed forces themselves have been one prong of the intervention against Angola; the other has been the ravaging band that calls itself UNITA, led by Jonas Savimbi. UNITA is armed, trained and equipped by South Africa, with the CIA playing a covert assisting role. It has the same objectives as the direct South African attacks—the terrorizing of the Angolan population, the destruction of Angola's infrastructure, and the general destabilization of that independent country. An avowed South African aim is to force the MPLA government to accept UNITA, its instrument, in a coalition to govern Angola.

On the other side of southern Africa, a nearly identical strategy and tactics have been carried out against Mozambique. Direct invasion by South African troops, except for home commando raids, has played less of a part in the assault on Mozambique, in which the main emphasis has been put on the arming, training and directing of a murderous bandit group, called the National Resistance Movement (MNR).

The MNR was originally organized by a Portuguese millionaire colonist and industrialist, Jorge Jardim, who virtually owned the port of Beira during Portuguese colonial rule. He fought FRELIMO with terrorist gangs and, after independence, moved to Rhodesia—which Ian Smith permitted him to use as a base for armed attacks against the new FRELIMO government. Jardim set up the MNR, using former members of the ruthless Portuguese security agency, PIDE, ex-counter-guerrillas of the notorious "Flechette" units, and one-time FRELIMO members ousted from the liberation movement for committing crimes. From Rhodesia, the MNR began its attacks into Mozambique in June 1976, but the FRELIMO government forces destroyed the main MNR bands by 1979. When Zimbabwe gained independence in 1980, the MNR remnants, along with the worst of Ian Smith's suppressive troops, fled to South Africa.[30]

Following the Southern Africa Development Coordination Conference in April 1980 and its adoption of a program to free its member countries from dependence on apartheid South Africa, the Botha government in Pretoria gave extensive assistance to the rebuilding of the MNR. By 1981 its raids into Mozambique were resumed.

The clandestine war against Mozambique's FRELIMO government has been more destructive than the attacks on Angola. Transportation (especially railways and bus lines), communication, power lines, industries, farms and their equipment, government buildings, bridges, and in particular the oil pipeline from Beira to Zimbabwe, have suffered massive destruction, gravely damaging Mozambique's economy. Destruction of crops has disrupted agriculture and contributed to famine conditions. The MNR makes no attempt to organize among the people, but has resorted to indiscriminate killing of peasants and workers or their literal enslavement as burden bearers. The destabilization of Mozambique became nearly complete.

In coordination with this subversion, South African military bases were built along the border with Mozambique in a threatening manner, and Mozambique was accused of permitting itself to serve as a base for the ANC and its Umkhonto we Sizwe to attack South Africa. Mozambique's Foreign Minister Joaquin Chissano firmly answered the charge: "The ANC is a liberation movement which is recognized by the Organization of African Unity and the United Nations. There is no reason why we should not have an ANC office in Mozambique. We fully support the struggle against apartheid. That is why it is only reasonable for us to have an official office of the ANC in Maputo."[31]

Said Mozambique's President Samora Machel in June 1982: "Prior to 1975, our main enemy was Portuguese colonialism. Between 1975 and 1980 imperialism attacked us through the agency of the racists of Rhodesia. Since 1980 it has been using the fascist apartheid regime as the main strike force against us."[32]

By the beginning of 1984 the increasingly harassed government of Mozambique felt compelled to negotiate an agreement with South Africa, for which South Africa had pressed, an agreement that amounted essentially to submission to South African terms. Known as the Nkomati Accord, after the place on the border between the two countries where it was signed on March 16, 1984 by President Machel and Prime Minister P.W. Botha, it obliged Mozambique to concede the expulsion of all but half a dozen ANC representatives from Mozambique while South Africa promised to cease giving aid to the MNR. In this agreement, Mozambique bent over backwards in order to obtain an arrangement that would end the terror and destruction it was enduring.

Mozambique lived up to its part of the Accord, South Africa did not. As events quickly proved, South Africa had sent huge stockpiles of arms and supplies into Mozambique for the MNR before the Accord was signed. Training and infiltrating of reinforcements for the MNR went on without letup. It was reported in October 1984 that 18,000 MNR recruits were in training camps in the Transvaal. Sabotage and killing within Mozambique were accelerated rather than reduced.[33]

South Africa, in fact, used this continued intervention to try to wring further concessions out of the FRELIMO government, demanding that MNR forces be allowed not only to return freely to Mozambique but to be given places in the country's army, civil service and even government ministries. As in the case of UNITA in Angola, the demand was in effect for FRELIMO to accept the MNR in a coalition. It was even proposed that South African troops be allowed into Mozambique as the "peacekeeping" force. Portugal came into the picture with a demand that Portuguese ex-colonists who had gone back home (the "retornadoes") be permitted to return to Mozambique to reclaim their properties.[34]

When it became plain that South Africa had engaged in deceit and trickery, Mozambican leaders denounced the betrayal of the Accord. President Machel said that "violence and terrorism are continuing to claim lives and spread destruction in Mozambique." If the situation had gone on deteriorating "it is because South Africa is not f. 'filling the agreement."

The president of FRELIMO, Marcelino dos Santos, was more specific: "Our enemy is called imperialism and in this part of the world its spearhead is South Africa. We are continuing to detect radio communications transmitting orders to the bandit gangs and reports from the bandits back to their leaders." South Africa, he charged, was endeavoring "to give political status to the bandits and criminals which it created in the first place."

Declared President Machel: "The real architects of the conspiracy against Mozambique are based in certain Western European capitals" and rely on "neighboring countries from whom they receive the necessary logistic support and who infiltrate terrorists, saboteurs and mercenaries."[35]

III THE U.S.-SOUTH AFRICAN ALLIANCE

It is too abundantly substantiated to be denied that the apartheid system has persisted so long because of an economic and military alliance between South Africa and the leading capitalist countries. All of the capitalist powers have been involved, both openly and covertly, in funding, arming, protecting and profiting from the racist South African white dictatorship. Above all, however, as the issue of apartheid has grown to become one of the central moral and social questions before the world in the contemporary period, the leading role in reinforcing and defending apartheid has been assumed by the United States.

This trend, occurring over the past 30 years, since the 1950s, has paralleled the global imperialist spread of the United States, the penetration of its transnational companies and bank capital into every part of the world where private capital still remains dominant. As the most powerful capitalist country, economically and militarily, the U.S. has been in a better position to pour investments and loans into areas of its choice, and to erect the military bases and logistical systems to protect them.

The assertion of U.S. dominance that this has embodied has collided directly with the upsurge of national liberation, of anti-colonialism, in all the once colonial regions of the earth. Virtually all of the wars and uses of military power engaged in by the U.S. since WWII—in Korea, Vietnam, Laos, Kampuchea, Guatamala, Cuba, Philippines, Grenada, Nicaragua, Lebanon and others—have been directed against liberation forces seeking full independence and self-determination. This has been the direction of U.S. foreign policy in general, and of the various agencies, like the CIA, which help to carry it out. The policy aims—to preserve the complete freedom of U.S. corporations to operate, to maintain unrestricted access to cheaply obtained raw materials, and to retain or develop anti-democratic structures of local rule amenable to such foreign control—have been most often disguised as "opposing Soviet imperialism" of "helping friends to fight the communist threat" or similar pretences. These claims are identical to those used by the South African racist rulers in suppression of anti-apartheid movements.

It has been in pursuit of its global imperialist policy that the U.S., leader of the capitalist power bloc in the world, emerged as the main partner of apartheid South Africa. Significantly, the development took place as South Africa—hemmed in with its anachronistic racist system as the forces of liberation swept across the rest of the African continent—also resorted to military force and other ruthless means to preserve its way of life. The U.S.-South African relationship that has resulted has become the core of the imperialist-apartheid alliance. It is also the cornerstone of U.S. policy in Africa in general.

The U.S. Penetration of Africa

U.S. links with South Africa need to be seen in the context of the overall U.S. policy in Africa. The Washington-Pretoria axis is directed by the African Affairs section of the State Department, which oversees Africa as a whole.

Historically, the U.S. penetration of Africa came at a relatively late date. In the main, this was due to the nearly complete division of the continent in the 19th century among the European colonial powers, on which the seal was set by the Berlin Conference of 1885. Britain, France, Belgium, Spain and Germany had vast colonial shares of African territory, covering the continent from the Mediterranean to the Cape of Good Hope. This colonial rule involved control of investment policies, trade and local resources, freezing out the interests of other powers, including the U.S., which had not yet reached the industrial and financial point of challenging, or needing to challenge, the other powers in Africa.

In the latter 1950s the winds of change began to blow, bringing independence to 6 African countries in that decade, 32 in the 1960s (17 in 1960 alone), 8 in the 1970s. Today there are 50 independent countries in the Organization of African Unity. Self-government and management of national affairs by Africans themselves essentially meant a weakening of the position of the former colonial powers, even in those countries where neocolonialism occurred. Into this breach moved U.S. interests.

What happened can be read in the investment tables. Total U.S. investments in Africa in 1957 were $664 million, and of these $301 million were in South Africa.[1]

In the following seven years, by 1964, the African total had almost tripled, to $1,701 million and in the succeeding seven years, by 1971, they had more than doubled again, to $3,833 million. By 1972 U.S. direct investments by volume in the whole of Africa had exceeded those that had been built up for more than a century by both Britain and France.[2]

The primary purpose of the U.S. attention to Africa has been obtaining control over the continent's natural resources. These are enormous. It is estimated that over 50% of the raw material needs of the capitalist powers is supplied by Africa, which is believed to have 90% of the world's deposits of diamonds (575 million carets), platinum and palladium (12,700 tons), and chrome ore (1.6 million tons); 25% of the world's bauxite (4 billion tons), 15% of copper ore (44 million tons), 14% of natural gas (5,300 billion cubic meters), 13% of iron ore (30 billion tons), 12% of oil (9.2 billion tons), and large amounts of lead, zinc, tin, columbite, lithium, beryllium, graphite and other minerals. The greatest amount of most of these is in South Africa.[3]

By the early 1980s transnational corporations (TNCs) had put over $11 billion directly into their African operations, outside of South Africa. In a general imperialist pattern that includes the activity of U.S. capital, nearly 60% of all foreign investment in Africa has gone into the exploiting of natural resources. Another 34% has been for creating new markets for the finished goods of the western powers, and scarcely 6% has been for manufacturing or other industrial processes. Thus after three decades of investment and lending in newly independent Africa by the U.S. and other capitalist powers, Africa, with 10% of the world's population, accounts for less than 1% of the world's industrial output.[4]

The profits extracted from this pattern of investment have exceeded those from any other region of the world. In the years 1970-1978, when $4.3 billion of TNC capital went to Africa, their profit outflow was $15.92 billion. U.S. earnings from Africa that were a mere $33 million in 1960 (from areas outside South Africa), had jumped to $684 million by 1971, and reached an annual rate of $1 billion in 1975. For U.S. companies this represented a rate of profit 50% higher than in other developing countries and 120% higher than in developed countries.[5]

A Conference of Communist and Workers Parties of Tropical and Southern Africa, held in the summer of 1978, declared: "International imperialism and its principal weapon—the TNCs—are the main enemy of the African peoples today more than ever before. Africa's economic, social and technological backwardness is the aftermath of the overthrown colonial domination and the present imperialist policies of plunder and exploitation of African peoples." By the 1970s, although the book value of TNC investments continued to rise, the amount of new capital from outside the continent was dwindling. This was because investment was being financed from profits and from drawing on local African savings or capital sources. U.S. corporations were taking 40% of their investment needs from local sources. This was a process that further drained African capacities for development.

An even greater drain developed from another phase of foreign profit-taking to which increasing emphasis was given by imperialist powers from the 1960s onward, that of loan capital. Developing countries in general were persuaded to rely heavily on foreign loans, both for development programs and for offsetting deficits created by the unequal trade terms embodied in the relationship with western countries—between the unstable, often steeply dropping prices of their raw material exports and the constantly escalating prices of finished goods imports. For Africa, the loan policy was projected by Robert McNamara, former Ford Motor Company executive and ex-U.S. Defense Secretary, when he assumed the presidency of the World Bank. In his first public speech in that capacity on September 30, 1968, he said that the greatest expansion of the World Bank's activity should occur in Africa: he proposed to triple the Bank's lending to African countries. In the World Bank the dominant interest and major fund contribution is by the U.S., and the Bank's policies have usually reflected U.S. foreign policy aims.

Between 1967 and 1978 U.S. loans, credits and subsidies to African countries (not counting South Africa) totalled $6,846 million (of which $829 million was for military aid).[6] This did not include funds channeled through international finance agencies. The consequence was that foreign debts of independent African countries that were $7 billion overall in 1965 had jumped to $70 billion by 1979, and had soared to $150 billion by 1985. Nearly 50% of these debts were owed in one way or another to U.S. banks and lending agencies.

For imperialist interests, the advantages of loan capital lay in the lever they provided for exerting control over developing countries and their economies. Besides interest and repayment terms, concessions and conditions could be demanded concerning the way loans should be used, the areas and directions of development, and the nature of both domestic and foreign policy. Discouragement of industrialization, of a public sector, and of raised living standards that affect TNC wage bills are all part of the lending terms, howsoever subtly presented. Loans are also calculated to be a corrupting influence on governments and on recipients of loan funds.

U.S. penetration encountered sharp rivalry from the European powers; Britain through the Commonwealth and France through its special ties with its former colonies. Western Europe in general through the multination trade and aid agreement known as the Lome Convention, sought to fend off the U.S. drive and to tie most African countries to their old colonial rulers. However, a number of "dollar allies" appeared in Africa: Liberia, Kenya, Morocco, Sudan, Tunisia, Somalia, Zaire, Egypt, and Ivory Coast.

Effects of the U.S.-led investment and loan policies were clearly evident in the case of Kenya, which was selected after its independence from Britain in 1964 as one of the main U.S. bases of operation in Africa. Kenya was persuaded to shift its mainstay of agriculture from food production to production for export, especially coffee, tea and sisal. At first the gross national product went up by 6% a year between 1964 and 1977, until the crisis-prone conditions of western markets hit Kenya's exports. In the 1978 collapse, Kenya's receipts from coffee fell 66% and from tea 75%. Kenya now imports over half its food needs, at high prices. Over 180 TNCs operate in Kenya, but their investments have gone, along with loan capital, not into industry or balanced forms of development, but into quick and easy profit areas like tourism, insurance and wholesale trade. A Kenyan journalist said in 1982: "We have been caught in a trap. After independence we were tempted with illusory wealth and well-being, and we fell for the bait, we were caught. I doubt very much that we shall ever get out of this capitalist trap." A Kenyan MP, J. M. Kasuiki (who was later murdered for his nationalist stand), said in 1983 that U.S. and British neocolonialism had created "ten millionaires and ten million beggars." In August 1982 the first reaction came in a rebellious upheaval involving air force officers, students and the urban poor in Nairobi and other centers.[7]

The strategic aim of the U.S. (and of Britain and France in particular among other powers) was the creation of neocolonial client states in Africa. Their main fear has been the growth of a nationalist independence by African countries, of trends toward social emancipation among their peoples, and of a socialist orientation. This has been reflected in a generally anti-imperialist stance by the Organization of African Unity. In the 1970s measures to restrict the operations of TNCs began to be adopted in Nigeria, Ghana, Gabon, Togo and elsewhere, while state control of oil and mineral ores has been undertaken in Algeria, Nigeria, Libya, Zambia, Sierra Leone, Tanzania, and others.

Most worrying of all for U.S. interests has been the adoption by more than 10 African countries of a socialist orientation, including Ethiopia, Angola, Mozambique, Peoples Republic of the Congo, Benin, Tanzania, Algeria, Guinea. The majority of African countries, furthermore, have formed diplomatic, trade and cultural relations with the Soviet Union, the German Democratic Republic and other socialist countries. In the view of U.S. imperialist interests and governments such tendencies have converted Africa into an arena of the global ideological conflict, of the struggle between the two systems of capitalism and socialism, of the cold war.

In the alignments seen from this outlook, South Africa is an important, if not the most important, element in an alliance against "communism" and all socialist-oriented and anti-imperialist trends in the rest of Africa.

Along with economic penetration, the U.S. has carried on major programs for tying African countries to the west, particularly to the U.S., and to the free enterprise system. In these programs the concentration has been chiefly on influencing and indoctrinating the educated African elite, civil servants, teachers, technicians, trade union leaders, and public figures.

From 1961 the Ford Foundation appropriated at least $10 million a year for various "African programs," aimed especially at executive personnel in the business and state sectors. In some cases the Ford Foundation has been in competition with British and French program agencies. For example, its greater financial resources enabled Ford to win out over the British Commonwealth Fund in the mid-1960s in rivalry to build the Ibadan Agricultural Institute in Nigeria. The Ford Foundation has financed the holding of a series of conferences in African cities broadly termed "Afro-American Dialogue" which have brought together scientists, intellectuals, congressmen, businessmen, government officials, journalists and others, and African presidents, prime ministers, public leaders, scientists, intellectuals. Begun in 1968, the conferences have ostensibly been organized by the Afro-American Institute in New York, backed by the State Department, but the preparation has actually been made by the CIA and other special agencies to carry out U.S. policy aims in Africa. The 13th conference, held in Harare, Zimbabwe in July 1983, had on its agenda, for example, the role of private investment in national development, the importance of U.S. economic aid, and U.S. policy in Southern Africa (especially a defense of the "linkage" of Cuban troop removal from Angola with the granting of independence by South Africa to Namibia).[8]

A training program to educate Africans to a U.S. orientation has been carried out by the U.S. Agency for International Development to the tune of $200 million a year. A phase of this has been the sending of thousands of Peace Corps Volunteers to Africa, with the training of teachers as one of their main tasks. In 1970-1971 it was estimated that about ten million African children were being taught by teachers trained by Peace Corps workers. The AID has promoted as well the African Scholarship Program of American Universities (ASPAU) which has drawn African students to the U.S. In the academic year 1954-1955, before the major U.S. investment drive occurred, there were but 1,234 African students in the U.S., or 3.6% of the total of foreign students. By 1964-1965 the number had risen to 6,865 (8%) and in 1969-1970 it had jumped to 15,000 (18%). The aim in this field has been to shape the outlook of civil servants, politicians, technicians, teachers and media workers, in particular, in accordance with U.S. anti-communist views.[9]

For the population in general, the U.S. Information Agency has been the vehicle of indoctrination, setting up libraries of carefully selected volumes, distributing masses of free literature in various languages, holding seminars and lecture series. By 1979 there were over 70 U.S. information centers in Africa, and the U.S. was estimated to be spending $32 million a year on propaganda in Africa.

U.S. radio and television programs have filled the African air waves. The central Voice of America transmitting station has been in Liberia, beaming not only into Africa but the Middle East as well. In 1981 a new powerful VOA transmitter was set up in Botswana for concentration on southern Africa. Considering that the British BBC Overseas Service and the French broadcasting system also give major attention to Africa, the African listener can hardly escape the bombardment of pro-western propaganda.

Leaving no avenue of influence untrodden, the U.S. penetration has included an expansion of religious missionary work. In 1945 there were but 3,000 U.S. religious workers in Africa. By 1965 there were 10,000. Both Catholic and Protestant U.S. denominations issue a plethora of journals, have their own schools, and operate radio stations.

In 1965 the U.S. launched another sector of its African offensive, a drive to gain control of the developing African labor movement. This was carried out through the African-American Labor Center (AALC), set up in that year by the AFL-CIO. As in the case of all of the international labor activities of the AFL-CIO in the post-World War II decades, the African sector was under the direction of the CIA. It was headed by Irving Brown, who gained notoriety for being in the pay of the CIA, and of AID. The AALC by the early 1980s had links with trade unions in every African country but Angola, Mozambique and Ethiopia. Although Nigeria had ordered AALC representatives out of the country for detrimental interference (as it had also done in the case of the Peace Corps), Nigerian labor leaders still continued to be invited on all expenses paid visits to the U.S. through AALC channels. An AALC specialty has been the organizing of seminars for African trade union members around such themes as the need for stable and harmonious industrial relations, especially in foreign-owned or managed plants and mines. The selection and nurturing of anti-communist and pro-western trade union leaders is one of the main aims of the AALC.

All of these various activities have been tied in with the enormous expansion of CIA operations in Africa. In 1984 it was reported that there were 40 CIA stations and 3,500 CIA agents on the continent. The CIA was detected in plots against the governments of Ghana, Zambia, Benin, Mozambique, Nigeria and Seychelles, and its agents were involved in attempts to split trade unions in 35 countries.[10]

In operating its varied economic and ideological levers in Africa, U.S. imperialism has had a number of key objectives: to project a private enterprise viewpoint and the importance of the private sector as against reliance on the public sector in many of the countries; to emphasize western capitalist values while denigrating socialist principles and practice in both advanced socialist and developing countries; to forge a pro-western group of African countries in order to disrupt the solidarity of the Organization of African Unity and to prevent the OAU from taking an effective anti-imperialist stand; and, especially, to prevent the growth and consolidation of national liberation movements with a socialist orientation.

Numerous attempts were made, during virtually every summit meeting of the OAU, to disrupt African unity on liberation issues. In January 1976 when the OAU, meeting in Addis Ababa, was deliberating the recognition of the MPLA government of the People's Republic of Angola, U.S. Assistant Secretary of State W. Shauffele toured Zaire, Ivory Coast, Senegal, Cameroon and Gabon in an undisguised campaign to persuade them to withhold support for recognition. He did not succeed. In August 1982 the OAU summit scheduled to be held in Tripoli, Libya was actually wrecked by U.S. intervention: the legitimate government of Prime Minister Goukouni in Chad was overthrown by the invasion from Sudan by the rival Hussein Habre group that was armed and financed by the CIA, and Libya's support of Goukouni was made the means of persuading enough conservative members of the OAU not to go to Tripoli, preventing a quorum for a meeting. Subsequently backing for Morocco to oppose OAU recognition of the Polisario liberation movement against Moroccan occupation of the Western Sahara and Polisario's Sahrawi Arab Democratic Republic caused disruption of the 1983 OAU summit.

Frustrations of U.S. Policy in Africa

Despite, or perhaps because of, its intensive penetration effort in Africa, the U.S. failed in its main aims of holding back the liberation process and of pressing African countries along a path of capitalist development in partnership with the west. Major miscalculations were made by U.S. policymakers.

As an emphasis on shaping client states in north and sub-Saharan Africa prevailed in the 1950s, 1960s and early 1970s, the U.S. perspective was to maintain full western control of southern Africa in alliance with the hard core state of South Africa. With that rich region as a secure base, pressures could be kept up on the rest of Africa.

In 1969, during the Nixon administration, special adviser Henry Kissinger and the National Security Council created a special interdepartmental group for African affairs and commissioned it to prepare a report on perspectives particularly in southern Africa where liberation struggles were occurring in the Portuguese colonies and in Rhodesia [see p. 32].

In pursuit of the NSSM39 recommendations, greater U.S. military aid was given to Portugal for its colonial wars, the Nixon administration lifted the U.N. embargo on its importation of Rhodesian chrome ore (although the U.S. had large stockpiles of the ore), and U.N. Security Council resolutions for sanctions on South Africa were systematically vetoed.

A shock was caused among U.S. policymakers when Angola, Mozambique and Guinea Bissau won liberation in 1974 and when the Patriotic Front forces compelled the capitulation of both Ian Smith and British colonial rule in Rhodesia in 1979-1980. The shock for U.S. African policy became more profound with the Ethiopian revolution of 1974. Even capitalist-oriented Nigeria proved to be prickly in its independence, while the fragility of Kenya as an ally was driven home by the revolt of August 1982.

The U.S. policy of creating client states in Africa and of shaping "a union of white and black states" under U.S. influence that would serve to safeguard the interests of U.S. corporations had essentially failed.

U.S. limitations at the time in trying to cope with the collapse of the racist "Tar Baby" expectations were driven home in Angola in 1975-1976. Here CIA aid to the UNITA-FNLA counterrevolutionary elements and support for South Africa in its invasion of Angola to overthrow the MPLA government were frustrated by the arrival, at the Angolan government's request, of effective Cuban fraternal military aid. Coming at a time of great U.S. popular opposition to the Vietnam war and of humiliating defeat for U.S. imperialism at the hands of the Vietnamese people, an involvement in Angola could not be sustained. Anti-intervention sentiment caused the adoption in the U.S. Congress of the Clark Amendment, forbidding CIA or other military assistance to UNITA or similar bands in Angola.

For a time under the Carter administration, the U.S. attempted to alter the image of its African policy and to distance itself publicly from colonial and racist regimes. This was under the influence of an international planning institution set up chiefly by the Rockefeller interests, called the "Trilateral Commission." A sizeable body of transnational corporation and political leaders of the U.S., Western Europe and Japan, it sought to project policies that would enable secure and stable environments in various regions of the world, in particular in what was called the "third world" of developing countries. Although the "Trilateralists" were committed to blocking socialist influences and trends, they talked of gradual social change, of permitting limited social justice in order to forestall more radical changes that would seriously affect their interests.

President Carter himself was a member of the Trilateral Commission. Speaking in Nigeria in April 1978—during the first-ever U.S. Presidential visit to Africa—he said that U.S. policy in Africa was a commitment to "majority rule and individual human rights . . . to economic growth and to human development . . . a commitment to an Africa that is at peace, free from colonialism, free from racism, free from military interference from outside nations, and free from the inevitable conflicts that can come when the integrity of national boundaries is not respected." He added that "in the name of justice we also believe that South African society should and can be transformed progressively and peacefully."

The early years of the Carter administration were a period of relatively soft rather than hard-line foreign policy; the climate of detente still prevailed in international relations and reflected Trilateralist positions. In Africa, the policy was one of emphasis on peaceful processes of change or reform, urging, for example, an "orderly nonviolent transfer of power in Rhodesia." The position in regard to

South Africa was stated by Carter's Assistant Secretary of State for African Affairs, Richard Moose, in evidence given to the House of Representatives' African subcommittee; on May 1, 1980. He said:

> Today, more than at any other point in its history, the South African government should have the confidence to embark fully on the process of reform. Other countries, including the United States, are ready to support such an effort made in good faith, as are many South Africans . . . . Such a reform process should be comprehensive, eventually including an end to racial discrimination, equal social services for all South Africans, freedom for blacks to participate in all sectors of the economy, and essential steps towards reforms to bring all South Africans into full political participation.

Stressing that the U.S. wanted this to be achieved through "peaceful change," Moose said: "It is crucial that we demonstrate to the South African black majority they have Western support for their aspirations for equal rights and full political participation in the life of their country."

The Carter administration did not actively encourage investment in or trade with South Africa, and halted the sale of arms and military equipment in conformity with the 1977 U.N. arms embargo. It was the period when the Sullivan Code, of supposed equal treatment for black workers, was devised for U.S. companies in South Africa. It was the time when the Polaroid Corporation withdrew from South Africa (at the end of 1977) due to anti-apartheid pressure from its employees in the U.S. In 1978 the U.S. went through the motions of working for the implementation of U.N. Resolution 435 on the independence of Namibia, taking the initiative of setting up a western Contact Group allegedly to press South Africa to abide by the Resolution.

This line of policy was a temporary stance. In part it was utilized to create a "human rights" image for the U.S. while a propaganda assault on the Soviet Union for supposed "human rights" issues was mounted. The early Carter years proved to be but an interlude while U.S. imperialist interests prepared a counterattack against the liberation movements and social emancipation trends in the developing countries. Supporting an intensive campaign against detente on grounds that it was opening the way for "Soviet imperialism" in the "third world" and was putting the U.S. globally on the defensive, the most aggressive sectors of the U.S. military-industrial complex became dominant in policy-making circles. In the latter Carter years, the corresponding policy shifts were already taking place.

Elected in 1976 on peace pledges to fit the popular U.S. mood aroused by hopes over the nuclear arms limitation agreements with the Soviet Union (SALT I and SALT II), and by desires for "No more

Vietnams!", the Carter administration swung within two years to the greatest increases in arms spending up to that time in U.S. history (jumping from $89.4 billion in 1976 to a $175 billion arms bill in the last Carter budget for 1981). SALT II approval was blocked in the Carter congress, bigger arms programs were pressed upon Western European countries, NATO approval was gained for stationing U.S. Tomahawk cruise and Pershing II missiles in Western Europe, a new Pacific Alliance stretching from Japan to Australia was projected, a U.S. Indian Ocean military presence anchored on a massive Diego Garcia Island base was established, and a 110,000-strong Rapid Deployment Force to protect U.S. "national interests" in Africa and the Middle East was conceived of and given maximum emphasis.

Policy toward South Africa altered as well. In September 1979 South Africa exploded a tactical nuclear weapon from a naval vessel on which a sanctions-breaking U.S. howitzer had been installed, and U.S. intelligence agencies participated in a coverup, pretending that the detected flash could have been "natural phenomena." In November 1979 a U.S. House Armed Services Committee visited South African military bases, including the naval base at Simonstown. The chairman of the Committee, Melvin Price, said that South Africa is vital to U.S strategic interests, "otherwise we wouldn't be here." In December 1979 a special State Department mission was dispatched to Kenya and Somalia to explore the obtaining of bases for the U.S. Rapid Deployment Force.

For Africa, the aggressive U.S. policy steps meant the essential abandonment of less direct efforts pursued since the 1950s to make use of client states and neocolonial arrangements to gain U.S. objectives. The establishment of a direct U.S. military presence on the African continent was deemed necessary to check the spread of national liberation, anti-imperialism and social emancipation. For Rapid Deployment Force use, military bases were acquired over an arc from Northwest to Northeast Africa: in Morocco five U.S. bases were made operational, accompanied by a trebling of U.S. military aid from $30 million to $100 million between 1980 and 1982. Egypt, receiving combined military and economic aid of $3.5 billion, provided RDF bases in Sinai. Two bases were obtained in client-state Sudan, another in Somalia (which was armed and encouraged to use the arms against socialist-oriented Ethiopia). In Kenya three important naval and air bases were acquired. East Africa could also be further targetted from the Diego Garcia base in the Indian Ocean. Besides these RDF steps, military aid went to Liberia on the African west coast to facilitate a U.S. military outpost and the expansion of the already huge Voice of America transmitting station.

As forms and direct means of U.S. intervention were installed in northern areas of Africa, the role of South Africa as an imperialist ally and strike force was given increased attention in U.S. policy, serving in effect as the southern arm of the pincers being applied upon independent Africa. This became a key part of the global strategy of the Reagan administration that took office in January 1981.

The U.S. Investment Stake in Apartheid

As in the case of the African continent as a whole, U.S. investment and trade began to grow in South Africa at a more rapid rate after the loosening of ties from 1948 onward with the long-standing colonial power, Britain. U.S. interest in South Africa, however, developed earlier than in most other African countries and was prompted not by opportunities such as those in the independent Black states but by the U.S. desire to take advantage of the ruthless exploitation of Black workers kept in abysmal colonial conditions by apartheid.

Prior to 1948, major U.S. corporations already had a presence in South Africa. Morgan, Guggenheim and others had acquired holdings in mining early in the century. More serious attention was paid to South Africa during World War II. In part this came from a quest for minerals to feed the enormously enlarged U.S. war industries, but not absent in the process was the seizure of an opportunity to penetrate a mainly British preserve while Britain was occupied in a back-to-the-wall struggle for survival against Nazi Germany. The O'okiep Copper Co. Ltd., for example, largest of its kind in South Africa at the time, with 57% of its shares owned by the U.S. Newmont Mining, opened its Namaqua mines in 1940. Other large U.S. mining investments occurred subsequently in chrome, vanadium and other mineral ores. These accounted for most of the increase in South African exports to the U.S. from 1938 to 1954, from $2 million to $58 million. In the same period U.S. exports to South Africa went up nearly five times, from less than $50 million to $233 million.

Despite this foothold in South African investment and trade, U.S. interests did not seriously increase their stake until the racist regime had put its police-state machinery of apartheid laws into place. In 1957 Charles W. Engelhard, Jr. of Newark, New Jersey, chairman of one of the largest mineral and ore companies in the world, the Minerals and Chemicals Corp. (assets in 1967 of $471 million), joined with the South African Anglo-American Corp. of Harry Oppenheimer in a coup to take over Central Mining, one of the big South African holding companies.

In 1958, the American-South African Investment Corp. was set up by U.S. interests, with Engelhard as its chairman and with M. D. Banghart, vice-president of Newmont Mining, as a director. Within a few years it had invested $40 million in a wide range of industries. Mining shareholdings alone of this corporation were located in the East Driefontein, Kloof, Southvaal Holdings, President Steyn and Helena gold fields, the Transvaal Consolidated Land platinum-chrome-coal conglomerate, Palabora copper, and De Beers diamonds.

In the same year of 1958, a branch of the First National City Bank of New York was opened in South Africa, and in the following year, 1959, the Chase Manhattan Bank began operations there. Chase Manhattan undertook in 1965 to merge its branch with the British Standard Bank, second largest in South Africa, which has in-numerable branches all over the country. The extent of this link, which has tended to conceal the U.S. bank's lending activity, may be seen in the jump of Standard Bank's assets between 1964 and 1968 by 40%, from $1 billion to $1.4 billion.

Total U.S. direct investments in South Africa, which had stood at $288 million in 1956, had just begun to climb at a quickened pace when the Sharpeville massacre took place on March 20, 1960. This brutal episode, in which 69 Blacks were killed during a peaceful demonstration against the pass laws, was followed by the arrest of 22,000 people and the banning of anti-apartheid organizations. A wave of international revulsion occurred, mingled with fears among foreign investors about political instability in South Africa. An exodus of capital began, reaching as much as $222 million in the months after March 1960.

At this point it was the U.S. banks that stepped in and acted to reverse the tide of withdrawal. The First National City Bank took the initial aid step with a $5 million loan. At a plea from Harry Oppenheimer, a $30 million loan was extended to Anglo-American Corp. by a group of U.S. banks. Then a $40 million revolving loan was made available to the South African government by a consortium of 10 U.S. banks: Bank of America, Chase Manhattan, First National City Bank, Manufacturers Hanover Trust, Morgan Guaranty Trust, Chemical Bank of New York, Bankers Trust, Irving Trust, Continental Illinois Bank, and First National of Chicago. Together with this was the maintenance of a flow of direct U.S. investments, averaging over $30 million a year from 1960 to 1966. It could be claimed, literally, that U.S. capital saved the apartheid system at a crucial point in its history.[11]

In this critical period, U.S. direct investments doubled, rising to $692 million by 1968. Other western powers—Britain, West Germany,

France—followed suit, but the U.S. rate of investment increase was five times faster than that of any of the others. Furthermore, during this important decade the nature of U.S. investments altered significantly. A shift occurred from the earlier concentration on mining toward manufacturing, the growth sector in the South African economy. Whereas manufacturing represented but 37% of U.S. investments in 1963 or $158 million, this had gone up to 48% in 1968 or $332 million. This rapid industrialization occurred only in South Africa, with western assistance, and helped to make South Africa economically strong—a major trading country and expansionist force in Africa. It helped to make the apartheid state self-sufficient in a widening range of both consumer and capital goods industries, able to a great extent to withstand sanctions, embargoes and boycotts.

During this time a campaign was carried on in U.S. business and financial circles to encourage investment in South Africa. M. D. Banghart (Newmont v.p.) publicly urged U.S. companies to go to South Africa, where an average profit of 27% could be realized. John W. Snyder, former U.S. Secretary of the Treasury, issued this statement in 1960: "South Africa is worthy of our closest association in building up a strong world economy, and also in the protection of the world against the encroachment of Communism."

The latter claim was to become one of the principal propaganda justifications for relations with South Africa and the main reason given by the apartheid regime for suppressing resistance internally and for committing aggression against its neighbors. It was also voiced by Snyder in his capacity as a lobbyist for the South Africa Foundation. Set up in 1960 just after the Sharpeville massacre and its repercussions, this organization of South African businessmen, with Harry Oppenheimer in a leading role, was designed to promote South Africa's "image" so as to offset and smother anti-apartheid response abroad. In the U.S., one of its main points of concentration, a number of leading U.S. businessmen, including Charles Engelhard, Charles B. Randall of Inland Steel, Snyder and others, lent their support to it.

Between 1968 and 1975, when the apartheid system reached its fullest development and the anti-apartheid forces were at an ebb, direct investments by U.S. companies attained their most intensive flow, increasing by more than three times to an estimated $2,397 million. A U.S. House Subcommittee estimated in 1971 that South Africa was the last place in the world where a company could recoup 100% of what it invested "in no time." The majority of U.S. firms in South Africa, the subcommittee found, paid African workers below the official Poverty Datum Line.[12]

In 1976 the revolt in Black townships, particularly in Soweto, checked the growth of foreign investment temporarily and threatened to provoke another exodus of capital as had occurred after Sharpeville. This threat receded as the regime's armed forces brought their firepower to bear against the unarmed demonstrating Black and Colored peoples. However, in 1977 the United Nations arms embargo against South Africa was adopted, also having its effect on the flow of long-term foreign capital. This period in the mid-1970s was further affected by the short-lived shift in U.S. foreign policy during the early years of the Carter administration, a shift away from open confrontational policies globally and toward a more subtle effort to blunt national liberation struggles by advocating "peaceful evolutionary change to majority rule," "human rights," and the "reform" of apartheid. A noticeable discouragement of trade and investment in South Africa occurred.

By the latter 1970s the most aggressive sectors of U.S. imperialism were resuming control, a trend that became fully dominant with the election of the Reagan administration in 1980. The Reaganites openly associated themselves with the apartheid regime to a degree not previously seen in U.S. policy. U.S. investment, loans and trade rose at a rapid rate.

In November 1984 the president of the South African Federated Chamber of Industries, Ron Ironside, reported that the total of U.S. private assets in South Africa had reached 26.5 billion rands (or $14.4 billion at the current exchange rate) and that U.S.-owned shares accounted for 60% of all foreign holdings on the Johannesburg Stock Exchange. Other surveys put the U.S. stake at over 28 billion rands or about $15.5 billion, asserting that "over 350" U.S. companies were involved in direct investment with subsidiaries (other estimates placing the total at as many as 500 companies), while 6,000 U.S. firms were participating in U.S.-South African trade. The U.S. holdings represented 20% of all foreign investment in apartheid, the major British stake making up 40%.[13]

The U.N. Special Committee Against Apartheid published a study in May 1981 that charged that 65 international corporations based in 11 countries had "contributed significantly to the maintenance of apartheid in South Africa." Of these, 22 were U.S. corporations: Amax, Burroughs Corporation, Caltex, Citicorp, Control Data, Exxon Corporation, Firestone, Fluor, Ford Motors, Foxboro, General Electric, General Tire, Honeywell Inc., IBM, Mobil, National Cash Register, Newmont Mining Corporation, Phelps-Dodge, Sperry Corporation, Union Carbide and U.S. Steel.[14]

Aid to apartheid by these companies had to do with their presence in key areas of the economy. As for size of investment, 75% of the U.S. total was accounted for by 13 big U.S. transnational corporations: General Motors, Ford, Texaco, Standard Oil of California, Mobil, General Electric, ITT, Chrysler, Firestone, Goodyear, Minnesota Mining and Manufacturing, and IBM . Bank loans came chiefly from: Citibank, Chase Manhattan, Morgan Guaranty Trust, First National City Bank of Boston, First National Bank of Chicago, and Bank of America.[15] Mining companies like Newmont and Engelhard Minerals and Chemicals had important investments, but the U.S. role in South African mining has been mainly through shareholdings in the big South African mining companies.

Direct investment, in any case, does not reflect the extent of U.S. involvement in the apartheid economy. Engelhard Minerals and Chemicals Corp. in the early 1980s owned 11% of the common stock and 7% of the preferred of the huge Anglo-American Corporation, which owns or controls about 1600 companies in South Africa. The assets of Anglo-American were the equivalent of one-fourth of the entire South African gross national product in the mid-1970s, and in the ever-increasing monopoly process in South Africa is one of the three big corporations expected to control virtually the whole economy by 1990.[16] Other U.S. transnationals tied in with Anglo-American are U.S. Steel, American Metals Climax, the Guggenheim interests' American Smelting and Refining Co., Foote Mineral Co., Roan Selection Trust, Citibank and Morgan Guaranty Trust.

Anglo-American, in turn, in part through its interlocking links with U.S. corporations, has become the biggest foreign investor in the U.S. For example, Anglo-American owns 29% of Engelhard Industrial Materials, 50% of Inspiration Consolidated Copper, and 51% of Terra Chemicals International (fertilizers), besides outright ownership of Amcon Group (mining, steel and scrap metal), Arc America Corp. (construction materials), Skytop Brewster Rig (oil rig manufacturing), King Oil Tools (oilfield equipment), and Mechanical Seal and Service (oilfield equipment). Particularly through its major stake in Engelhard Minerals and Chemicals, Anglo-American in 1980 controlled $19.2 million in sales in the U.S. In 1981 the South African corporation embarked on a stepped-up international expansion through its Boart International Group (100% owned by a subsidiary, Anglo-American Industrial Corp.) which manufactures tools and general equipment for exploring and exploiting natural resources. Boart set up facilities in Minneapolis and Detroit, besides Toronto and North Bay in Canada (as well as Mexico City, Sao Paulo, Niederthellen in West Germany, and Adelaide in Australia).[17]

These extensive operations are still only a portion of the Anglo-American move into the U.S. economy. In 1982 it was reported that Anglo-American had transferred assets worth over $2 billion to a Bermuda-based holding company, Minorco. Between 1980 and 1982, hundreds of millions of dollars had been invested through Minorco in U.S. and Canadian coal, uranium, gold, copper and other minerals, making Minorco one of the biggest foreign investors in the U.S. in those years. In addition to the Minorco activities, "a total of 144 separate investments in North America by the Anglo-American group have been identified." Of these, 106 were in the U.S., spread over 37 states, including chemicals, energy, agriculture, mineral processing, investment banking, marketing, and various trading and holding companies.

Minorco is the largest single shareholder (27.2%, worth $450 million) in Phibro, a huge New York commodity trading company that had worldwide sales of $25 billion in 1981. Phibro happens to be a spinoff from the former Engelhard Minerals and Chemicals Corp. which changed its name to simply Engelhard Corp. in the early 1980s. Minorco is also the largest shareholder in Engelhard (27.5% of the shares). The president of Minorco, H. Ronald Fraser, is on the Phibro board of directors. (Other Minorco board members are: Harry Oppenheimer as chairman, Walter B. Wriston who is chairman of Citicorp, Felix G. Rohatyn the head of the investment banking firm of Lazard Brothers, Robert Clare of the Shearman and Sterling law firm that represents Citicorp, and Cedric Ritchie, chairman of the Bank of Nova Scotia.)[18]

The connection with Phibro is very significant for South Africa because Phibro is the largest trader in the world in oil on the spot market: South Africa gets most of its oil through spot market trading.

A report by the American Committee on Africa said in 1982: "Anglo-American has placed itself in the position to become an important broker between the U.S. and South Africa . . . . Anglo's investments significantly strengthen U.S. economic and political relations with South Africa and its undemocratic system."[19] Anglo-American has been thought to be moving its holdings abroad in a long-range preparation for the collapse of apartheid in South Africa, but as long as it remains as a bulwark of the South African economy, it is a vehicle for U.S. companies to extract profits from the apartheid system, while its large presence in the U.S. reinforces those interests opposed to any break with the apartheid regime.

Although the greater amount of the U.S. stake in South Africa is indirect, in the form of shareholding and loans, U.S. direct investments are highly important for their location in key sectors of the economy. One of these sectors is energy, oil and nuclear.

A U.S. oil company, Standard Vacuum, built the first oil refinery in South Africa, near Durban, in 1954. Caltex, in 1967, erected a $24 million refinery in the Western Cape, the nucleus of a large petrochemical complex. Caltex and Mobil Oil, together, provided South Africa with 44% of its oil in the 1970s, when the anti-apartheid movement internationally was demanding an oil embargo on the apartheid state. A consortium of Caltex and Mobil with British Petroleum and Shell had 73% of oil distribution within South Africa in the same period. After the 1978 imposition by the Arab countries of their own oil embargo, U.S. oil companies, particularly Esso, obtained extensive offshore exploration concessions in the Western Cape to assist in the creation of a self-sustaining South African oil supply.

For the apartheid state, a pressing need has been the development of a substitute source of oil to enable self-sufficiency in case of effective international embargoes. Close U.S.-South African cooperation has existed in a crash program for extracting oil from coal. It began in the 1960s, conducted by the state corporation SASOL. Launching of SASOL was financed by a loan from the U.S. Export-Import Bank. The contract for building a SASOL 3 plant at Secunda in East Transvaal was given to the U.S. Fluor Co.—a $30 million project. Fluor completed the plant on schedule in 1982 and it had an initial production of 8,000 barrels of fuel a day.[20] The tie-up between U.S. and South African interests in the SASOL program was carried further in 1980 when the U.S. Department of Energy (under the Carter administration) made a deal with SASOL to acquire the know-how concerning the design work of synthetic oil extraction; the U.S. paid SASOL 46 million rands for the technology.[21] By mid-1985 SASOL plants were producing 70,000 to 100,000 barrels of oil a day, about one fourth of South African daily demand.

Contribution by U.S. interests to another South African energy supply came in December 1981 when the biggest ever South African contract to a U.S. firm was made to Combustion Engineering, a 780 million rand project to build six 600-megawatt boilers for the "C" power station of the state electricity corporation, ESCOM.[22]

U.S.-South African energy cooperation has been even more marked in the nuclear field. As early as 1950 an agreement was entered into for the supply of South African uranium to the U.S.; 50,000 tons were bought between 1953 and 1971. The agreement was expanded by the Eisenhower administration in 1957 to a broad range of nuclear cooperation. From 1955 to 1977 a total of 90 South African nuclear specialists were trained in the U.S., and over 150 U.S. experts visited South Africa. In 1958 the Allis Chalmers Corp. provided the South African Safari-1 project with a nuclear reactor along with enriched uranium (sufficient to make 10 bombs). In 1974 the nuclear cooperation agreement was renewed up to the year 2007. It was interrupted in 1978 when the U.S. adopted the Nuclear Proliferation Act with a provision banning export of enriched uranium to a presumably non-nuclear country like South Africa.[23]

However, as soon as the Reagan administration took office it began the resumption of nuclear cooperation with South Africa. This included the supply of Helium-3, used to make Tritium, a component of thermonuclear weapons. Five licenses of nuclear technology were approved for South Africa in 1980-1982, including vibration testing equipment that can be used to test warheads and ballistic reentry vehicles, computers (Cyber 750/170), and analysers used in nuclear test blasts. The Reagan administration advanced a "dual use" theory to justify its action (i.e., nuclear technology that could be used for the dual purposes of civilian and military application should be allowed). A U.S. nuclear team was in South Africa in October 1981 to inspect uranium enrichment plants, and a South African team at the same time toured the U.S. Portsmouth, Ohio, enrichment plant. Westinghouse in 1983 signed a $50 million agreement with South Africa to supply nuclear reactor equipment.[24]

Carlton Stoiber of the U.S. State Department's Nuclear Export and Import Control Office said on June 25, 1982, that such a relationship "can serve as an inducement to the South Africans to be more forthcoming on non-proliferation issues" and that it "would be a mistake to limit our negotiating ability through further restraint on international commercial relations." In that same month the chairman of the South African Uranium Enichment Corp., Dr. Ampie Roux, said that by 1987 South Africa would be completely self-sufficient in the production of enriched uranium.

Equipping South Africa with a nuclear potential can only be viewed in relation to the arming of the apartheid state. It has gone hand in hand with U.S. participation in the supplying of conventional arms on a large scale to the apartheid rulers, a process that continued after the adopting of the international arms embargo by the United Nations in 1978. Both by smuggling and by selling indirectly through other countries, a large proportion of the armaments of the apartheid regime has come from U.S. sources. A report in September 1981 asserted that 37% of South African arms had come from the U.S., including 40 Starfighter bombers, 52 heavy bombers, 37 C-130

Hercules transport planes, 43 helicopters, 230 medium and light tanks, 400 self-propelled artillery mounts, 250 armored cars, and numerous Cessna-185, Swearingen-Merlin-4, and L-140 planes.[25]

The amount of smuggling of arms from the U.S. is difficult to estimate and can only be indicated by those instances in which operations have been detected. In 1980 two officials of the U.S. Space Research Corp., George Bell and Rodger Gregory, were convicted of embargo violations, after the event. Through an elaborate scheme in 1978, soon after the U.N. embargo, they employed fake shipping papers and a roundabout route by way of Antigua to export two 155 mm. howitzers, 30,000 howitzer shells, a radar tracking system and various other weapons, all of which eventually appeared in South Africa. The howitzers were believed used for the secret nuclear test from the deck of a naval vessel in 1979 in the South Atlantic. In another case, a shipment by air of 2,000 automatic rifles, bound for Durban, was intercepted by an alert customs officer in Houston, Texas in 1981.[26]

A little known area of U.S. direct investment operations in South Africa is the participation by many of the hundreds of U.S. subsidiaries in subcontracting for the government arms corporation, Armscor. Supply of vehicles for the South African Defense Force is believed to be done by General Motors and Ford.

In manufacturing the U.S. role has been most significant in motor vehicles. The Ford Motor Co. had built an assembly plant in Port Elizabeth as early as 1924, and General Motors had followed in 1926. Firestone joined the expanding auto-related industry with a tire plant in 1936, and Goodyear subsequently arrived with a similar plant in 1947.

A major injection of auto-making capital came in 1970, when General Motors invested $125 million in engine and assembly plants in Port Elizabeth ("The Detroit of South Africa"). Besides cars, General Motors manufactures parts and accesssories: batteries, sheet metal components, springs, radios, spark plugs, earthmoving equipment, fridges. By 1973 it was utilizing 600 supplier firms and 773 sales and service outlets all over South Africa, affecting the jobs of tens of thousands of workers, and stood eleventh in total assets in the country.

Ford has the most modern auto assembly plant "in the southern hemisphere" in Port Elizabeth. It came into operation in 1973 and was producing 250,000 Cortina model cars in 1981 at the rate of 100 per day.[27] Chrysler Corp. completes the U.S. auto triumvirate in South Africa. Together the U.S. companies have controlled over one-half of the car market in South Africa.

The strategic location of U.S. investment capital has helped to give U.S. imperialism its strong position in the western alliance with the apartheid regime. An equally important factor has been the activity of U.S. loan capital, which has literally been the savior of the racist government at a number of crucial points in its history.

As previously stated, it was the extension of loans by U.S. banks that restored confidence in the apartheid system and checked the flight of foreign capital in the wake of the 1960 Sharpeville massacre. The loans, made to both the South African government and private sector corporations, the Anglo-American Corporation in particular, reversed the panic trend and also established the U.S. as the most significant ally of the racist state. This was soon afterward enhanced by the Export-Import Bank loan for launching the crucial SASOL coal-oil conversion plants.

Readiness of the U.S. to bolster the apartheid regime was explained in part by a spokesman of the U.S. metals industry, E. F. Andrews, vice-president of Allegheny Ludlum Industries: "We would have to revert 40 to 80 years in our standard of living and technology if deprived of the minerals and metals of South Africa, and southern Africa. Without these strategic metals, all production of steel, aircraft, missiles, tanks, naval vessels, autos and weapons of all kinds would cease."[28]

Invariably U.S. loan capital has played a vanguard role in creating financial respectability and stability for the apartheid regime. Up to 1980 South Africa had tended to obtain its loans from U.S. and Western European sources as quietly as possible, with the least fanfare, in order not to arouse anti-apartheid opposition. In 1980, however, an openly announced loan of $250 million was undertaken by a banking consortium headed by the U.S. Citicorp (together with the West German Dresdner Bank, the British Barclays , and the Swiss Commercial and Credit Bank). In order to "ease the passage" of this loan and to offset criticism, Citicorp spread it about that the U.S. money would be used by the South African government "to build schools and hospitals for the Blacks." This has since become a standard Reagan administration excuse for loans to the South African regime. The director of the Interfaith Center for Corporate Responsibility, Tim Smith, said, however: "I see it as a direct flow of capital that releases funds for the military and police. It is a cynical attempt to get South Africa back into the credit arena by waving the flag of both races, hoping that this can offset criticism."[29]

Indirect financing of the security measures of the apartheid state had become the main purpose of U.S. and U.S.-organized loans. In 1982 the International Monetary Fund, in disregard of United Nations resolutions condemning and urging sanctions against South

Africa, broke precedent and granted South Africa a $1.1 billion loan. It was widely known that the IMF decision was made at the insistence of the Reagan administration. Its spokesman, Donald Regan, then an IMF governor, asserted: "Politics is something that should be debated at the U.N. not in these multilateral lending institutions." In the U.N. it was indeed debated. Ghana's UN ambassador James Victor Gbeho denounced the IMF loan, saying that it was the U.S. which politicized the IMF by denying loans to Vietnam, Nicaragua and Grenada while backing a loan to South Africa. India's U.N. ambassador Kamal Nath condemned the loan, quoting a report of the U.N. Special Committee on Decolonization which showed that South African drawings from the IMF in 1975-1977 largely helped to meet expenditures on defense. He said: "Those in the IMF should have realized that voting in favor of this loan was not a vote for development and stability, rather it was a vote for suppression, subversion and aggression."[30]

Also in 1982, the U.S. itself extended loans totaling $623 million to South Africa. Observers pointed out that the IMF-U.S. loan totals were roughly identical to South Africa's military expenditures in the 1980-1982 period.[31]

The Reagan Administration and "Constructive Engagement"

The resurgence of an aggressive U.S. imperialist policy internationally in the latter years of the Carter administration was enormously expanded by the Reagan administration into a foreign policy of imposing U.S. "national interest" upon the rest of the globe.

An indication of the line to be pursued in regard to South Africa within this policy was brought out early in the 1980 election campaign by the national security adviser to Reagan, Dr. Joseph Churba, president of the Washington-based Center for International Security. In an address for the ears of the South African leaders made in Johannesburg on June 12, 1980, Churba said: "In the absence of U.S.-South African cooperation, the Cape sea route is defenseless and on the ground an incredible threat is posed by the so-called Front-Line states. In view of this it is imperative that there should exist greater security cooperation between the two countries. I do not believe that the USA can outbid the Soviet Union in gaining radical South African support.

"If a close South African-American alliance was formed, we would have to draw up a balance sheet. Such an alliance would probably mean facing an oil embargo from Nigeria. However, we have no credible sanctions option, and if it comes to a choice, America would have less to lose in forfeiting Nigerian oil than it would by disregarding an alliance with South Africa. The unqualified lifting of the U.S. arms embargo against South Africa and the immediate supply of increased technology aid are priorities."[32]

The election of Ronald Reagan was hailed in South Africa by government and business spokesmen. The Afrikaaner economist Johan Cloete said: "His election is good for South Africa in that a possible trade boycott of the country via the Security Council of the U.N. now looks even more unlikely."[33]

This proved to be a modest estimate. Projecting a policy of "constructive engagement" toward South Africa, the new Reagan administration proceeded to open the avenues of every form of alliance with the apartheid regime. No sooner had the administration occupied its offices than a team of five top-level South African military intelligence officers, including Admiral Willem du Plessis and Brigadier Nels von Tonder, arrived in Washington on an unpublicized visit. Their presence was revealed when they were observed in the lobby of the State Department: they confessed that they had been invited to pay a "courtesy call" to the Defense Intelligence Agency.[34]

Two months later, in May 1981, an official visit by the South African foreign minister, Roelof "Pik" Botha, occurred. The Lawyers Committee for Civil Rights Under Law said that by extending such an invitation the U.S. was removing the "polecat status" from South Africa, and that this was "a symbolic gesture which speaks loudly to all Africans."[35]

The Reagan-Botha talks resulted in the reinstatement (which the Carter administration had let lapse) of military attaches of the two countries, in Washington and Pretoria. On his return to South Africa, Pik Botha said that the U.S. "wants evolutionary change and the maintenance of law and order." Shortly afterward the U.S. announced an "adjustment" in its arms embargo, allowing the export to South Africa of military medical supplies "for humanitarian purposes" as well as equipment "to combat air piracy," no case of which had been reported in South Africa. At the same time the U.S. began the training of South African coast guards in the U.S.[36]

Coinciding with the Botha visit was a meeting in Buenos Aires on May 26, 1981 of U.S., South African, Argentine, Paraguayan and other South American representatives to discuss the setting up of a South Atlantic Treaty Oganization. It was sponsored by two Washington-based policy bodies, the Institute of American Relations and the

Council of Inter-American Security, and the Reagan representative was General Vernon Walters, former deputy director of the CIA. The outcome of these and similar discussions extended over several years has never been publicly revealed. A year later the *Johannesburg Times* reported that a secret pact had existed among these countries, and Israel, for many years.[37]

Resumption of U.S.-South African nuclear cooperation began as soon as President Reagan assumed the presidency.

In the early part of 1981 U.S. Assistant Secretary of State Lannon Walker was sent to Morocco where he held a secret meeting with Jonas Savimbi, chief of the South African-backed UNITA bands in Angola; the meeting was reported eventually by Reagan administration spokesman Larry Speakes as being "part of an administration review of Southern Africa policy." Walker said in explanation that "the region south of Zaire is of growing strategic, economic and political importance to the U.S." In March 1981 the Reagan administration proposed to the U.S. Congress the repealing of the 1976 Clark Amendment forbidding U.S. military assistance to the counter-revolutionary UNITA and it was proposed to bring Savimbi to Washington to lobby for aid.[38]

Promises made to Savimbi at this time came to naught when the House of Representatives Subcommittee on Africa rejected the Reagan proposal. However, on December 2, 1981 Savimbi was in Washington meeting with Assistant Secretary of State for African Affairs Chester Crocker and his deputy, Walter Stoessel.

It was reported that one of the main influences toward military cooperation between the U.S. and South Africa was the U.S. veterans' organization, the American Legion, which from the time of the U.S. arms embargo in 1978 had been calling for the U.S. to lift all sanctions and the arms embargo on South Africa and to enter into a full military alliance with the apartheid regime. General Neil Webster of the South African Defense Force said that "I do not know of any other organization in the world to come out so strongly and clearly in favor of South Africa."[39]

Another influence on U.S. policy at this time was the U.S. Chamber of Commerce in South Africa, which was set up in 1977 with 250 member firms. It issued a complaint in April 1981 that the arms ban was costing U.S. corporations extensive South African orders which it alleged were going to European, especially West German, companies. It was protested that a U.S. firm lost a 1.2 million rand order for electronic medical equipment for military hospitals to W. G. Siemens, and that others were losing chances on computers and communications equipment that fell under the arms embargo lists.[40]

The "constructive engagement" policy had a form of cultural tie as well. One of the entertainment personalities close to President Reagan, Frank Sinatra, flew to the casino-night club center at Sun City in the "independent" Bantustan of Bophuthatswana to perform, lending respectability to the segregated "homeland" in return for $2 million for nine concerts. Following the Sinatra lead, other U.S. singers and actors, at the U.S. administration's encouragement, were lured by apartheid money into cooperation with the South African efforts to break the international cultural isolation of the racist state.[41]

Consolidation of the Reagan alliance with apartheid came with the appointment of the officials who would implement it. One set of such appointments was the new U.S. ambassadorial team to the U.N., headed by the arch-imperialist Jeane Kirkpatrick, with Kenneth Adelman as her deputy and chief adviser. The Adelman selection in particular was publicly welcomed by the Botha government in Pretoria which said that it "considers the appointment of prime importance in setting the image of a new U.S. approach to South Africa."[42]

Most important of the appointments, however, was that of the new Under-Secretary of State for African Affairs, Dr. Chester Crocker. He had been the Director of African Studies at the Georgetown University Center of Strategic and International Studies. During the pre-election period that put Reagan on the road to the White House, Crocker had carried out a study for the Rand Corporation on policy options in regard to South Africa. His report, "The South African Security Apparatus and the Regional Balance," stressed the need for security over social priorities and predicted that the military and big business "can see South Africa through its troubles."[43] Crocker also made a study, "U.S. Policy for the 1980s," in which he admitted: "In political terms South Africa is not embraceable without our incurring massive diplomatic damage and risking severe domestic polarization." Nevertheless, he went ahead as a Reagan appointee with precisely an embracing policy.

At the time of the Crocker appointment it was claimed in the South African press by Cas de Villiers, former director of the Foreign Affairs Association that had served as a front for the South African government's Department of Information, that his section was "largely responsible for the present breakthrough in relations with the U.S." De Villiers said he had "intensively cultivated" key people in the U.S. in the years 1975-1978 and that these included Chester Crocker, Ernest Lefevre (who was put in charge of "human rights" by Reagan), and Ray Cline (formerly of the CIA and a Reagan adviser who urged that the U.S. should create an "all oceans" naval alliance in which South Africa should have a salient role in "defense of the Cape sea route").[44]

Crocker's ties with South Africa went further. For some time his confirmation as under-secretary was held up in the U.S. Senate because he and his family held goldmining shares in South African mining companies.

Even before his confirmation Crocker was laying the ground for the kind of policy he would carry out. His advice was seen in the position projected by Reagan in a television interview in which he praised alleged efforts in South Africa to remove apartheid. "As long as there is a sincere and honest effort being made, we should be trying to be helpful," said Reagan piously. "Can we take the other course, can we abandon a country that has stood beside us in every war we ever fought, a country that is essential to the free world, that has minerals?" This was identical to the line voiced by Crockers in statements to the press as he waited approval by the Senate of his post: he asserted that South Africa was moving away from apartheid and that the U.S. should back it.

Alfred Nzo, secretary general of the African National Congress, in a press statement on June 4, 1981, replied to this Crocker stance:

"The American Assistant Secretary of State-designate for African Affairs, Chester Crocker, is reported to have told the Chief Editors of American newspapers and other media that the racist regime in South Africa is 'making a serious and honest effort to move away from apartheid' and because of that 'the United States backs it.' This shameless lie underlines the anxiety of the Reagan Administration to whitewash the bloodstained apartheid regime.

"Crocker has the guts to make a public admission that this same racist Pretoria regime, which is sowing so much strife and suffering, including murdering scores of those who oppose it, is 'a friend of the United States.' Such statements are made by leaders of the American Administration notwithstanding the fact that the genocidal policies of the apartheid regime have earned nothing but condemnation and isolation from all over the world."[45]

A full-scale presentation of the Reagan administration policy he intended to pursue was set forth by Crocker, as a formally confirmed Under-Secretary of State for African Affairs, in a major speech delivered in Honolulu in September 1981. In this he set the scene by declaring, "We are concerned about the influence of the Soviet Union and its surrogates in Africa," which tends to "undermine the basic American interest in Africa." He said: "This Administration aims to meet this threat," but hastily sought to fend off alarmed criticism: "The U.S. has no desire, for that matter no mandate, to act as the policeman of Africa. But let there be no misunderstanding: this country will not hesitate to play its proper role in fostering the well-being of its friends in Africa and resisting the efforts of those whose goals are opposite."

After stressing that U.S. interests are heavily concentrated in the southern third of the continent, which contains "immense deposits of many strategic minerals which are vital to industrial economies like ours . . . vital to Western defense and high technology industries," Crocker pointed to "a combination of local and external pressures that could lead to expanded conflict and polarization." He said that "the USSR and its clients have shown every interest in keeping the pot of regional conflicts boiling," and therefore "it is imperative that we play our proper role in fostering the region's security and countering the expansion of Soviet influence."

Having set up the argument that the Soviet Union and not apartheid was the real threat in southern Africa, Crocker then laid out the meaning of "constructive engagement," saying that "we must have a realistic strategy, one that assures our credibility as a regional partner. Our task is to maintain communication with all parties and to pursue our growing interests throughout the region. In South Africa, the region's dominant country, it is not our task to choose between white and black. The Reagan Administration has no intention of destabilizing South Africa in order to curry favor elsewhere. South Africa is an integral and important part of the global economic system and plays a significant economic role in its own region. We will not support the severing of those ties. It does not serve our interests to walk away from South Africa any more than it does to play down the seriousness of domestic and regional problems it faces.

"The U.S. seeks to build a more constructive relationship with South Africa based on shared interests, persuasion and improved communication."[46].

The "constructive relationship" quickly proved to be many-faceted, the "shared interests" being economic, political and military. In 1981, as a consequence of the "confidence" stirred in U.S. business circles, the U.S. outstripped Britain to become South Africa's leading trade partner in both imports and exports, a 50% jump over 1980, a trade position it has maintained to the mid-1980s. From January 1981 to December 1982 four sets of relaxations were declared by the Reagan administration on exports to South Africa. These included, in September 1982, the removal from the list of banned goods of air ambulances for the South African Defense Force and the police. A policy was adopted of permitting "non-military goods" to be sold to the South African armed forces and police. Under this, permission was given for Sperry Univac 1100 series computers to go to an

Armscor subsidiary, Atlas Aircraft Corp. By the end of 1981 over 100 South African orders for computers were lined up for approval. The new "constructive" spirit extended to the security firm field: in December 1981 the U.S. multinational security firm, Wackenhut Corp., entered a cooperation deal with Securitas of South Africa for "the exchange of expertise and information." One of the export items sold to a South African corporation was 2,500 "shock sticks"(i.e., the cattle prod used for "crowd control"in the southern U.S. states during the 1960s civil rights struggles).[47]

In the year following President Reagan's inauguration, the value of U.S. direct investments in South Africa went up by 13.3%, including both retained profits and the infusion of new capital from abroad. According to the U.S. Department of Commerce investments of $2,320 million at the end of 1980 had risen to $2,630 million at the end of 1981.[48]

U.S. loans were increased, to become the main form of U.S. capital for sustaining the apartheid regime. Prior to the Reagan election, U.S. bank credits had dropped from $2.2 billion in 1978 to $1.4 billion in 1980, but these quickly recovered in 1981. The total that stood at $1.8 billion in June 1981 soared to $3.7 billion by December 1982. Besides this was the exceptional IMF loan of $1.1 billion arranged with U.S. connivance. Most of the loans came from major banks—Citibank, Chase, Morgan Guaranty, Manufacturers Hanover, Bank of America.[49]

The acceleration of economic links with South Africa was accompanied by massive advertising and lobbying campaigns by the South African government in the U.S. in this period. In the latter part of 1982 an extensive advertising drive, financed by the Information section of the South African Department of Foreign Affairs, placed large ads in U.S. newspapers, including the *Wall Street Journal* and *Washington Post*, and in glossy magazines, with pictures of white and black South Africans working and playing together, captioned and sloganed "Changing Face of South Africa," and "South Africa is Changing." To lobby for South Africa, the same Information section hired a former campaign manager for Reagan, John Sears, of the Banks and Sears law firm, and the law firm of Smathers, Symington and Herlong, at a total cost of $800,000.[50]

Shielding South Africa from boycotts and sanctions was a major feature of "constructive engagement." On April 30, 1981, the U.S. joined with Britain and France to block by a triple veto the application of a wide range of U.N. sanctions against South Africa, including an oil embargo, in order to compel the racist state to agree and to assist in the implementation of the U.N. decision on the independence of

Namibia. In August 1981 the U.S. alone vetoed a U.N. decision to condemn South Africa and to demand its withdrawal from Namibia. On December 17, 1981 the U.S. voted against U.N. General Assembly Resolution 36/172B which declared 1982 International Year of Mobilizatior. for Sanctions Against South Africa. Out of 14 anti-apartheid resolutions in the U.N. in the latter part of 1981, the U.S. voted "no" 12 times (3 times alone) and abstained twice.

Military cooperation with South Africa matched this intensified political relationship. In the first three years of the Reagan administration, more arms and equipment flowed from the U.S. to the apartheid regime, it was reported by observers, than in the previous 30 years. The embargo list was extensively revised: military transport planes ceased to be considered weapons, light aircraft used against guerrillas (in Namibia) were freely sent, computers for both army and police were relaxed, military medical equipment was removed from the lists, extensive arms smuggling operations occurred without serious interference, military attaches were exchanged, top South African officers (especially intelligence officers) went to Washington, coast guards and police from South Africa were trained in the U.S.[51]

There was another aspect of "constructive engagement." In March 1982 the Reagan Congress undertook special hearings on the anti-apartheid movements in South Africa and southern Africa which smeared the ANC and SWAPO as "terrorist" organizations, allegedly under the control of the Soviet Union and the Communist Party.

The effect of the Reagan "constructive engagement" policy was summarized by a professor of law at the University of Witwatersrand in South Africa itself, John Dugard. He said that "the Reagan policy toward South Africa encourages the Nationalist Party government to go back to extreme forms of apartheid repression." He pointed to no legislative reform in the 1981 parliamentary session, the enforcement of racial laws with a new vigor, the intensification of Group Areas Act prosecutions, an increase in tortures, and the abandonment of restraint by the riot police in attacks on black demonstrators.[52]

U.S.-South African Collaboration In Aggression

Collaboration between the CIA and the South African intelligence agencies and the South African Defense Force had been carried on for years, especially in the repeated South African invasions of Angola from 1975 onwards. Before and during the 1975 invasion CIA chiefs met with BOSS (Bureau of State

Security) representatives regularly in Kinshasha, Zaire, and the BOSS director visited Washington secretly twice to confer with the CIA's African Division Chief, James Potts.[53]

Within weeks after the election of President Reagan these links had a stepped-up development in one of the bloodiest acts of aggression by South African armed forces, the raid on the Matola district of Maputo, Mozambique, on January 30, 1981. The homes of South African refugees, some of them members of the African National Congress, were attacked and 12 of them were killed, along with Mozambican citizens. Following this raid, the government of Mozambique expelled from the country on March 5, 1981 four CIA agents on the staff of the U.S. Embassy: second secretaries Frederick Boyce Lundahl and Louis Lem Olivier, communications officer Arthur Russell, and political secretary Patricia Russell. The CIA agents were charged with having pinpointed the homes of ANC people in Maputo for the South Africans. Olivier, posing as an American liberal, had attempted to recruit into the CIA one of the ANC members, Mursa, offering him $300 at a time, radios and consumer goods.

The Maputo newspaper, *Noticias,* said: "Once again it makes clear that the American secret services have acted in our country for a long time as allies of South Africa. It demonstrates once again that American imperialism and apartheid work together when it comes to preventing the liberation of southern Africa." It was asserted that the CIA-South African operation had been orchestrated from the U.S. Embassy in Maputo. In addition, a U.S. official in a company called Mabor, a subsidiary of the U.S. General Tire and Rubber Co., was also expelled from Mozambique for using Mabor as a front for the CIA.[54]

This episode of CIA-South African collaboration against an independent African country was followed by the organizing of an attempted coup in Seychelles, the newly independent island republic off the eastern coast of Africa that had a progressive nationalist government and is a member of the Organization of African Unity. The coup, to be carried out by a band of mercenaries flown to Seychelles in the guise of a holidaying beer club, was frustrated on November 26, 1981 and most of the mercenaries arrested.

The commander of the mercenary group, Col. Mike Hoare, a South African, had had a previous link with the CIA when he commanded the brutal mercenary unit in the Congo (Zaire) that drowned in blood the anti-imperialist government initially headed by Patrice Lumumba. In the trial that occurred after the Seychelles incident, Hoare was revealed to have told his mercenaries that he had had the assistance of the CIA and that he had negotiated an arrangement with President Reagan and

U.S. Secretary of State Haig for a successful coup to be recognized by the U.S. within hours. At least one member of the mercenary group, Charles Dukes, was an American. Another, Martin Dolincheck, confessed during the trial that he was a senior officer in the South African National Intelligence Service (successor to BOSS). The group's second in command, Tullio Moneta, testified that the CIA gave support: "I was under the impression that a Mr. Manning was the CIA representative and was giving the coup support. He was going to tell us about the movements of warships mainly from Russia, but also possibly from Cuba, Mozambique and other countries whose ships would be hostile to us."[55]

U.S.-South African collaboration in aggression in southern Africa was raised to a higher level with the visit to South Africa at the end of September 1982 of the director of the CIA himself, William Casey. (A secret CIA directive had been circulated by Casey in May 1981, "The Draft Plan of Operations in Africa and the Near East," in which a program of subversion against "unfriendly countries" had been projected.[56]) A leading South African newspaper commented: "A visit, albeit secret, from a man of his stature points to either a strong need to persuade Pretoria to a particular course of action or to coordinate agreed policies."[57]

The Casey visit occurred shortly after the murder in Maputo, Mozambique on August 17, 1982 of Ruth First, a leading white member of the African National Congress. She was killed by a parcel bomb that was in an envelope with U.S. Embassy markings and carrying the name of a U.S. magazine (SADEX) published in Washington.[58] That South African intelligence agents were behind the assassination was obvious, and the complicity of the CIA was charged by anti-apartheid leaders.

It was not long before the purpose of the CIA director's visit became plain: it was to map out a campaign for the expulsion of the ANC from the countries bordering South Africa which gave ANC members refuge. This was to be done through every conceivable means including armed aggression, individual assassination (as in the case of Ruth First, which was followed in 1983 and 1984 by a series of similar murders of ANC cadres in Zimbabwe, Angola and Zambia), subversion, and intensive destabilization. It was evident from succeeding events that the apartheid regime was given the green light to carry out such policies.

On December 9, 1982 South African commando troops stormed across the border of Lesotho and attacked sections of the capital city, Maseru. In the murderous raid 41 people were killed in their homes, 29 of them Black South African refugees (including five former political prisoners who had been confined for years on Robben Island), and 12 Lesotho nationals. All those killed were civilians, working in Lesotho. As customary, the South African government proclaimed that it had destroyed a base of the ANC's armed force, Umkhonto we Sizwe.

In the subsequent period apartheid commandos and agents killed ANC and other refugees in Swaziland, Zimbabwe, Zambia and Bostwana. On June 14, 1985, in a raid identical to that upon Maseru, South African troops invaded Botswana and devastated a section of the capital city, Gabarone, killing 16 people, including Botswana and Netherlands nationals and several South African refugees who were working in civilian jobs in the city.

The avowed intention of the South African attacks has been to destroy alleged ANC bases from which it was claimed that the ANC was staging guerrilla attacks on targets in South Africa. This was disclaimed by the ANC which has asserted that its bases are in South Africa itself. Independent observers visiting the raided sites immediately after the attacks have confirmed the absence of any military features in the homes or of any sign of defending fire to have come from them.

Aside from the assassination and terrorizing of ANC cadres and supporters, the South African campaign of aggression has had the strategic aim of undermining and controlling the independent countries of southern Africa, a process that fits in fully with U.S. goals in this mineral-rich region of Africa. The prime examples of this coordinated U.S.-apartheid policy have been Mozambique and Angola, which have received the brunt of South African invasion and subversion.

In Mozambique, U.S. cooperation with South Africa produced the Nkomati Accord, which the FRELIMO government was forced to sign on March 16, 1984. This agreement was negotiated chiefly behind the scenes by Chester Crocker, who persuaded President Machel of Mozambique that it would end the South African-backed sabotage by the MNR bandits, and that the U.S. and South Africa would restore the ruined Mozambique economy.

The pressures on Mozambique, however, did not end with the Nkomati Accord. Instead of subsiding, MNR attacks increased, with obvious extensive aid from outside. Finally, in September 1985, combined FRELIMO-Zimbabwean troops captured the main MNR base and seized masses of documents and diaries proving not only continuous South African heliocopter-borne arms aid but repeated visits to MNR camps by the South African deputy foreign affairs minister,

Louis Nel. The documented evidence showed that South Africa had supplied the MNR with six months of military supplies just before the Nkomati Accord was signed, to enable uninterrupted attacks to be made.[59]

Among the demands made on Mozambique after the Nkomati Accord was to accept the return of thousands of MNR members and supporters from exile and their placing in army, civil service and even ministerial posts, as part of a coalition government arrangement.

This was pressed for by the U.S., backing it up by offering to provide funds for MNR "resettlement centers." More important, in circumstances of ravaged fields and crops that were a key MNR target, the U.S. urged agricultural aid on Mozambique with the provision that it must go only to private farmers, i.e., larger peasant farmers including Portuguese owners who had either remained after the revolution or were ready to return with the MNR, while aid would be withheld from the state farms, cooperatives and small peasant farmers. Mozambique's desperate need to revive its MNR-ruined economy led it to accede to U.S. pressures and to join the IMF and World Bank in September 1984. The first targets of typical IMF "austerity" demands were the FRELIMO government's proudest achievements, its socialized health and education programs.[60]

A similar pattern of U.S.-South African coordination has occurred in Angola. Soon after the Reagan inauguration it was reported that a group of 14 U.S. military experts visited the headquarters of UNITA in Angola to discuss arrangements for supplying $100 million in arms aid. This had followed the lobbying visit by UNITA's Jonas Savimbi to Washington early in that year. The chief public maneuver by the U.S., however, was to insist on the "linkage" of an independence settlement in Namibia with the removal from Angola of fraternal Cuban troop assistance.

Most revealing of U.S. intrigues concerning Angola emerged with the publishing in January 1984 of a confidential document smuggled out of Zaire. It was a memorandum bearing the insignia of the Zairean National Security Council, addressed to President Mobutu, filed from the office of Seti Yale, Mobutu's special adviser. In it was a detailed account of a meeting in Kinshasha in late November 1983 between a U.S. "special envoy," three UNITA representatives, military and intelligence officers from South Africa, and an observer from the Israeli military mission in Zaire. The meeting was about the destabilization of the Angolan government.

The main report and plans at this gathering, said the document, were made by the U.S. official, who urged UNITA and other subsidized groups to "consolidate their authority and influence in the liberated areas" and to "speed up social and political measures to deepen the population's discontent against the regime of dos Santos [Angola's President Eduardo dos Santos], the Cuban and Soviet presence and aid from other Communist countries in Angola; destabilize the situation in the capital; organize acts of sabotage against principal economic installations, and seize strategic points as well as important roads." The U.S. official advocated that steps should be taken to disrupt joint Angolan-Soviet projects in particular, to infiltrate agents into the Angolan army, and to sow division in the MPLA leadership, all with the aim of compelling the Angolan leaders to negotiate with UNITA. It was promised that the U.S. would increase its "military and financial assistance" to UNITA, but South Africa was called upon to intensify its military attacks in Angola. (In December 1983 South Africa did in fact stage a deep military penetration into Angola.) When the UNITA representative in Washington, Marcos Samondo, was queried about the Kinshasha meeting, he declined to confirm or deny it, but admitted that UNITA had "contacts with U.S. officials at all levels on a regular basis."[61]

In the early part of 1986 the Reagan administration once again brought Jonas Savimbi to Washington as a lobbying presence, to help push through an administration proposal to supply Savimbi's UNITA with up to $100 million of military aid, including the Stinger ground-to-air missile.

South Africa's African National Congress condemned the policies of the Reagan administration in bolstering apartheid and in aiding and directing its aggressions:

"The intentions of the United States are clear to everyone, and that is to protect the Pretoria regime not only for the immense profits and riches the U.S.A. reaps from our people's exploitation and oppression, but also as the last bastion of the imperialist camp in Southern Africa, and indeed, Africa as a whole. The fundamental interests and security of the whole continent of Africa are being sacrificed on the altar of the so-called strategic considerations of the U.S. involving the protection of a regime that has not camouflaged its aggressive posture against Southern Africa and the rest of the independent African continent. This is indeed not only an outrage against Africa but it possesses also an urgent challenge against the rest of democratic, peace-loving humanity."[62]

IV NAMIBIA: APARTHEID COLONY

The clearest example oi apartheid South Africa's role as a colonial power and as an aggressor state is its behavior toward Namibia. In equal measure, the Namibia situation demonstrates most sharply the alliance of South Africa with western imperialist interests and governments.

Because the question of Namibia's independence and of South Africa's relation to it comes legally and intimately within the province of the United Nations and its procedures, the events and circumstances in this African territory have led to the most direct encounter between the international community and the apartheid rulers. The South African government's defiance of almost all other countries in the world to retain a colonial grip on Namibia is a further display of the ruthless, inhuman character of the apartheid system that sets it outside the rest of civilized society.

The inflicting of immense suffering and destruction on the people of Namibia and of neighboring countries has followed from the South African policy, but it is the alliance of the United States with the apartheid regime—in callous pursuit of U.S. aims of dominance in the region—that has been mainly responsible for the continued denial of freedom to Namibia.

South African Rule: A Betrayal of Trust

Occupying a vast area in the southwest corner of Africa, on the western border of South Africa, Namibia developed as a country under colonial conditions. For 400 years after the first Europeans landed on its shores, in 1484, Portuguese, Dutch and British traders visited the coast without establishing significant stations. The region was thought to be arid and without much wealth.

Semi-nomadic Bushmen inhabited parts of it at first but subsequently other tribes, the Hereros, Damaras, Namas and others, came to raise cattle, grow corn and engage in other settled occupations; most populous of them all, the Ovambos, an agricultural tribe, occupied extensive northern areas.

Encompassing 317,825 square miles and with a long South Atlantic coastline, Namibia has large desert regions that have limited its population, but it also has areas of good agricultural and grazing land. Abundant fish in the offshore waters have made fishing an important industry. Most important of Namibia's resources, however, are its very rich mineral deposits. These have been the main reason for both South African and western efforts to keep control of the territory.

The colonial process did not begin until after Britain took over the Cape Area from the Dutch in 1795. Missionary and trading stations were extended along the coast to the west, and in 1878 Britain annexed Walvis Bay, placing the port under its Cape Colony six years later. Germany, arriving rather late as a colonial power in Africa, moved in to contest control of the region in the 1880s, finally coming to an agreement with Britain that left Walvis Bay in British hands while Germany was left free to seize what else it could.

In a series of ruthless wars against the inhabiting tribes, during which up to 15,000 German troops were brought in, Germany grabbed the best land for its settlers. The Hereros in particular fought the invaders desperately until they were driven into the Omaheke desert and either massacred or left to starve: only 16,000 out of 60,000 Hereros survived. However, the German colonialists were never able to conquer Ovamboland and its people, largest of the tribes, in the north.

South West Africa, as it was then known, was lost by Germany during World War I when it was invaded by a South African army under British command and put under occupying military rule. Although British South Africa wanted to annex the colony outright as part of the redivision of colonial possessions that featured the imperialist war, the Treaty of Versailles declared it a mandated territory to be administered by South Africa in behalf of Britain, with reports on its progress to be made to the League of Nations.

The spirit of mandate was never observed by South Africa, which virtually made the territory one of its provinces. In particular, the rules laid down for the administrating country to prepare the territory for self-determination and to "promote to the utmost the material and moral well-being and the social progress of the inhabitants," were totally ignored by the South Africans. In a manner as ruthless as that of the German imperialists, South Africa seized land from the inhabitants, crushed any protest or resistance (including the first use in a colonial war of bombing from the air) and introduced all the racist features of the South African colony. The land of the Ovambos was brutally occupied, their chief killed by South African troops, and the Ovambo people themselves cruelly divided by an agreement with Portugal that ran the border between South West Africa and the Portuguese colony of Angola straight through Ovamboland.

A mandate status continued through the 1920s and 1930s until after World War II. League of Nations mandates were then transformed into trusteeships under the United Nations, to terminate in independence in a reasonable time. Petitions for independence came from the Namibian people from 1946 onward. At first the Union of South Africa demanded the absolute incorporation of the territory into itself, but the U.N. General Assembly rejected this bid. One of the acts of the Afrikaaner Nationalist Party when it won power in 1948 and proclaimed the Republic of South Africa was to refuse to recognize the trusteeship status of South West Africa or to submit reports on its mandate to the U.N. An appeal against this unilateral attempt to take possession was taken by Namibians to the International Court of Justice which in 1950 ruled against South Africa, declaring that the mandate/trusteeship was still in force.

These maneuverings over the territory began a long process of international efforts to free South West Africa from South African control. When the International Court of Justice evaded the question of declaring illegal South African acts of introducing apartheid in violation of its mandate/trusteeship, the U.N. General Assembly in 1966 adopted Resolution 2145 (XXI) which formally terminated the mandate and put South West Africa under U.N. control. The main reason for doing this was that South Africa had failed to fulfill its obligation to ensure the moral and material well-being and the security of the people. Endorsed in 1969 by the Security Council, which called on South Africa to withdraw immediately, this U.N. step was finally confirmed by an advisory opinion of the International Court of Justice in 1971. A General Assembly resolution, in June 1968, heeded the wishes of the territory's people and declared the name of the country to be henceforward Namibia.

All of these acts, constituting a position of international law, were spurned and defied by South Africa, which proceeded to extend its apartheid laws over the territory and to permit the exploitation of its people by both South African and western corporations. One of its moves was to effectively annex Walvis Bay, transferring it to Cape Province for administration and setting up military bases in the 434 square mile enclave.

South African defiance of international law, whether it be conditions of mandate or the U.N. order to withdraw control, has included the implementation of the same apartheid land divisions and Bantustan "homeland" policies that characterize the racist state in South Africa. A special commission prepared a report known as the Odentaal Plan in 1964 which divided the Namibian people into twelve population groups, relegating each to a "homeland."

In this Plan, the white sector of the population, a minority of less than 100,000 in a total population of nearly a million, was given 50.6 million hectares, comprising about two-thirds of the land area of Namibia, for its "homeland." This huge area included virtually all of the mineral wealth, the best agricultural land, and the main fishing sites, as well as almost all the towns in the country. The divided black people, making up nine-tenths of the population, were permitted 32.8 million hectares that included vast tracts of desert and semi-desert.

By dividing black Namibians along "ethnic" lines, keeping them in "homelands" and assuring that they are ruled by conservative tribal chieftans, as in South African Bantustans, the apartheid regime has sought to split them as a nation and to prevent the growth of national sentiment. In apartheid style, the various black groups are not permitted into white areas unless for specific work, as cheap hired labor from what amount to labor reserves.

In virtually every respect, apartheid has been carried out in Namibia—in education, in health facilities, in housing, in wage and job discrimination. In accordance with the Odentaal Plan nearly 30% of black people have been subjected to the ruthless removal procedures of being expelled from "white" areas and deposited in barren and alien places. To ensure imposition of the apartheid system and to crush protest against it, the whole panoply of repressive laws in South Africa has been applied to Namibia.[1]

The Western Stake in South Africa's Colony

The fact that Namibia is still not independent today, 20 years after the U.N. ordered the termination of South African control, is due only in part to the police measures used to maintain that control. Equally responsible for the perpetuation of Namibia's colonial condition are the big western transnational corporations that share with South Africa the exploitation of the country's rich resources.

Namibia's wealth was fully revealed in post-World War II surveys that brought the major transnational mining companies in an investing parade. Uranium, diamonds, copper, lead, iron, zinc, manganese, lithium, silver, vanadium, coal, sulphur, tin, cadmium, and tungsten were found in large deposits. Luxury karakul or astrakhan pelts, half the world's supply, are produced. Fish stocks were abundant (until overfishing nearly destroyed the pilchard grounds).

In the exploitation of these riches, in which the mining industry is the most intensive and most lucrative, two big corporations account for 90% of mining production. These are Consolidated Diamond Mines, a subsidiary of the De Beers division of the Anglo-American Corporation, and Tsumeb Corporation, which is jointly owned by U.S. and South African companies. Tsumeb, producing copper, lead, zinc, silver and cadmium, is one of the two biggest corporations in Namibia. Its two major U.S. owners, Amax (American Metal Climax Inc.) and Newmont Mining, have each had a 29% share holding. U.S. capital was also reported in 1983 to be "in the ascendency" as well in Consolidated Diamond Mines, which controls 93% of Namibia's diamond output.[2]

Exposure of how Consolidated has operated in Namibia was made in November 1985 in a report compiled by a South African judge, Justice P.W. Thirion of the Natal Supreme Court, who was appointed to investigate "irregularities" in the diamond industry that were depriving the territorial administration of revenue. Consolidated was charged with "uncontrolled stripping" of the richest diamond ores at its main mine at Oranjemund in southern Namibia. Through illegal swapping of high quality Namibian gemstones with lesser-quality stones from South Africa, the administration in Namibia was alleged to be defrauded of over $400 million in a period of five years. The stripping operation accompanying this was said by a Consolidated technician, Gordon Brown, to be intended to "get as much out of the ground as possible before a change of government" (i.e., before independence), and the declining diamond reserves that were the consequence have been visible in the fall of extraction from 1.9 million carets in 1978 to 930,000 carets in 1984.[3]

South Africans own about 40% of the shares in the mining industry, nearly all of the fisheries, most of the construction industry and the majority of the commercial enterprises. In addition, South African government corporations run the railroads, ports, airlines and airports, radio, post office and telegraph systems. Commercial agriculture is dominated by about 5,000 white-owned farms, mostly Afrikaaner and German.[4]

In the Namibian economy, however, the main feature is the presence of the transnational corporations. Out of 15 of the principal

TNCs operating in Namibia, 5 are U.S.-owned. Besides Amax and Newmont Mining, U.S. TNCs include Falconbridge Nickel Mines (shared with Canadian capital), Bethlehem Steel and Nord mining, which control tungsten and tin mines. Britain has Charter Consolidated, Rio Tinto Zinc, Consolidated Gold Fields, and Selection Trust. From West Germany, Metallgasellschaft, Urangesellschaft AC, Otari Mining and Railways Corp. Canadian firms, besides Falconbridge, include Oamites Mining Co., Rio Algom, Consolidated Mining and Smelting, Etosha Petroleum. The French: Minatome, Total and Aquitaine. In sum, these companies make up the strategic economic base of the country.

Profits of U.S. companies in Namibia have been enormous. It is estimated that each Tsumeb share with a nominal cost of 0.5 rand realized a profit of 2.5 rands in 1978 and that this jumped to 4 rands in 1979, an 800% profit rate, highest in the mining industry. In the meantime, the average wage of a black worker in Tsumeb mines was $30 a month, while a white worker was paid $550.[5]

The western hand in Namibia's retarded independence is best seen in the case of the Rossing Uranium Ltd., which was established in 1968 after the U.N. resolution ending South Africa's mandate. Its existence was not publicly known until 1970; when a $25 million contract entered into by the British Labor Party government for Britain's Atomic Energy Authority to receive 7,500 tons of uranium ore from Rossing between 1973 and 1980, was revealed. The Rossing shareholders subsequently became known: 60% owned by the British Rio Tinto Zinc, and other shares held by Canada's Rio Algom, France's Total, West Germany's Urangesellschaft; and South Africa's Industrial Development Corp. and General Mining.

U.S. corporations played a key part in the Rossing venture. A consortium of U.S. banks including Bank of America, Chase Manhattan, and the First National City Bank provided $20 million of financing to get production going, and the contract for designing, engineering, materials procurement, and construction of the mine went to Western Knapp Engineering Division of Arthur G. McKee Corp. of San Francisco.[6]

Located near Swakopmund in Namibia, Rossing has uranium ore reserves of 100,000 tons and is the largest open cast uranium mine in the world. By 1984 it was producing one-sixth of the uranium in the capitalist part of the world, and the discovery of new deposits promised to increase that amount. The lucrative nature of the mine has been indicated by the report that Rio Tinto Zinc makes 40% of its profits from Namibia with but 7% of its investments there.[7]

Uranium from Rossing is intended for use in the Trident submarine enrichment plant for Rossing ore has been erected at Capenhurst near the city of Chester.

This entire mining operation has been carried out in direct disregard of U.N. resolutions and directives issued since 1966. Furthermore, most of the big mining transnationals have continued to engage in intensive prospecting for uranium and other minerals, and for oil and gas, applying for and receiving their prospecting grants from the South African government. Western companies have continued in flagrant disregard of U.N. resolutions and the decree of the U.N. Council for Namibia (September 1974) for protection of Namibia's resources. It was specifically aimed at warning TNCs to stay away from Namibia and not to exploit its wealth, the income from which in taxes, licensing fees and other revenue has gone not to the people of Namibia and their welfare but to South Africa.

As U.S. and other transnational companies have continued business as usual in an essentially colonial Namibia, western governments have adopted the stance of giving lip service to the idea of Namibian independence while blocking steps to bring it about. The tone was set by President Richard Nixon in 1970. On May 20 of that year the Nixon administration announced that it would officially discourage further U.S. investment in what was then South West Africa. No investment interest took it seriously. In London on May 21 the *Financial Times* said: "Mr. Nixon's decision will not be translated into any formal ban on new investments and will not affect existing U.S. investments in the territory." Not only did this prove to be the case (the financing and constructing of the Rossing mine went ahead, for example) but on December 10, 1970, a U.N. General Assembly resolution condemning South Africa for its refusal to withdraw from Namibia, and calling for "effective measures" to compel it to do so was vetoed by the U.S. together with Britain, France, Portugal, and South Africa.

The most pertinent fact about the investment stake and the operations of U.S. and other foreign corporations in Namibia is that their entry occurred almost wholly after the establishment of the apartheid state in South Africa in 1948 and especially after the United Nations in 1966 declared an end to the South African mandate. There can be no doubt, in the circumstances of an international spotlight being focused on the illegality and racist nature of South African rule, that the corporations involved have been taking calculated advantage of apartheid and colonial policies to gain maximized profits.

SWAPO'S Struggle for Namibia's National Liberation

The combined South African-western exploitation of Namibia would perhaps have drawn less international condemnation if the Namibian people themselves did not resist it. However, an alternative has existed: the Namibian people have demanded and fought for independence, for freedom from foreign control and exploitation, and their struggles have been officially recognized by the United Nations.

Petitions for independence were sent to the U.N. in the latter 1940s by some of the tribal leaders in Namibia, such as Chief Hosea Kutako of the Hereros and Chief David Witbooi of the Namas. A more important, mass-based movement developed in the 1950s, among Ovambo contract workers. It led to the 1957 Ovamboland People's Congress in Cape Town and then to the creation of the Ovamboland People's Organization in 1958. The movement began with protests against contract labor conditions but when in 1959 the OPO set up an organization in Windhoek, the Namibian capital, it launched a campaign against the forced removals from the city under the segregationist "homeland" laws introduced by the South African authorities. During an OPO demonstration against removals on December 10, 1959, police attacked the demonstrators, killing 11 and wounding 54.

This repressive act caused the OPO leaders and others to take the further step of setting up the broader South West Africa Peoples' Organization (SWAPO), a national liberation movement for complete freedom from colonial rule, specifically South African rule. It was founded on April 19, 1960, and in 1961 held a national congress in Windhoek. Although SWAPO has drawn its main support from the Ovambos, that is because they comprise one-half of the population of the country; it also has support from among the other tribal groups, including members from the white minority.

From the outset, SWAPO has not limited itself to any one form of struggle for independence, considering that methods depended on the conditions set by the colonial rulers. The likelihood of armed struggle was recognized, and in 1962 SWAPO created a People's Liberation Army of Namibia (PLAN), began training and established its first base, inside the country. An external wing of SWAPO was formed to lead a possible armed struggle if called for and to conduct international relations for support of the Namibian independence struggle. An internal SWAPO wing has persisted with open, legal, peaceful activities within Namibia.

When the International Court of Justice declined to rule on the question of South Africa's illegal apartheid policies in 1966, SWAPO decided it had no alternative but to launch an armed struggle for national liberation. For two decades the armed struggle has continued, concentrated mainly in the northern part of the country but extending well down into the central part on occasion. The savage repressive military campaigns employed by the South African Defense Force against PLAN, the SWAPO organization as a whole and its support groups among the people have been a major factor in arousing international support for SWAPO.

The U.N. General Assembly in 1973 formally recognized SWAPO as the authentic representative of the Namibian people. That recognition has never been challenged by anyone but South Africa's apartheid rulers and their closest western allies.

Although South Africa has never formally banned SWAPO's internal wing, it has used harsh methods to deny it campaigning rights, and has harassed, arrested and detained masses of its members and supporters. In 1971-1972 a general strike by SWAPO and worker organizations paralyzed the Namibian economy and was met by brutal South African reprisals.

In the attempt to put down the SWAPO armed struggle, the apartheid rulers have turned the whole of northern Namibia into a military zone of control, dotted with bases for an estimated 100,000 or more regular and part-time South African troops. The people of the region, mainly Ovambos, have been subjected to massacre, torture and forcible removal into fenced-in encampments, their homes burned and crops destroyed.[8]

Foreign mining companies within or bordering on the zone, while able to call on South African troops, have set up their own armed means to oppose SWAPO activities. This includes the U.S.-owned Tsumeb mines and the Rossing uranium mines. SWAPO obtained a secret Rossing document in 1980 that detailed an arrangement for installing three armories on its premises "for defense against civil, labor or terrorist attacks."[9]

Western governments, in particular the U.S. government, and corporations have joined with the South African regime in branding SWAPO as "Marxist" and as ready to drive out white settlers and foreign investment interests. However, the president of SWAPO, Sam Nujoma, said in January 1981:

SWAPO has stated time and time again that it is committed to the creation of a democratic and non-racial society in which the rights of all citizens, regardless of race, religion or ethnic origin, will be specially protected. But we make a clear distinction between rights and entrenched privileges. On this basis the rights of whites in Namibia will be protected under the law of the land. SWAPO's concept of a social order in a liberated Namibia is that all who want to live in Namibia and are prepared to obey the laws of the country will be welcome to stay. [10]

This was repeated by President Nujoma in December 1981:

> We have made it clear that the people of Namibia are not fighting against the minority white settlers, because under a future independence of Namibia the white settlers will be welcome to live with us.[11]

Toward foreign corporations that have defied United Nations calls to withdraw from a South Africa-controlled Namibia, SWAPO has had an attitude that is in keeping with that internationally arrived-at position, calling upon foreign economic interests to quit the country and declaring that those failing to do so will be presented with a "bill of indictments" demanding compensation for their plundering of Namibian resources. Rio Tinto Zinc is singled out for special warning for its Rossing uranium mining operations.[12]

Further elaboration on the SWAPO attitude toward the foreign companies concerned was made by President Nujoma in an interview in Paris with a representative of the South African *Financial Mail:*

> *Q.*What will be your attitude to multinationals?
> *Nujoma.* Multinationals, which are now exploiting Namibian mineral wealth, are bound by the South African laws to pay taxes and royalties to the regime. According to the information we have, they also pay South African white employees who are in military service for up to a year, which means they have become part and parcel of the South African war machine.
> *Q.*SWAPO has recently stated that the big mining companies, like RTZ, which operate against U.N. decrees, will be made to pay indemnity after independence. Does this mean they will be nationalized?
> *Nujoma.*Nationalization would depend on the decision of the Namibian parliament. It is not something I can say now. We will adopt a new approach towards foreign investment. It is possible we will guarantee whatever is required for them to continue their operations in our country, but we would not allow them to continue the present system which is geared to benefit the minority white settlers. Of course, new agreements and treaties will have to be entered into.[13]

SWAPO, confident of its support among the people of all Namibia, has declared itself ready to participate in any free and fair elections to determine Namibia's future and the government to prevail under independence. In 1980 the South African National Intelligence Service conducted a detailed study in Namibia of the probable results of such an election. It concluded that SWAPO would receive 83% of voter support. During the subsequent period signs have pointed to a further growth of pro-SWAPO sentiment. South Africa has therefore clutched at every straw to prevent democratic elections.

Western "Contact" with South African Rule in Namibia

In the 1970s the South African government came under increasing pressure over its Namibia policy. Repeated U.N. resolutions demanding withdrawal from the territory and calling for sanctions to compel South African compliance were negated by the vetoes and abstentions of the U.S., Britain and France, but the work of the U.N. Council for Namibia, set up in the latter 1960s, and of the U.N. Committee on Decolonization helped to strengthen the independence movement and its international backing.

A U.N. Fund for Namibia was established in 1970 to finance the Council's program for training Namibian personnel, aiding refugees and rendering varied forms of technical assistance. A U.N. Institute for Namibia was opened in Lusaka, Zambia in 1976, where Namibians have been trained for civil service and administrative functions in an independent Namibia, especially in the organization of the economy, an educational system, and a labor policy.

A critical point in the trend toward international support for Namibia came in 1974 with the liberation of Angola from Portuguese colonial rule. This was a strategic turning point for SWAPO, which now had a vast safe support base adjoining its home territory. SWAPO had been able to maintain logistical routes through Angola during Portuguese rule itself, but the MPLA government was an active ally of SWAPO, raising the prospects for the liberation war in Namibia. The South African invasion of Angola, with CIA support, in the latter part of 1975 was motivated to a considerable extent by a desire to eliminate this threat to apartheid rule, and South Africa's humiliating defeat by MPLA-Cuban forces and retreat to Namibean bases heightened its fears for the future.

In September 1974, within a few months after the Portuguese collapse, South Africa had moved to block a genuine Namibian independence. Through the white South West African National Party in the colony, virtually a duplicate of the ruling National Party in

South Africa, a call was made for a Constitutional Conference, ostensibly to prepare for independence. Such a Conference was held in September 1975. It was organized around delegations from "population groups," i.e., from the eleven tribal "homelands" and the white sector, a device that preserved the apartheid structure of the colonial society. All those who refused to accept this arrangement were denied the right to attend or to take part in preparing the constitution or the independence. SWAPO and other groups, representing the bulk of population, refused and were excluded.

Called the Turnhalle Conference after the building in Windhoek in which it was held, the constitutional gathering was a puppet show manipulated from Pretoria. Despite the careful selection of delegations, it was marked by intense dissension in and among the tribal groups, and by the dominant role of the minority white grouping. It took nearly two years of slow, stalling sessions to map out a constitution as desired by South Africa. The draft provided for eleven separate ethnic governments and an appointed National Assembly which would have very limited powers and would be fully under the control of Pretoria. Provisions were made for holding an election for an "interim government," and "independence" was projected for December 1978.

The Turnhalle maneuver was condemned internationally and even the western powers were compelled to support a U.N. decision (Resolution 385) in January 1976 calling on South Africa to take steps for the transfer of power to the people of Namibia and to agree to free elections under U.N. supervision. Backing for SWAPO internationally increased in this period, particularly support for a SWAPO offer to negotiate a settlement with South Africa, providing the South African army and police would withdraw as insisted by the U.N., the repressive emergency regulations in the country would be lifted, and South Africa would accept the principle of Namibian sovereignty. Sympathy for SWAPO was augmented by the arrest and detention without trial, in the course of the Windhoek Turnhalle Conference, of hundreds of the members of the SWAPO legal internal wing.

At a September 1976 U.N. Security Council meeting on South Africa's failure to abide by Resolution 385, developing country representatives moved for an arms embargo against South Africa to compel it to relinquish its hold on Namibia. This was vetoed by the U.S., Britain and France. Again, in December 1976 similar attempts to obtain a Security Council arms embargo resolution were vetoed by the U.S., Britain, France and West Germany. By the early part of 1977, however, with South African counterinsurgency campaigns going on in Namibia, the pressure was building so strongly, especially among

African countries, for not just an arms embargo (which was finally adopted in that year) but for sweeping sanctions against new loans and investments in South Africa, that the western partners of the apartheid state felt it necessary to shift to other tactics to forestall effective anti-apartheid measures.

The tactical move was an offer for a "Contact Group," organized at U.S. initiative, to be the mediating/negotiating vehicle to deal with South Africa for free elections and independence in Namibia. A five-member Contact Group was created, made up of the U.S., Britain, France, West Germany and Canada—the countries with the main investment stake in - the apartheid system and in Namibia. Beginning with the spring of 1977, the Contact Group shuttled about southern Africa conducting an endless series of talks with the South African government, the Turnhalle grouping, SWAPO, and the governments of the frontline states, ostensibly aimed at achieving the implementation of U.N. resolutions. In truth, the Contact Group talks, stretched out over nine years to the present time, have constituted an elaborate maneuver to get nowhere, to stall a Namibian independence settlement, and to permit South Africa the time to conduct its war of suppression against SWAPO and to set up the puppet colonial structure it wanted in Namibia.

After an entire year of shuttle talks, the Contact Group, under U.N. pressure, produced a "Proposal for a Settlement in Namibia" in March 1978, submitting it to then U.N. Secretary General Waldheim. Using the Proposal as a working basis, the Secretary General dispatched his own mission to Namibia in August 1978 to investigate the situation. The report of that mission and its findings were synthesized with the western proposals in a final report to the Security Council on August 29, 1978. It was formally adopted by the Security Council on September 29, 1978, as U.N. Resolution 435.

Resolution 435 comprises the basic document for the transition to independence for Namibia. It sets forth an outline plan for the holding of free and fair elections under U.N. supervision, calling for the setting up of a United Nations Transition Assistance Group (UNTAG) with a civilian and a military component to carry it out. The military component would number 7,500 including seven infantry battalions totalling 5,000, plus 200 monitors and a logistical force of 2,300. The civilian component would be made up of approximately 360 experienced police officers to prevent intimidation and interference during the election period and 300 professional officers to be in charge of the polling, together with a supporting staff of approximately 1,200.

In the stages up to the election, hostilities would be ended by both the South African armed forces and SWAPO's PLAN, both of which would be confined to bases. South African troops would be with-drawn by stages from Namibia until reduced to 1,500, which would remain only until the election results were certified, and would then withdraw. SWAPO personnel in exile would be permitted to return to the country to participate in the electoral process.

The election would be for a Constituent Assembly, which would meet, draw up a Constitution, and set a date for independence. Upon inde-pendence the Constitution would come into force, with future elections and forms of representation to be in accordance with its provisions.

It soon became apparent that agreement by the Contact Group to the procedures in Resolution 435 was a tactical step in the face of growing international pressure and not a readiness to push through Namibian independence. Between the adoption of Resolution 435 and its implementation stood arrogant South African intransigence and a Contact Group attitude of permitting South Africa the fullest and most prolonged benefit of doubt and objection.

While the Resolution and its independence procedures were being worked out, South Africa had already thrown serious obstacles into the path of the process. In June 1978 it unilaterally undertook to register voters in Namibia for an election of its own. Registration was conducted under the guns of the apartheid army and police, with SWAPO barred from taking part. Rejecting the U.N. proposals, South Africa announced a week before the adoption of Resolution 435 that it intended to go ahead with its own election in Namibia before the end of the year.

The apartheid election was held on December 4 to 8, 1978, in defiance of the U.N. plan. It was won by the Democratic Turnhalle Alliance, a party organized by the white minority together with the most conservative Black tribal chiefs from the "homelands" who had participated in the Turnhalle Conference. The DTA was heavily financed by the South African government and, pertinently, by rightwing parties in West Germany, which also provided the DTA with ten special vehicles equipped with cinema projectors and screens, a potent means of propaganda in the rural "homelands" during the election campaign.[14] Winning 41 out of 50 seats in the apartheid Assembly, the DTA formed a colonial government headed by its leader, a white farmer named Dirk Mudge. A National Assembly was proclaimed in May 1979, recognized by South Africa.

This internal structure was wholly the creature of the South African government, which appointed an Administrator General as the top-most authority in Namibia. No laws could be passed by the Assembly without ratification by the Administrator General. South Africa kept full control over foreign affairs and international relations, over defense matters and over planning. In the civil service that was set up, South African citizens were appointed and sent in to hold the top positions. Apartheid practices were instituted, from the ethnic dividing of the country to the composition of the various services. A "South West African" (South Africa has refused to recognize or use the name "Namibia") armed force was established for "security," officered by South Africans, serving as an auxiliary of the SADF. In 1980 a Council of Ministers was set up as the effective ruling body, composed wholly of DTA members, reducing the National Assembly to an even more negligible status.

To the international community, one of the most objectionable aspects of the South African unilateral move for an internal "settlement" of the Namibian question was the creation of armed forces to be used for "security" and repression. Tribal "armies" were first established in each "homeland," amounting to little more than the private armies of the chiefs. In August 1980 these were drawn upon to form a South West Africa Territory Force (SWATF), the main task of which was to fight against SWAPO.

The vast majority of countries in the world condemned the South African defiance and its insistence on behaving as a colonial power. Demands for sanctions to compel compliance by the racist state to Resolution 435 were raised repeatedly in the U.N. General Assembly and Security Council as well as in broadly supported international conferences on Namibia. U.N. action was blocked by the vetoes of the U.S., Britain, France and West Germany.

Instead, the Contact Group resumed its role of delay, moving to deflect vigorous action aimed at ending South African arrogance. A Contact Group statement was presented to the U.N. General Assembly in May 1979 by then U.S. Ambassador to the U.N., Andrew Young. It said: "The governments of the Western Five have every intention of continuing to work towards a peaceful settlement of the Namibian problem under the auspices of the United Nations." The statement then purported to display impartiality, on the one hand chiding South Africa for creating its internal authority in Namibia ("The Five will not accept that that assembly truly represents the people of Namibia"); while on the other hand rebuking SWAPO for "loudly voiced mistrust of the West, baseless charges of malfeasance and absurd claims such as a call for a onesided ceasefire so that hundreds of their forces might pass freely into Namibia to establish themselves." Equating the oppressor and the struggling oppressed was a clever way of undercutting the independence forces.

Between 1979 and 1981, while South Africa went ahead with its puppet control system in Namibia, its campaigns against SWAPO's guerrilla PLAN during which the SADF and auxiliary troops were built up past the 100,000 level, and its repeated invasions of Angola with the excuses of eliminating SWAPO bases, the Contact Group solemnly went through the motions of negotiating with the regime in Pretoria. One objection after another to provisions of Resolution 435 was raised by South Africa: to the size of the U.N. peacekeeping force, to the presence of SWAPO bases in Namibia to which PLAN forces would retire during the election period, to the retention of arms by SWAPO. Every objection was seriously taken up and discussed at length by the Contact Group.

When President Neto of Angola broke a deadlock in the proceedings by proposing a demilitarized zone 50 kilometers wide on either side of Namibia's border with Angola, South Africa grudgingly accepted and then shifted to the making of unreasonable demands in implementation. Ignoring SWAPO, the Contact Group worked out with South Africa a demilitarized zone concept that virtually nullified the plan. It gave South Africa 20 military bases within the DMZ, each with its airfield and "population center," while SWAPO would have none, conceded the South African demand that five of the U.N. battalions out of seven would be stationed in the DMZ (thus reducing the U.N. presence in the rest of Namibia), and agreed that South African troops (but not SWAPO) would accompany the U.N. forces in the DMZ. Despite the weighting of this arrangement in South Africa's favor, SWAPO, Angola and the other frontline states, bending over backwards to overcome South African excuses for not proceeding with Resolution 435, accepted these South African conditions.

Other demands, however, were also made by South Africa. It insisted that the U.N. must withdraw its recognition of SWAPO as the sole and legitimate representative of the Namibian people, and that other "internal parties" in Namibia (meaning those created by South Africa), as well as UNITA in Angola, must be brought into negotiations. These demands were rejected by the U.N.

Throughout this period of stalling and endless delay by South Africa, the Contact Group voiced no criticism of South African tactics or the constant attacks upon Angola by South African troops. Between March 27, 1976 and June 11, 1979 there had been 193 armed mine-laying operations by the SADF in Angola, 7 bombing raids, 21 border provocations and one large-scale air and ground attack. These had killed 612 Namibian refugees (147 men, 167 women and 298 children) and wounded 611; killed 12 Angolan soldiers and wounded

63; and killed 3 Angolan civilians and wounded 15. Destruction in Angola in that period reached $293,304,000. Between June 1979 and December 31, 1980, there were 81 bombing raids, 33 attacks by helicopter troops, and 925 air space violations, resulting in 400 civilians killed and 640 wounded, while 85 Angolan soldiers were killed and 95 wounded, the destruction toll being $230,796,805. In the year 1981 there was a stepping up of South African attacks. Up to August 23 alone 100 bombing and 50 strafing raids occurred along with 1617 air space violations, 4 paratrooper landings, 34 ground attacks, 26 ground reconnaissance operations, 7 shellings and 9 mine-laying operations. On August 23 a major invasion with 11,100 troops, 36 tanks, 70 armored cars and 200 armored troop carriers occurred. In the course of it 206 Angolan soldiers and 158 civilians were killed. Destruction costs were over $400,000,000.[15]

Instead of pressing South Africa to end its war in Angola and its brutal war of repression in Namibia, the Contact Group applied its pressure upon SWAPO, trying to get the liberation movement to cease its armed struggle against illegal South African rule. At an international conference in solidarity with the people of Namibia in Paris in September 1980, organized by the African National Congress and UNESCO in coordination with SWAPO, this role of the Contact Group was assailed. It was reported that "SWAPO's president, Sam Nujoma, has repeatedly in the last two days bitterly accused the Western Five of secretly backing Pretoria. In his opening address Mr. Nujoma accused the West of deceit and said it would have the blood of Namibian people on its hands if Western countries refused to implement sanctions against South Africa."[16]

While the Contact Group went on with the limitless negotiations that fitted in with the South Africa tactics of delay, large corporations from all five of the Contact members continued to operate in Namibia in disregard of U.N. directives, and to pay their taxes and fees to the South African authorities. No effort was made by any of the five to persuade the companies of its nationals to withdraw in furtherance of U.N. decisions. On July 7, 1980, the head of the SWAPO mission to the U.N., Theo Ben Gurirab, demanded that all foreign interests quit Namibia, declaring that after independence a SWAPO-led government would compile a "bill of indictment" and demand compensation from companies plundering the nation's uranium and other resources in collaboration with the South African regime.[17]

The U.N. General Assembly in November 1980 endorsed the SWAPO position and that of the ANC. By a huge majority it adopted a resolution condemning all foreign interests in Namibia and South

Africa, calling them "a major obstacle to political independence and to the enjoyment of the natural resources of the territories by the indigenous inhabitants." This resolution was opposed by the Contact Group members and other western countries including Israel and Japan.

The Reagan Administration Blocks Namibian Freedom

Up to the latter part of 1980, the tactics of the western powers making possible a prolonged South African control over Namibia had centered on "negotiating" on objection after objection by the apartheid regime in regard to Resolution 435. The election of President Ronald Reagan in November 1980 marked a shift in such tactics: the U.S. openly assumed the role of changing the terms and the established ground rules for the transition to Namibian independence. Changes proposed and terms demanded were blatantly in favor of South Africa and against the liberation movements in southern Africa.

The new U.S. policy and its effects were felt even before the Reagan administration was sworn into office. A U.N. sponsored conference in Geneva in January 1981 on the implementation of Resolution 435 was wrecked by the belligerent non-cooperative attitude of South Africa. Although the SWAPO delegation that was present agreed to abide by the ceasefire terms of the Resolution and to the U.N. supervisory role in the elections, South Africa refused on the grounds that the U.N. was "not impartial" because of its recognition of SWAPO as the legitimate representative of the Namibian people. The intransigent South African stance was widely understood to arise from assurance that the Botha regime could now rely on much stronger backing from the Reagan government.

South Africa's apartheid leaders were confident that a new U.S. position on Namibia would be part of the overall "constructive engagement" policy that included increased trade, investment, loans and general ties of cooperation between the U.S. and the apartheid regime. An architect of that policy, Assistant Secretary of State for African Affairs Chester Crocker, visited South Africa in April 1981 and confirmed the new stance and its features regarding Namibia.

Crocker told Prime Minister Botha in Pretoria that Resolution 435 provided "a basis but perhaps not the complete basis" for a settlement. What Crocker put forward was the idea of an "all-party" conference to write a Constitution for an independent Namibia *before* the holding of elections for an Assembly. Furthermore, the mediator in such a

conference would not be the U.N., but the U.S. [18] This kind of arrangement would reverse procedures for independence laid down by the
U.N. In other words, the white minority-dominated Democratic Turnhalle Alliance and its puppet tribal chiefs would sit down with SWAPO
at a table with the U.S. presiding and devise a Constitution, instead of
an elected Assembly certain to have a SWAPO majority. Subsequently
it was revealed that Crocker had discussed with Botha a "solution" in
Namibia that would "safeguard U.S. and South African essential
interests and concerns."[19]

In July 1981 the U.S. argued for and obtained agreement from the
Contact Group to a new formulation insisting on "constitutional safe-
guards for minority groups" in Namibia, and in particular "reasonable
security for the 100,000-strong white minority."[20] There were several
features to the new Contact Group position, endorsing the U.S. proposals: "These are to ensure that the U.N. acts impartially in dealing with
SWAPO on the one side and the DTA on the other; the need for
constitutional restraints to be built into the independence arrangements to prevent a 'winner takes all' result in the elections; and the
composition of the proposed U.N. force which would supervise the
run-up to the election." On the last point the U.S. was insistent that, to
meet the South African complaint that the U.N. was not "impartial", an
"independent body" should supervise the election instead of the U.N.[21]
In sum, the Reagan administration proposals meant nothing less than a
scrapping of Resolution 435 and a resort to arrangements heavily
weighted in favor of South Africa and western interests in Namibia.

One of the obvious reasons for this U.S.-led maneuver lay in the
detailed study made by the South African National Intelligence Service
(formerly BOSS) in the latter half of 1980, which concluded that
SWAPO had at least 83% of voter support in Namibia. An election,
fairly held, would bring an overwhelming majority for SWAPO in an
independence Assembly.[22]

The Reagan administration policy was pursued in the face of overwhelming opposition internationally. Following the frustrated Geneva
conference in January 1981, the frontline states, the OAU, and Nigeria
(as head of the U.N. Special Committee Against Apartheid) issued a
joint statement saying: "We are left with no other alternative but to
support the escalation of the armed struggle being heroically waged by
SWAPO. In this regard the OAU member states as a whole pledge their
full backing. Africa pledges increased material and financial assistance
to SWAPO until final victory and total liberation of Namibia."[23]

In April 1981 a move in the U.N. Security Council for a range of
sanctions including an oil embargo against South Africa was blocked

by the U.S. together with Britain and France in a triple veto. In May 1981 the U.N. Special Committee on Apartheid held an international conference at UNESCO House in Paris attended by delegations from 124 governments as well as international agencies, non-governmental bodies and liberation movements; the issue of Namibia was included in the indictment of apartheid. A Paris Declaration of Sanctions against South Africa was adopted, calling for comprehensive mandatory sanctions. In the following month the 18th summit meeting of the OAU, held in Nairobi, fully endorsed the comprehensive sanctions declaration.

There was, however, a more central aspect of the U.S. policy shift yet to be revealed. An indication of it appeared in a memo prepared by Assistant Secretary Crocker for Secretary of State Alexander Haig, for Haig's meeting with South African Foreign Minister Pik Botha when the latter visited Washington in May 1981. Saying that the U.S. should work to "end South Africa's polecat status in the world, and seek to restore its place as a legitimate and important regional actor with whom we can cooperate pragmatically," Crocker went on: "The problem of Namibia which complicates our relations with our European allies and with Black Africa is a primary obstacle to the development of a new relationship with South Africa. It also represents an opportunity to counter the Soviet threat in Africa." The aim of a Namibia solution, in the U.S. view, should be to "engage with South Africa in security" and to include South Africa in the "general security framework" which the Reagan administration was erecting globally to serve U.S. "national interests."[24]

When Haig subsequently put forward the administration foreign policy position, he said: "It is in our interest that the solution we find should not put into jeopardy the interests of those who share our values—above all, our interests in a broad strategic sense." He was referring particularly to South Africa.[25]

Assistant Secretary Crocker finally unwrapped fully the "strategic interests" of the U.S. at a special session of the U.N. General Assembly in September 1981, called to discuss the future of Namibia. Said Crocker, there is an "intimate relationship between the civil war in Angola and the Namibian conflict." He declared that a Namibian settlement must be linked with the departure of Cuban troops from Angola.

By introducing the "linkage" issue into a solution of the Namibian question the U.S. dealt a crippling blow to hopes of the Namibian people, and of the rest of Africa, for independence. South Africa eagerly seized upon the demand, which had not previously been made a condition of a Namibian settlement, and, to the present time, is still using it, together with the U.S., to thwart the transition to independence.

The presence of Cuban troops in Angola has been irrelevant to Namibian independence from colonialism. Cuban troops are in Angola at the 1975 request of the MPLA government to help defend the country from South African invasion and armed subversion. At no time have they constituted a threat to Namibia in any way, or to any neighbor of Angola. Similarly, Angola has never threatened Namibia or South Africa.

It was revealed in the latter part of 1982 by the foreign minister of Angola, Paulo Jorge, that an agreement had been reached between Angola and Cuba as early as 1976 for Cuban troop withdrawal and that a phased pullout had actually begin in 1979, but attacks on Angola by South Africa had forced a halt to the process. Said Jorge, withdrawal would take place "as soon as Namibia attains independence and there is no likelihood of any further aggression against Angola."[26]

It is true that Angola has given sanctuary to Namibian refugees from repressive South African campaigns, and has given assistance to SWAPO. That assistance has been rendered not just as the fraternal relation of one liberation movement to another but as part of international support for SWAPO. Angola is acting both as a member of the frontline states which as a body have formally declared a policy of material and financial aid to SWAPO, and as a member of the OAU which also fully supports SWAPO's armed struggle for independence, especially through the OAU's Liberation Committee which was set up to give material assistance to all liberation struggles in southern Africa (including that of the African National Congress in South Africa). SWAPO, after all, is officially recognized by the U.N. as the sole representative of the Namibian people, and is permitted permanent observer status at the U.N. itself.

The issue of the Cuban troops was not intended by the U.S. to contribute to a solution of the Namibian question, but to serve the African phase of the Reagan administration's global strategy—to halt and reverse national liberation movements and trends in Africa, Asia and Latin America, and to confront and set back the Soviet Union, the other socialist countries, and Communist-influenced forces in every part of the globe, which are the main allies of national liberation. Forcing the Cuban troops out of Angola would gravely reduce the capacity of the MPLA government, engaged in the mammoth task of development out of colonialism, to withstand the assault by South Africa and its instrument, UNITA, would make possible a retrograde settlement in which UNITA would share and be in a position to seize power, and would throw Angola back to a neocolonial status, opening the country again to TNC plundering. At the same time SWAPO would lose a key ally; Namibian independence could be either delayed indefinitely or delivered to the puppet creations of South Africa, also to the benefit of U.S. and other western interests.

U.S. policy around the Namibia question amounted to a major stepping-up of the imperialist strategy of using its alliance with South Africa to roll back African liberation. As the pressures were applied to Angola, they were applied equally to Mozambique. Crocker's deputy, Assistant Secretary for African Affairs Frank Wisner, visited Mozambique and bluntly told President Machel not to "internationalize the war" being waged by the FRELIMO government against the South African-backed MNR; i.e., not to request the assistance of Cuban or other fraternal troops. Wisner impressed on Machel that the U.S. did back South African demands for a treaty with Mozambique under which the African National Congress presence must be removed from Mozambique.[27] The Nkomati Accord embodying this demand that was signed in January 1984 was negotiated behind the scenes by Chester Crocker and Wisner. After a pressure visit by Wisner to President Machel in November 1983, the U.S. envoy reportedly flew directly to Pretoria to inform South African Foreign Minister Pik Botha that the time was ripe for negotiating an agreement with Mozambique. According to *Time* magazine, much credit belongs to Crocker for the Nkomati Accord, which "raises American prestige."[28]

This kind of diplomacy was one of the key aspects of "constructive engagement." Chester Crocker and his team roved over southern Africa to pave the way for a revived "constellation of states" arrangement for South Africa. Crocker literally inserted himself as the chief mediator in the issues involving South Africa regionally, from Namibia and Angola across to Mozambique. Although the Contact Group remained in being and continued as the vehicle for keeping negotiations on Namibia in the control of western countries, outside the purview of the United Nations, the contact with South Africa was assumed almost entirely by Crocker, who merely reported back to the other Contact Group members on his talks with the Botha regime.

U.S. efforts to introduce obstacles to a settlement, outside the stipulations of Resolution 435, eventually produced conflict within the Contact Group. France and West Germany in particular disagreed with the U.S. stand on linking the presence of Cuban troops in Angola with Namibian independence. Early in 1984 France finally went to the extent of ceasing to participate in the Contact Group activities, over the Cuban troops issue.[29]

While the U.S. kept insisting on Cuban withdrawal as the prime condition for a Namibian settlement, repeated South African attacks on and incursions into Angola made the MPLA government feel that the retention of Cuban troops was essential. The situation had the earmarks of a cynical game. On the basis of wholly unsubstantiated claims that the SWAPO-PLAN units were "preparing" to infiltrate into Namibia from "bases in Angola," South African troops would invade Angola, "to eliminate SWAPO bases." The U.S. would then intervene in behalf of South Africa to bring about negotiating procedures with Angola for a withdrawal of South African troops. The stretched-out negotiations on that issue in turn held up negotiations on implementing Resolution 435.

A large-scale South African invasion of Angola in December 1983, supposedly to forestall SWAPO infiltration, typified the tactics of the apartheid regime and its allies. When proposals for negotiations on South African withdrawal were initiated, South Africa demanded the inclusion of UNITA in the talks. Angola and SWAPO strongly opposed the proposal. Said the Angolan government, "we categorically reject any kind of a dialogue or negotiations with the criminal band of traitors who are today in the pay of the Pretoria regime which is vainly trying to legitimize it as a participant in the proposed conference."[30]

Talks that opened in Lusaka in February 1984 saw South Africa glibly agreeing to withdraw as well as to cease giving support to UNITA. However, withdrawal, supposed to start in March did not begin in a small way until May, and then South African troops adopted the procedure of drawing back a mile or so and halting for three weeks to "consolidate the area," which invariably meant bringing in its UNITA puppets to establish themselves.[31] The bulk of South African troops in this invasion were not finally withdrawn until the first half of 1985, and units were still retained in Cunene province. In all this extended delaying action, no U.S. statement was made to criticize the apartheid regime or to hasten its compliance with an agreement, nor did Chester Crocker's shuttling about southern Africa indicate any effort in that direction.

The scarcely concealed U.S.-South African aim in this period was to press upon Angola and the other southern Africa countries Nkomati Accord type agreements with South Africa. In the case of Angola this was to embody the inclusion of UNITA in the Luanda government and a commitment to expel SWAPO and ANC people from Angolan territory. Throughout 1984 constant pressure was exerted upon Lesotho, Botswana, Swaziland and Zimbabwe for such accords.

Swaziland yielded, but the others did not, Lesotho going to the point of establishing diplomatic relations with the Soviet Union and welcoming a Soviet embassy on its South African-surrounded soil.

By the beginning of 1986, however, Lesotho had been forced to give in to South African anti-ANC demands. In May 1986 helicopter-borne South African troops raided Botswana's capital, Gabarone, South African jet bombers attacked Zambia, and commandos struck in Zimbabwe's capital, Harare, claiming to be hitting ANC targets.

South African invasions of Angola, made under the pretense of destroying SWAPO bases, were exposed in their true motivation in the latter part of September 1985. At that time the Angolan army, FAPLA, in a successful offensive, had defeated UNITA forces and was driving them toward the border with Namibia and to expulsion from the country. South Africa thereupon sent its air force into Angola in heavy bombing and strafing attacks that stopped the advancing Angolan motorized column, and sent its mercenary 32 Battalion over 150 miles into Angola to stiffen UNITA defenses.

Prime Minister Botha and his Defense Minister, General Magnus Malan, cast aside pretenses in this action. Malan admitted for the first time officially that "material, humanitarian and moral support" was being given to UNITA for its "opposition to communism." He said: "Our policy is to combat Marxist expansionism. In Angola, it concerns a Soviet-controlled offensive against all of southern Africa. Angola is Moscow's springboard into southern Africa." Botha, in his turn, proclaimed: "If the Russians and Cubans succeed (in Angola), the next target will be South West Africa (Namibia). If they succeed there, their next target will be Botswana. When they succeed there, their next target will be the Republic of South Africa."[32]

While UNITA was receiving shattering blows at this time from the Angolan army, the U.S. Congress, pressed by the Reagan administration, rescinded the 1976 Clark Amendment that forbade providing UNITA with U.S. arms. By October 1985 moves were made in the U.S. Congress to legislate large-scale military aid to UNITA. The consequences of such a step could only be the worsening of conflict in that region of southern Africa and erecting higher obstacles to independence for Namibia.

Resort to this type of South African-U.S. action and to this kind of wild anti-Soviet, anti-communist propaganda which had no relation to reality was tantamount to an admission of failure in the design of U.S.-South African strategy. It coincided with the publishing in Maputo, Mozambique of documentary evidence of South African treachery and non-compliance in the Nkomati Accord, including the continued extensive supply and reinforcement of the MNR rebels by South Africa, operational visits by South African cabinet members to MNR camps in Mozambique, and general efforts to overthrow or reduce to total subservience the FRELIMO government.[33] The U.S. remained silent about this outcome of the Crocker diplomacy.

Imperialist-apartheid strategy in southern Africa, with one of its main aims the cutting off of the ANC and SWAPO from their African and other international allies, prolonged the thwarting of Namibian independence. From the time the Reagan administration assumed its "constructive engagement" mediating role through its emissary, Chester Crocker, the implementation of Resolution 435 became stalled.

In October 1982 Foreign Minister Pik Botha announced that South Africa would hold onto Walvis Bay regardless of a Namibian independence. "Walvis Bay," he said, "belongs to us." South African troops were moved in to erect military installations around the area, which is the port linked by rail to the capital, Windhoek, and is the only really adequate import-export site on the Namibian coast. The introduction of the Walvis Bay issue and claim provided another contentious problem for blocking progress toward independence.[34]

SWAPO's Sam Nujoma revealed in September 1984 that South Africa was dismantling railroad lines in Namibia connecting Keetmanshoap and the smaller port of Luderitz, which would make the country wholly dependent on the port of Walvis Bay, in South African hands. "As far as SWAPO is concerned," said Nujoma, "Walvis Bay is an integral part of Namibia. SWAPO fights to liberate every inch of Namibia, including Walvis Bay."[35]

Plans were also announced by South Africa to make the South West Africa Territory Force, set up in 1980 to draw Namibian collaborators into an auxiliary role with the South African army in suppression of SWAPO, the basis for the defense force of an independent Namibia. Over 30% of SWATF was made up of South African troops. Its reactionary character as a South African instrument showed how it would "defend" Namibian interests.[36]

Attempts by the Pretoria regime to establish a puppet administration in the territory in the form of a "National Assembly" controlled by the white-dominated Democratic Turnhalle Alliance collapsed, however, within two years. In February 1982 the figurehead president of the DTA, Peter Kalangula, leader of the small National Democratic Party based among a small minority of Ovambos, quit the DTA and took his party with him, protesting against the indiscriminately ruthless behavior of the South African army in his region.[37] His resignation began the disintegration of the DTA and of the Assembly. The Damara tribal grouping, comprising 10% of the population, next walked out. Dirk Mudge, himself, wanting greater authority as the main DTA leader, quarreled with the Soutn African government and resigned on January 18, 1983. DTA rule was then replaced by the return of direct rule by South Africa, under an appointed South African general administrator.[38]

While South Africa maneuvered to frustrate implementation of Resolution 435, invaded Angola, and sought to create anti-SWAPO groupings within Namibia, its military campaigns against SWAPO-PLAN went on with mounting ferocity. A feature of these was the setting up in 1983 of a special police-army counterinsurgency unit called Koevet. Composed of 1,000 men, 200 of them South African and the rest drawn from the colonial South West African police, it operated under the South African Ministry of Law and Order and was known as "the killing machine." Koevet was trained to "show no mercy" to members of SWAPO or its PLAN guerrillas. Reports from Namibia told of peasants being slow roasted over fires by Koevet to extract information or made to run in 40° C heat until they fell dead. Shooting of women and children and the elderly and the burning of homes were reported as regular behavior by the South African army as well.[39] Said a leading Johannesburg paper: "South Africa's position is weakened because the army is not seen as a gentle giant protecting the people. There is a perception of the SADF as an occupying army and a destructive force. This is definitely increasing and is now well established."[40]

Far from cutting down SWAPO strength and influence, military suppression and political machinations against independence brought greater support for the Namibian liberation movement. A secret document leaked from a two-day military conference in Windhoek of South African counterintelligence officers in August 1984 reported "deep concern about SWAPO's presence in virtually all walks of life in the territory," saying that SWAPO was "so well organized that it is responsible for a growing feeling of insecurity."[41]

SWAPO's growing international prestige and worldwide demands for action on Resolution 435 forced South Africa in 1984 to go through the motions of talks with SWAPO. South Africa, however, refused to negotiate with SWAPO directly or alone. The Botha regime tried to maneuver SWAPO into negotiating not with South Africa but with its puppet creation in Namibia (which after the collapse of the first puppet Assembly was renamed from Turnhalle Democratic Alliance to Multi-Party Conference or MPC). When talks were finally held in Lusaka, Zambia in May 1984, the MPC was brought into the picture and South Africa sought to make it appear that it was an MPC negotiation with SWAPO, with South African representatives merely "observing." SWAPO denounced this maneuver, saying that it did not consider the internal parties a threat and was not fighting them. SWAPO was directly fighting South Africa and would meet with South Africa and no other.

The Lusaka meeting was attended by a 60-strong SWAPO delegation that disconcerted the apartheid team with its breadth. It included the Damara Council which went over to SWAPO at the beginning of 1984, a large part of the South West African National Union which had a Herero base, the Namibia Christian Democrats, and representatives of the Namibian Council of Churches, and virtually the whole of the Ovambo people. When the MPC, voicing the South African position, tried to set aside Resolution 435 as a deadlocked matter and said it was time to "seek a counter-strategy, not an alternative, based on new ideas to break the deadlock," SWAPO charged that this was a thinly disguised effort to replace the U.N. plan with a formula for indefinite delay and to try to give credibility to the puppet MPC (which tried to propose a conference in Windhoek, in the shadow of the South African army). The Lusaka meeting collapsed after three days.[42]

South Africa continued to persist in its policy of thwarting the independence of Namibia, assisted by the pretence at mediation by the Reagan administration's envoy, Chester Crocker. On April 18, 1985, the apartheid regime announced the creation of a second puppet government in Namibia. Botha said that it "should be seen as an interim mechanism for the internal administration of the territory pending agreement on an internationally acceptable independence." He appointed a South African administrator general with the power to veto any measure not approved by South Africa and with control over the police forces. In addition, as before, the South African government retained control of defense and foreign affairs. After a perfunctory murmur of disapproval by the U.S. and other Contact Group members, South Africa's latest colonial device in Namibia was accepted by them as fact.

Said a SWAPO statement: "We condemn the outrageous contempt for international opinion, as expressed in U.N. Resolution 435, and for the wishes of the Namibian people for true independence."

V THE CRISIS OF APARTHEID

The leaders of all the white-ruled racist regimes who have tried to prevail in southern Africa against the liberation process that has moved across the continent in the past quarter of a century have tended to think of their systems as permanent, able to endure indefinitely. In Rhodesia, Ian Smith, propping up his colonialist, "unilateral declaration of independence" with a counterinsurgency army, envisioned that the one man, one vote demand of the Black liberation movements would not come to pass for a thousand years. The Portuguese colonies of Angola and Mozambique, in the racist estimates of the policy-makers of the Nixon administration, could not be overturned by the liberation movements and could go on unlimitedly with some minor adjustments and with U.S. guidance.

Perhaps most convinced of all of their system's immortality have been the architects and officialdom of South African apartheid. The manner in which the apartheid state, with its structure of laws and security measures, and the divisions of people and land under separate development, were put into effect, indicated a belief that a lasting society of this type could be maintained. If necessary, some asserted, apartheid South Africa could withdraw into its laager and remain there, indestructible. Its allies in the capitalist countries, on their part, regarded it as capable of surviving as an aggressive state, sustained indefinitely by their investment and trade and extending its ideology outward. The leaders and apologists of apartheid have been the most arrogant, the most convinced of their system's durability, and the most self-deluded, of all the latter-day colonial rulers.

As it has happened, the apartheid system has had only a comparatively brief period of seeming stability and feasibility. In the decade of the 1960s, with the opposition anti-apartheid organizations believed to have been crushed, with the Black and other nonwhite majority believed to be submissively under control as low-paid labor, with Afrikaaner capitalism in a condition of burgeoning growth, and with funds pouring in from all the main capitalist countries, it looked as if the system was viable and strong. It was an illusion. Within a few years, historically overnight, there was crisis. From the early 1970s South Africa has been racked by a crisis of growing proportions and ramifications.

That crisis has two main interlocking features—economic and social—both rooted in the nature of the apartheid system itself.

Together they demonstrate the failure of apartheid and point to its inevitable collapse.

The Costs of a Racist State

In September 1985 the lending institutions of the western capitalist countries were jolted and swept momentarily by panic as a result of reports from South Africa of a grave economic situation. The Botha government had revealed that it could not repay the installments on foreign loans due at the end of the year and that it was resorting to tight exchange controls to check further deterioration of the economy. Two months earlier the government had felt sufficiently alarmed by a growing mass protest movement against its apartheid policies to declare a state of emergency in a number of key districts. South Africa's image as a secure and profitable bastion for imperialism was being transformed into a frightening picture of developing economic and political crisis.

The panic in the west came from concern over the safety of around $25 billion in direct and indirect investment and of loans that were variously estimated to total from $21 billion to $31 billion (of which about $14 billion were short term). Furthermore, a decline of the rand since the beginning of 1984 by more than 50% of its value meant that the profit returns of western subsidiary companies would be severely reduced.

To a considerable extent the economic circumstances of South Africa were due to the prevailing worldwide capitalist economic crisis, which was impinging on all the countries, developed and developing, tied to capitalist market relations. In particular a decline in the world price of gold and of other strategic minerals contributed to a South African balance of payments deficit; in turn, that caused a reduction of imports of both capital goods and consumer items.

In South Africa, however, the ordinary effects of capitalist crisis have been immensely aggravated by the apartheid system, in which the features of exploitation have been greatly intensified by racist oppression and its extreme inequalities. No other capitalist country has had such a gigantic gap between a monopoly minority of the wealthy and the vast majority sunk in and pressed down in abject poverty. What seemed ideal to the white capitalist—a huge reservoir of very low-paid Black labor without rights—proved to be the precise factor preventing an expanding capitalism: limiting the growth of the domestic market, impeding the accumulation of savings for investment (as in the case of bank deposits, insurance and shareholding by workers and middle class sectors in developed capitalist countries), hampering the development of productive forces in all sectors of the economy. Coupled with this has been the diversion of economic means from productive processes to the vast cumbersome apparatus of the apartheid state with all its special agencies, departments and segregated "homelands," its police forces and punitive institutions, its repressive army and huge arms budget. As the strains in the system have increased, so has the need for diverting ever greater resources to maintaining it.

The two key pillars of "separate development," the homelands system and its related devices of influx control, have risen precipitously in cost. By 1984 the price tag for these was over 3.5 billion rands a year, spent for the following (in rands):

Commission for Cooperation and Development	98,000
Commissioners General	235,000
Consolidation	126,500,000
"Development towards self-determination"	288,223,000
Assistance for governments of self-governing states	1,013,030,000
"Foreign Aid and Development" (includes aid to independent homelands)	637,790,000
Regulation of labor	3,086,000
Residential Control	2,309,000
Repatriation	3,964,000
Population Registration and Identification of Persons	8,233,000
Transport Subsidies for Public Passenger Transport (commuting from townships)	130,424,000
South African Transport Services Losses on Passenger Services	750,000,000
Decentralization Incentives	267,600,000
Total	(R)3,534,500,000 [1]

These expenditures and costs, made directly on the apartheid structure, comprised about 14% of the 1984 South African budget of 25.3 billion rands. The four "independent" homelands alone (Transkei, Ciskei, Venda and Bophuthatswana) accounted for an accumulated cost of 8,489 million rands up to the end of 1982.[2] To keep the "homeland" or Bantustan leaders in power as collaborators with apartheid was costing one billion rands a year by the 1982-1983 budgetary year (in the above list, this payment of salaries, subsidies and benefits is termed "assistance to governments of self-governing states").

However, this is not the whole direct cost of apartheid segregation. The establishment of Black townships for those working away from the homelands in white areas has caused an incalculable expense for construction, roads, rail extension and other needs. In 1983, as a means of deflecting Black protest from white authority, local town councils were created for 26 of the main townships. Financing these cost the Botha government 300 million rands a year, chiefly because the Black councils had meager sources for raising revenue to operate and had to rely on central government funds. Local government normally relies on property taxes in the main, but Black township residents were barred from owning land or living quarters and therefore could not be taxed.[3] When the Botha regime in 1984 sought to pass the local operating costs off onto the townships' people by insisting that the councils finance themselves through raising of rents, electricity prices and other services, the result was a mass boycott movement by Black residents that led to militant confrontation.

Township costs for the apartheid government was illustrated by the payout of 2.8 million rands in Soweto alone for riot squads and other security police.[4]

Apartheid institutions and implementation of apartheid laws have required a huge bureaucracy with a continual addition of state employees and civil service workers to run the system. These totalled 340,723 in 1982, an increase of 16,000 over 1981. The bill for these employees was 514,642,000 rands in 1982, which embodied a jump of nearly 100 million rands in a single year.[5] An example of the distortions and waste in the system is the maintanence of several departments of education, one for the white minority, one for "Bantu" education, and others for Colored and Indian minorities.

Innumerable other costs are connected with maintaining the apartheid state. South Africa's 242 prisons, built to hold a maximum of 72,892, have an overcrowding of 106,000 daily. The majority are Black, confined for pass law violations and other influx control offenses. Prison costs were 700,000 rands per day in 1983, or 255.5 million rands a year.[6]

The amount spent on developing the Sasol plants for extracting oil from coal, undertaken to counter the international oil embargo against apartheid, is not known but it is a huge government investment. Together with it can be calculated the extra costs occasioned by importing oil by surreptitious means to evade the embargo, costs over and above the price on the spot market where the South African government obtains most of its oil through the big western oil companies. In 1978 western oil company heads met secretly in South Africa with government officials to ask for a higher price because of risks and difficulties. South Africa agreed to set up a special Equalization Fund to "compensate" the companies, paying $39 a barrel in 1979 when the official price was $26. The major firm engaged in this trade has been Shell; it is known to have profited by an extra $200 million in the single year of 1980 just from the premium paid by the apartheid regime.[7]

In the same way the South African Chamber of Mines has spent large sums recruiting skilled white miners overseas, due to the job reservation laws that prevent the training and employment of Black workers for the skilled mining jobs. In the typical year of 1981 the Chamber spent 750,000 rands on its recruiting drives abroad.[8]

White farmers have had to be financed or subsidized to remain in areas of the Transvaal bordering on neighboring countries where it is feared that Umkhonto we Sizwe guerrillas may pass in transit or base themselves. In 1982-1983 government payments to prevent farm evacuation came to 5 million rands.[9]

These are all costs associated with the operation of the apartheid system, constituting a vast diversion of resources that could otherwise have been used for economic development and the improvement of the lives of all South Africans. The survey does not take into account the colossal waste of human resources—the Black productive power kept unemployed in the homelands.

The greatest drain of all, however, has been caused by the militarization of the apartheid state in order to hold down internal revolt and to conduct external aggression. Architects of the apartheid system perhaps did not visualize the extent to which this factor would grow. South Africa's military spending in the year the Nationalist regime left the Commonwealth and severed ties with the British crown, 1960, was a mere 44 million rands.[10]

In 1974, as Black workers began to stir, the arms budget was still only 707 million rands, but by 1979, after the collapse of the Portuguese colonies, the revolt in Soweto, the guerrilla war in Namibia and the rise of Black trade unions, defense allocations had vaulted to 2,189 million rands. Since then the increase has been in leaps, up to 2,465 million rands in 1981 and, with a massive 21.4% jump in a single year, to 3,750 million rands in the 1984-1985 budget. In 1986-87 it is 5,123 million rands.

The war in Namibia, a direct effort to maintain an apartheid colony, was costing 320 million rands a year in 1982.[11] A 1983 estimate put it at 2 million rands a day.[12] By 1985 it was approaching 1 billion rands yearly.

All told, the extremely heavy costs of running and trying to defend the apartheid system have been consuming well over one-third of the South African governmental budget. Not only have they gravely weakened the country's economy, but they have caused the apartheid regime to turn increasingly to foreign borrowing to sustain its spending pattern. Ostensibly government borrowing has been done to finance education, housing, transport and other innocuous items, but this has actually enabled the shift of resources from such areas to military spending and to the purely apartheid-running features of the budget. In the main, the mountainous foreign debt that began to topple over in 1985 was piled up to support the racist system. South Africa's crisis is essentially a crisis of apartheid.

The Failure of "Separate Development"

The debilitating and self-destructive cost of maintaining white domination in a segregated society has been but one aspect of the failure of the apartheid system.

Undoubtedly the architects of that system considered that it could be workable and permanent, that a master-slave relationship in the modern world could produce growth and development, at least for the white minority. Theoretically, "separate development," while preserving and augmenting the prosperity and high living standards of the 4.5 million whites, was supposed to enable enough well-being for the 26 million Black and other nonwhite sectors of the population to keep them from rebelling or upsetting the arrangement. For the Black "homelands" or Bantustans, however, development has been almost nonexistent.

A measure of that lack of development, in the years when South Africa as a whole was registering 6% to 8% growth rates, are the figures on per capita Gross Domestic Product in the homelands in the years 1975 to 1980. In six of the Bantustans taken together (Kwazulu, Lebowa, Qwa Qwa, Gazankula, KaNgwana, and KwaNdebele) per capita GDP rose merely from 44 rands in 1975 to 47 rands in 1980. The rise was slightly better in the four "independent" homelands (Transkei, Ciskei, Venda and Bophuthatswana) but there, as in all of the homelands, over one-half of what was counted as GDP came from the wages of migrant workers. These wages were actually a consequence of production in the white areas.[13]

In a relentless application of the homelands policy by the National-ist government, a grand total of 3,522,900 Black people were uprooted from where they had been living and relocated in the Bantustans. Between 1960 and 1980 the proportion of Blacks living in the Bantustans jumped from 40% to 54%. A Surplus Peoples Project study in 1983 found: "Living conditions in relocation areas are generally very poor and most people suffer material loss when they are relocated, particularly those moved from where they had agricultural land to where they do not."[14] A better way of putting the segregationist policy is to call it "separated from development."

Thus, in 1980 over 5.2 million out of the 6.2 million Black residents in the six "self-governing" homelands had no measurable annual income. In the four "independent" homelands only about 1 million out of 4.6 million were classified as economically active. Between 1960 and 1980 a mere 75,000 jobs were created in the Bantustans, although due to both relocations and natural increase their populations had risen by 7 million. The true "development" function of the Bantustans, whether "self-governing" or "independent", lay in the figures on migrant or commuted labor from these areas to the industrialized white areas: 2,074,000 in 1981.[15]

For the great majority of people in South Africa, "separate develop-ment" has meant a descent into worsening poverty. A more brutal effect has been the destruction of family life by the migrant labor system. Absence of the working husband or suitor has left a 3 to 1 ratio of women in the Bantustans and widespread one-parent family situa-tion. One survey made in South Africa concluded that for many Black women marriage is no longer an attractive proposition. These unsta-ble circumstances have fed the discontent of the oppressed.[16]

Only in 1982, as crisis and unrest were growing, did the Pretoria government undertake to stimulate some investment in the Bantus-tans. Incentives were offered for both foreign and South African businesses: cash refunds of 95% of Black wages, interest rates on loans one-third of those normally required for setting up industries, a cash grant of 125% of the cost of training Black workers, rebates of 40-60% on rail costs and harbor charges on transported or exported finished goods.[17] Despite these incentives the response was slight: the remote, mostly barren Bantustans, landlocked and for the most part without resources, power or infrastructure, had meager access to ports, air-ports or railheads, and were distant from markets. However, by 1985, after Black trade unions had spread and conducted militant struggles for higher wages in the white urban areas, a trend began from white businessmen to set up industries in or near the borders of Bantustans.

This was not merely a matter of drawing upon the cheap unemployed Black labor in the Bantustans, which could be paid for less than in the urban areas, but had to do with the fact that trade unions are banned in the Bantustans.[18]

Families, one-parent or otherwise, have had to look upon their children in serious states of malnourishment. The director of the South African Institute of Race Relations, John Rees, said in 1980 that 3 out of 4 urban and 8 out of 10 rural Black children were malnourished.[19] It was reported in 1983 that 96 children die of malnutrition every day in South Africa.[20]

Above all, the Bantustans are incapable of being self-sustaining. If not for the handouts of the Pretoria government, which constitute a drain on the central regime and which are mainly to sustain the narrow ruling groups, these "states" would disintegrate. As it is, they cannot carry on the responsibilities of administration. As late as 1982 over one-half of the population in the six "self-governing" Bantustans (i.e., 3.3 million people) had no education or "unspecified" education.[21]

Migrant employment, however, has far from absorbed the labor power pent up in the Bantustans, the bulk of which is left economically inactive. No precise figures are revealed or known about unemployment in South Africa, but estimates have run between 19% and 31% of the labor force, in the neighborhood of 3 million. Of these, only about 75,000 are white. Most of the unemployed are in the Bantustans. Such a massive waste of the country's productive forces (aggravated by the policy, especially in the mining industry, of importing contract labor from the neighboring countries) renders the true verdict on South Africa as a developed country.

It may be asked, if these are the conditions, why the upheavals occurring in South Africa have not taken place in the Bantustans. In part it is due to the social structure in these areas, which is largely rural and lacking in the intense collectivity of the urban townships and their industrial life. The absence of large numbers of adult men, as migrants, is a factor, as is the resultant age composition of those remaining: 60% are below the age of 20. Together with these circumstances is the semi-dictatorial rule of the tribal chiefs who accept the apartheid divisions embodied in the Bantustans. Political parties that oppose apartheid are either forbidden or severely harassed, trade unions are banned and migrant workers who join trade unions at work places in the white areas or become leaders in them are frequently arrested, and in some cases special counterinsurgency police forces trained by mercenaries have been set up to threaten and terrorize anti-apartheid activists.

The intolerable conditions of the Bantustans, however, have tended to act against and to disrupt other features of apartheid, in particular the complementary Group Areas Act and the influx control measures to enforce it. As relocation and the cramming of Blacks into the Bantustans has gone on, thousands have seeped back into the townships in the white areas, driven by poverty, returning illegally in violation of the Group Areas Act, and prepared to accept lower wages from exploiting employers who turn a blind eye to the lack of proper passes or labor permits. The actual population of townships like Soweto is unknown because of the presence of so many "illegals," a mounting phenomenon as the economic crisis has worsened.

In reaction, the Botha government has devised stricter methods of influx control, fitting it to the electronic age. Influx control has become computerized:

> Computers in all areas now controlled by the main administration boards, linked to each other and to a central computer in Pretoria, would enable the Government to combat unemployment by providing instant information on where jobs are and where workers are who can do the jobs. The system would also enable the Government to tighten up severely on influx control. A wide array of personal details—including "relevant" criminal offenses—would be fed into computers . . . there are fears that the system could be abused by the authorities and that it could give the Government unprecedented control over the lives of black people in urban areas.[22]

Pass laws have been tightened up, with raids staged in the townships to catch offenders. From 1980 to 1981 a 20% increase in pass law arrests occurred, the total going well above 200,000. This arrest rate has continued, rising higher in subsequent years. In 1982 the Botha government resorted to the adoption of a new influx control law, the Orderly Movement and Settlement of Black Persons Act, more severe than past measures. The previous renewable 3-month visitors' permits for relatives and friends coming from the homelands were scrapped, with visitors now allowed a nonrenewable 14 days a year. Punitive provisions of the Act fell heaviest on employers of "unauthorized" Black workers or "illegals": they can now be fined 5,000 rands instead of the previous 500 rands. Those giving accommodation to "illegals" may be fined 500 rands.[23]

Nevertheless, the unauthorized drift from the Bantustans to the townships has continued. The chairman of the Anglo-American Corporation, Gavin Relly, a critic of influx control, said in September 1984: "Movement to the towns is going to take place whether we like it or not and however draconian the measures we take to prevent it."[24]

South African Capitalists and "Reform"

Within South African ruling circles themselves, indications that the apartheid system had been built on unstable foundations began to emerge in an organized manner soon after the Soweto revolt of June 1976. One of the early manifestations of such a trend was the conference of big businessmen in Johannesburg in November 1976. It was called at the initiative of Harry Oppenheimer, then chairman of the Anglo-American Corporation, and Anton Rupert, head of the large Rembrandt conglomerate. The conference set up the Urban Foundation, with Oppenheimer and Rupert as its chairman and vice-chairman. It has served as a voice of an important sector of South African capitalists and of a number of foreign companies that together reportedly employ about 70% of the labor force in the private sector.

At this conference Anton Rupert declared: "We [capitalists] cannot survive unless we have a free market economy, a stable black middle class." Another prominent figure in the group, Judge Jan Steyn, told the conference that an Urban Foundation would have "the fundamental aim to improve the quality of life of the urban (black) citizen" and to attain "ordered advance to urban tranquility."[25]

Those associated with the Urban Foundation had, in fact, profited greatly and rapidly gained their corporate power from apartheid.

However, they had soon become aware that the restrictions of apartheid eventually meant limitations on the processes of capitalist growth. Influx control negated Black labor mobility. The migrant labor system, as practiced, meant an unstable labor force of inadequate productivity, affected by the disruption of family life. Job reservation and meager Black education operated together to create a growing shortage of skilled labor without which economic and technological growth were gravely hampered.

One of the most outspoken of the South African capitalists has been Harry Oppenheimer (who has also been one of those most intertwined with foreign capital). "I do not believe the private enterprise system can ally itself with apartheid without destroying apartheid," he said, implying that free enterprise must inevitably burst the bonds of apartheid.[26] On another occasion he said: "Time is running dangerously short and if our problems are not faced now they will have to be faced in a much more aggravated form in the future."[27] In 1981 he asserted that South Africa must make "substantial efforts toward social change within five years to avoid revolution."[28] Again, in 1984; "the undoubted risks involved in accelerating the rate of internal change are risks that ought to be taken."[29] Oppenheimer called it extremely important for changes to be effected in Black education, township housing, the influx control system, and the country's constitution.[30]

The calls for reform raised by the Urban Foundation and its chief spokesmen were not isolated demands. They came in one form or another from the South African Chamber of Industries, the Association of Chambers of Commerce (Assocom) and individual business executives. The Assocom urged the government at the end of 1982 to enshrine in the constitution labor mobility and a common citizenship for all races.[31]

In 1980 the Anglo-American Corporation commissioned a study on migrant labor. Written by Merle Lipton, formerly of Britain's Royal Institute of International Affairs, it concluded that migrant labor should be replaced by a policy of allowing black workers to settle with their families near their places of work.[32]

By the latter 1970s these capitalist interests understood that the features of apartheid that had made it possible for them to accumulate vast wealth were now acting as fetters on their further development. This was particularly the case as development of the economy along capital intensive lines became more pronounced. The need for skilled labor in high technology industry became acute. The white labor force was increasingly unable to make up the shortage.

A root of this phase of the crisis was in the system of Black education, which was deliberately not designed to produce the vocationally skilled or the technically proficient, or to provide the grounding for advanced training. Job reservation for whites further restricted the skilled labor force, and apprenticeship programs were nonexistent for Black workers.

By 1980 there was a national shortage of 15,000 to 20,000 professional and technical staff workers in the country. There was reportedly a need for 4,000 to 5,000 more managers than were available. Skilled manpower, from electrical and mining engineers to computer programers, was said to be "dangerously thin on the ground." The then outgoing president of the Chamber of Mines, Dennis Etheridge, warned of a shortfall of skilled labor in the industry equivalent to the complement of skilled personnel in two gold mines employing 20,000 workers, including a lack of accountants, engineers, metallurgists, computer programers, and draftsmen.[33]

Barlow Rand, the country's biggest industrial conglomerate, estimated at the time that it alone could absorb the country's entire annual output of electronic engineers.[34] A year later, in 1981, the corporation said it would have a skilled labor shortfall of 30% in three years. The executive chairman of Barlow Rand said that his corporation's call for reform measures to solve the skilled labor problem was not a political statement but a "business imperative."[35]

It was estimated that in South Africa in the 1970s professional and technical workers comprised only 4.5% of the economically active sector of the population (compared with 14.2% in the USA).

The overwhelming number of these were white: there were 13.5% of whites in this category, bringing the white population close to the saturation point for this type of labor.[36] Efforts by South Africa to bring in skilled white immigrant workers were made increasingly difficult as the crisis of apartheid and its explosive possibilities were made glaringly evident to the rest of the world. In fact, the crisis was causing a depletion of the skilled and professional groups through emigration. The only possible source of skilled labor was from among the Black and other nonwhite workers.

However, in 1981, out of 11,964 apprenticeship contracts made, only 495 were Black, while among those attending technical training courses of any kind 47,302 were white and only 2,632 Black. By April 1982 there were a mere 40 indentured Black artisans in the entire country. In the meantime the educational basis for developing Black skills was being destroyed by an educational system in which 84% of Blacks with schooling had gone no further than the primary level, while 30% had no education at all.[37]

These circumstances have affected foreign companies as well as South African, and account for the urging for reform that has come, at times, from western quarters. Expansion and the introduction of advanced productive means are hampered for all capitalist sectors by apartheid relations.

Demands from the Urban Foundation and other business organizations persuaded the Vorster government to set up special commissions to study and make recommendation for changes or improvements in the labor force situation. The Riekert Commission of Inquiry into Manpower Utilization and the Wiehahn Commission on Industrial Conciliation and others took limited steps towad increasing the number of skilled Black workers. Technical and vocational training was made more available. However, the steps taken, such as a 1981 law establishing technikons were all in accordance with the segregated education policy that permitted only meager funds for Black education, resulting in the usual poor and very inadequate training facilities. The consequence was the turning out of an increasing number of semi-skilled Black workers while the posts requiring highly skilled labor were left for whites, or unfilled. The problem, therefore, continued to exist and to grow.

Coupled with this issue was a question of equal if not more pressing gravity for the economy: the growth of Black workers' militancy, of strikes, and of trade union organization.

Throughout most of the 1960s Black workers' struggles were barely visible, subdued by the post-Sharpeville repressions and outlawings. A few Black trade unions remained in being but they were not legally recognized unions. In the years 1962-1968 less than 2,000 Black workers per year took part in strikes. Their demands were not won.

The consequences of the ruthless exploitation that enabled boom-style prosperity for white South Africans and foreign companies in the 1960s could not be repressed, however. In April 1969 the first break from these pent-up conditions came when 2,000 Durban dock workers stuck for a wage increase. It was unsuccessful and most of the workers were "relocated" from the Durban area to homelands and replaced. In 1970 there were 17 strikes of small size, involving but 615 Black workers. In October 1972 the Durban dockworkers, after threatening to strike for over a year, again walked out, this time shutting down South Africa's second largest port. At that time the poverty datum line for a weekly wage was 18 rands but the dockworkers were receiving a minimum wage of 8.5 rands. As a Wage Board promised to examine their case, usually a device for stifling a strike, their demands were reinforced by an overtime strike by thousands of Black and Colored dockworkers in Cape Town, filling the harbor in a month with unloaded ships. When the Wage Board hastened to render its decision in November, minimum wages were boosted by 40%.[38]

This landmark victory by the dockworkers stirred Black workers all over South Africa. An even greater impact, however, had been spreading from a seminal strike in Namibia that began in December 1971. Over 3,000 Ovambo contract workers in Walvis Bay struck against the migrant labor system, the restrictions on movement and freedom of employment, and for higher pay. (The action followed widespread protest demonstrations against South African rule, in the wake of the June 1971 International Court of Justice ruling declaring South African occupation illegal and calling for withdrawal.) Within a week the strike had expanded to virtually every mining and industrial center in Namibia. Over 12,000 workers were out by December 20, and by mid-January 1972 the number had grown to over 13,000. The Namibian economy was literally brought to a halt for a month, and was reactivated only by a government agreement to scrap the contract migrant labor system and to permit labor mobility, while granting some wage rises. Subsequently the South African authorities reneged on the agreement and repatriated the Ovambo workers who had struck, but the significance of the strike action, successfully forcing the government to yield, even temporarily, was felt across South Africa as well as Namibia.[39]

From January 1973 to the middle of 1976 over 200,000 Black workers went on strike in South Africa. Over 800 strikes occurred in this period. Beginning in the Durban-Pinetown-Hammarsdale industrial complex in Natal province, where 160 walkouts occurred in 146 enterprises in the first three months of the upheaval, the strikes spread to the Transvaal and Cape provinces, affecting textile factories, pulp and paper plants, sugar mills, aluminum, rubber, food, plastics, engineering, construction, transport and other sectors. Wage increases were won in most cases. It was the biggest strike wave in South Africa since the early 1940s, prior to the advent of an apartheid government. Furthermore, despite their illegality, unregistered Black trade unions compelled employers to negotiate.[40]

It was this comparatively rebellious upheaval against the apartheid labor and wage system that stirred South African capitalists to reexamine the system and to advise reforms. While the questions of the shortage of skilled labor came to the fore simultaneously, the critical factor in the strike phenomenon was Black worker organization, the emergence of trade unions on a wide scale. During the strike period at least 22 unions had sprung up with a membership of around 30,000.[41]

For the management of struck plants, a major problem arose over how to negotiate with strikers, to discuss demands or to settle grievances. Most often demands were made anonymously, and even where trade unions had been formed, leaders were not inclined to come forward due to the bans on organization. An anarchic state of labor relations prevailed that could become uncontrollable.

The product of this, at businessman's demand, was the setting up of the Wiehahn Commission in August 1977. Composed of 11 whites, 1 Colored, 1 Indian and 1 Black, it was headed by Prof. Nic Wiehahn, head of the Institute of Industrial Relations at the University of South Africa, and a member of the Broederbond. The Commission's findings and recommendations were published in May 1979.[42]

Reform embodied in the Wiehahn Report was the first serious change forced out of the apartheid rulers in the developing crisis of their system. Its recommendations amended one of the pillars of the apartheid state, the 1956 Industrial Conciliation Act which forced existing trade unions to split on racial lines, excluded Black workers from registered trade unions, thus denying them bargaining and negotiating rights, and extended job reservation on the basis of color to all sectors of the economy.

Stating that "unless African trade unions are brought into the statutory register as soon as possible, African workers may well be drawn into informal organizational structures which might in the long run not be possible to dismantle or restructure," the Wiehahn Report deplored this "trend toward uncontrolled and disorderly development" and called for trade unions to be registered regardless of the color of their members; for individuals and trade unions to be allowed full freedom of association, and for any trade union meeting normal requirements to be registered and to have the right to participate in bargaining and the settlement of disputes.

The Commission said the Report was being made for "economic reasons" with the "preservation of industrial peace as the primary objective." More pertinent was the declared intention "to bring the Black worker organizations under institutional control." According to the pro-government press, the Wiehahn proposals would assure the continued influx of foreign investments that were being affected by industrial unrest, comprising "a new labor strategy." Anxious to reassure its own members, the National Party prepared slide and tape show propaganda to present to its provincial party congresses in September 1979, stressing that there were dangers in a situation in which Black unions existed in "a legal limbo" where they could "do as they please, keep their membership lists confidential, accept foreign funds and spend them as they like, and even get involved in politics . . ."[43]

Wiehahn recommendations were included in an Industrial Conciliation Amendment Act which came into effect in October 1979. Its recognition of Black trade unions through registration, however, was hedged with a thicket of restrictions. Black workers were divided up by definition into "permanent residents" (i.e., in urban townships), "migrants" and "frontier commuters." Migrants and commuters (the latter being those living in Bantustans and commuting daily across the borders to work in white areas) were excluded from eligibility of registration and trade unions were supposed to divest themselves of such members to qualify for registration. Membership lists and accounts had to be submitted for registry. Furthermore, a clause prohibited trade unions from engaging in political activity or supporting political parties and candidates.[44]

As the Minister of Manpower Utilization, Fanie Botha, subsequently pointed out, "the purpose of the new dispensation is to bring Black unions under statutory control."[45] A Wiehahn recommendation acted upon was the setting up of a National Manpower Commission that was to exercise total control over labor supply and trade union activity. It sought to set up Works Councils for negotiations at plant level, a step that tended to negate the role of trade unions. The Manpower Commission had extensive powers to control education of workers, industrial relations, training, the registration of trade unions, trade union elections, and the prohibition of political activity; its powers included the deregistration of trade unions as well, enabling it to clamp down on unions exercising independence and too much democracy.[46]

Control over the Black drive for union organization came from other quarters: the white trade unions that had job reservation as one of their main purposes. The general secretary of the white Underground Mining Officials Association, Doc. Coertze, said: "Today whites are skilled and most blacks won't be able to compete for many years. There would be only a few of them and we're prepared to treat them as honorary whites. I would rather have them in our union than in a separate one. That way we can protect our interests. If they are in a separate union they would be outside our control."[47]

The government White Paper on the Wiehahn Report was a more or less clear statement of the realities of the economic pressures on the apartheid state: "The government's general goal in respect of manpower is that the country's labor, regardless of race, color or sex, must be developed, used and conserved to the optimum extent. The development of manpower implies the continuous upgrading to the highest possible level of the abilities of the entire work force with proper regard for industrial ability and interests and the present and future needs of the economy."[48]

However, as in all moves by the South African government toward what it termed "reform," the amendment of the apartheid labor laws tended to be contradicted by built-in limitations and restrictions. On the one hand, employers took advantage of the Works Council device for their dealings with workers, ignoring unions; the appointed Works Councils were invariably controlled by the employers, and thus were boycotted by the unions, producing further disputes. On the other hand, the 27 Black unions then in existence opposed the membership ban on migrants and commuters and refused to register in protest. A period of new struggles began.

Nevertheless, the change inherent in the Wiehahn Commission recommendation was of major importance: the apartheid regime had accepted the principle of Black trade unionism. Those involved in setting up the Commission and in implementing its recommendations said in some trepidation that "the demands of the economy will force a pace of progress beyond the government's ideas of control."[49] This proved to be the case. In a short space of time the gate that had been opened slightly was forced apart by a flood of Black trade union organizations that refused to abide by the restraints placed upon them.

The White Rulers Hunt for Allies

The Wiehahn Commission was only one of a set of government-created bodies that appeared in the latter 1970s. Another was the Riekert Commission on Manpower Utilization. A third was the Schlebush Commission on amending the constitution. These were the products of a "Reformist" wing that had emerged in the ruling National Party, a grouping that was aware that adjustments had to be made in the apartheid system to enable it to survive. "Reform" in the South African context had little to do with the liberal connotations which it has in the political processes of the western capitalist countries. "Reform" of apartheid means making the system less rigid while preserving its essential aspects; it means recognizing the elements of the crisis of apartheid and trying to blunt them before they become too sharp to grip.

Increasingly the more realistic South African policy makers realized that not rigid separate development, but forms of integrated development, were mandatory for the country. Management and control of the actual labor force, making effective use of all its sectors for a growing economy was thus resorted to, albeit cautiously. Another realization matched this: that the white minority could not maintain its racist dictatorship indefinitely on its own and had to seek alliances across the lines of segregation.

One of the factors in the situation was the population crisis. A leading Afrikaaner paper, linked with the "reform" group with which Prime Minister P. W. Botha was identified, pointed it out in this way:

"In 1936 the Afrikaaners still made up 11.68% of South Africa's population. The percentage has fallen to a meager 7.23% in 1980. Over the same period the white group . . . has increased by 125.96%, the browns [i.e., Coloreds and Indians] by 23.46% and the black population by 230.33%.

"From such statistics a right-thinking person can form only one conclusion: Afrikaaners will very soon become altogether too few to man their own civil service, police force and army. And if we can't do it on our own, how on earth can we hope to dominate the other population groups."[50]

To reduce the odds, the white regime has undertaken a variety of steps since the latter 1970s. The most prominent of these has been a constitutional change, creating a three-tier parliament in which

Colored and Indian sectors of the population have been given a form of representation. In this arrangement, which excludes the Black majority, the Colored and Indian groups are given a kind of participation in government in which they presumably would feel their interests linked to those of the whites.

The constitutional change came from the recommendations of the Schlebush Commission, which also created the executive post of president in the government and a consultative presidential council with Colored, Indian and even a Chinese as members, but no Blacks. This change is in no way a relinquishing of power by whites. In the three-tier parliament that took effect in the September 1984 elections, Colored and Indian people have their own separate chambers which are little more than talk shops. Similarly, the presidential council has a merely advisory role. Power remains as before with the white chamber, and, ultimately, in the more highly centralized authority of the white president who can veto or overrule the nonwhite chambers.

Behind the constitutional move, which was played up particularly in the western countries as a "major reform," was the harsh reality of population trends and of the crucial problem of manpower in both the economy and the armed forces. The inability of the white sector of the population to provide sufficient skilled labor for the growing economy was being aggravated by the conscription needs of an army that had to be expanded to meet its external and internal operations. Under prevailing circumstances, increasing numbers of white workers had to be withdrawn from jobs in industry and elsewhere to fill the army ranks.

As early as 1977, when Prime Minister (now President) P. W. Botha was minister of defense under then Prime Minister Vorster, he had told an NP Congress in Cape Town that the inclusion of Coloreds and Indians in the South African Defense Force was acceptable in principle.[51] In 1978 even the extreme right-wing National Party branch in Transvaal province adopted a resolution at its congress calling on the government to institute compulsory military training for Coloreds and Indians.[52] The principle was accepted, but how to carry it out? As one National Party leader put it: "You can't ask a man to fight if he cannot vote."[53]

It was reported in the South African press that "the generals [i.e., the SADF commanders] were in favor of extending the call-up to Coloreds and Indians and for this reason they are believed to have put considerable pressure on the National Party leadership to 'extend the franchise to Indians and Colored.' Once the new Constitutional proposals are implemented, the pressure for conscription of Indians and

Coloreds will be increased not only by the demands of commerce and industry, by the depleting number of whites available for military service, but also by conservative whites who dominate the SADF."[54]

"There are several reasons," said a leading South African newspaper

why the South African state, under attack both externally and internally, is compelled to extend the basis of military service. Firstly there is the obvious manpower problem. There are fewer than a million white men on whom both the economy and the military could draw. The growing challenge to the South African state must inevitably push matters to the point where further military mobilization will seriously damage the economy with its endemic shortage of skilled labor. Yet the manpower constraint is not the only factor . . .

Equally important is . . . the public relations aspect. For propaganda purposes the state clearly needs growing numbers of non-whites in the Defense Force in order to project the view that the military build-up is not part of a racial and class struggle but rather a case of all South Africans preparing to fight shoulder to shoulder against the forces of "communism and chaos." A third reason for Colored and Indian conscription concerns the National Party constituency. All along, the Nationalist leadership has made it clear to its followers that the extended rights and privileges the Coloreds and Indians will receive in the new dispensation will carry with them increased responsibilities of "full citizenship." That means, quite simply, also sharing the burden of defense.[55]

This was the main argument with which the constitutional "reform" was pushed through against strong opposition by those whites not wanting any dilution of apartheid. A referendum on the change had to be held among whites, and one-third voted against it (1,360,233 "yes" to 691,577 "no").[56] Approval of the change was credited to "the National Party's 'total war' strategy." Among other motivations, like divide and rule, political manipulation, a principal motivation is to co-opt Indians and Coloreds as "junior partners in the white laager."[57]

To a certain extent, Blacks also have been recruited into the Defense Forces. Up to 1972 both the government and the SADF generals were adamantly against recruiting Blacks but by 1977 about 20% of the army was nonwhite.[58] They were recruited in "racially pure" units that were under white officers, and were paid lower, apartheid wages. Although Black troops have been kept to a 20% level in the army, it is reported that in combat against SWAPO in Namibia "an extremely high proportion" of Black troops is employed and "bear a disproportionate burden of combat," making them "a kind of cannon fodder."[59]

Aims of bringing the Colored and Indian communities into alliance with the whites were largely frustrated by mass boycotts by both minority peoples of the parliamentary scheme and of the 1984 election for the segregated chambers. The white regime has succeeded at most in gaining only a form of support from the upper well-to-do layers of the Coloreds and Indians, but this had been more or less the case previously and has marked no real shift of forces.

The white rulers' quest for allies also extended to the incorporation of Black sectors into support for the status quo. Black allies have been sought or deliberately developed in both the Bantustans and the urban townships. In the Bantustans the ruling groups, the tribal chiefs and their hangers-on, have been heavily subsidized to assure collaboration and loyalty. A very narrow stratum of Black businessmen and small industry has been encouraged to be part of this Bantustan elite, and a program of reducing the number of owner-farmers (from an initial 500,000 to 50,000) to produce a sector of relatively rich peasants with class interests tied to apartheid collaboration, has been pursued.[60] Bantustan strategy of the apartheid regime, however, has been more a matter of retaining the cooperation of the ruling groups than of widening an alliance: mass anti-apartheid struggles have tended to isolate those tribal leaders in or around the white camp. Among them, the leader of the Kwazulu Bantustan, Chief Gatsha Buthelezi, has played the most prominent role, organizing among Zulus the Inkatha movement in opposition to anti-apartheid bodies.

It is in the urban townships where the more significant efforts have been made by the government to divide the Black population and to win either the active or the tacit collaboration of a section of it. This has had to do with policies of fostering a Black middle class or Black petty bourgeoisie, and of creating other groups with relative privileges that they would be expected to want to protect.

The Wiehahn and Riekert Commissions, and the Orderly Movement and Settlement of Black Persons Act that incorporated some of their recommendations, give attention to encouraging the Black middle class outside the Bantustans. Under the original Bantu laws and Group Areas Act, Black businessmen could have enterprises only in Bantustans or in Black townships. Severe limitations had been placed on expansion, branching out or acquiring for a business any kind of a national character. A Black businessman in an urban area could not open an enterprise in a Bantustan without first dissolving his urban business. Black business possibilities were further curtailed by the Bantu Laws Amendment Act of 1963 that forbade Blacks to trade outside the townships, barred any further granting of trading licenses to Blacks, permitted a licensee to operate only one business and barred partnerships, companies or combinations; assigned the erection of all business premises to local (white-run) Bantu Administration authorities and put the ownership and control of all service enterprises (liquor stores, restaurants, hotels, cinemas and others) in local authority hands.

When Black businessmen in the Johannesburg African Chamber of Commerce, formed in 1953, sought to link up with Black businessmen in other areas in a National African Chamber of Commerce in 1964, the government's Ministry of Bantu Administration and Development stepped in to force an abandonment of such a structure because the government would recognize only 9 separate African ethnic communities and forbade a "national entity." NACOC had to change itself into NAFCOC (National African *Federated* Chambers of Commerce.

When Wiehahn-Riekert "reform" concessions were made after 1977, some of the restrictions on Black business activity were lifted. Forms of enterprise were increased, trading sites enlarged, and a 99-year leasehold on land for business allowed. Supermarkets could be opened, and white managerial skills could be employed. As a result, a considerable increase in Black enterprises occurred. In Soweto alone, for example, the 1,223 Black licensed business in 1977 went up to 1,535 in 1980.[61]

The shift of attitude by the apartheid regime toward relaxing the limits placed on a Black petty bourgeoisie and toward allowing some proliferation of its opportunities had the aim of tying this sector in with the white economy. It had deeper motivations as well. These have been most openly expressed by Dennis Etheredge, chairman of the Vaal Reefs Exploration and Mining Company and president of the South African Chamber of Mines in the 1970s. In a speech to white South African and foreign industrialists and businessmen in Sun City, Bophuthatswana, in May 1980, he pointed to a survey taken in Cape Town which had shown that those participating blacks equated capitalism with the apartheid system and felt that its benefits were enjoyed only by whites. Said Etheredge:

Private enterprise, capitalism, is held in low regard by blacks in South Africa. They are not standing ready to accept it with open arms. In fact, they appear to reject it because it is identified with whites and a system which they believe is oppressing them. It is associated in their minds with selfishness, greed and exploitation. Literate, urbanized blacks in South Africa do not associate capitalism with democracy. Capitalism is seen as the opposite pole to democracy and Christianity. This is a very unhealthy situation and we ignore it at our peril.[62]

A few months later Etheredge returned to this theme in another such speech, declaring that it was important to involve blacks in the capitalist system:

> If blacks do not become involved we face the possibility that capitalism will be overthrown in the years ahead. Blacks do not see themselves as part of the system. It is important that we turn our minds to these matters as quickly as possible.[63]

The development of a black middle and entrepreneurial class has been one of the main means of dealing with this apartheid problem. Besides the opening up of wider areas of enterprise, an encouragement of black/white partnerships has occurred, particularly in the case of supermarkets and other retail trade businesses. Distrust on the part of NAFCOC has limited this tendency, because it was found that even in such partnerships with a Black majority share, the drift was toward the acquiring of greater power and control by the more experienced white managerial elements with easier access to white economic areas. White monopoly interests, however, have endeavored with success to draw NAFCOC into association. Six white monopolies have become associate members of NAFCOC, and the NAFCOC president, Sam Motsuenyane, has been invited onto the boards of three major corporations (Anglo-American, A.E.C.I., and Permanent Life Assurance). Motsuenyane revealed in June 1983 that NAFCOC had developed links with the British Embassy, the U.S. AID Agency and the West German Konrad Adenauer Foundation, all interested in fostering this channel for the enhancement of capitalism in the eyes of Black people.[64]

Part of the U.S. "constructive engagement" policy has been the nurturing of an expanded Black business and professional sector. An education program funded by the U.S. AID and administered by the U.S. Institute of International Education was reported by Lawrence Eagleburger of the State Department in 1983 to be rapidly overtaking South Africa itself in the training of black South African engineers, computer scientists, chemists and business personnel. By 1985 it was said that more black South Africans would be studying business and technical subjects in U.S. universities (400) than in South Africa.[65]

Some black graduates of such courses are to be drawn into low-rung managerial positions in the subsidiaries of U.S. and other foreign corporations in South Africa, forming another strand of Black community links to capitalism.

Attention to the development of a black middle class has been one phase of urban township policy to divide the black population. Influx control laws, by excluding Bantustan inhabitants, by strictly limiting relations and contacts between Bantustan and township, and by giving special privileges to township dwellers, have deliberately aimed at creating divisions of privilege between the two types of community. The extension of 99-year leasehold rights to those able to buy a house created a property-owning stratum in the townships, although this has grown slowly: by March 1981 there were only 1,881 99-year leases held by Blacks in the country. Nevertheless the emergence of clearer class divisions in the Black townships have been evident.[66]

By the end of 1983 the Botha government considered it feasible to introduce the concept of elected Black local councils in townships, in place of the Bantu Administration. A total of 38 were created by early 1985, with a perspective of eventually setting up 103. Inevitably the candidates for mayors and councillors came from middle class elements who had the approval of the central apartheid government. The factor of patronage, the administration of services, the collection of rents (all housing not privately owned is controlled by local authorities) and of charges for utilities, created a political structure that was merely an adjunct of the national apartheid structure.

In sum, the various crisis measures called "reform" set in motion a process of establishing allies from the white minority among the black majority. In 1983 the director of the Institute for Strategic Studies at the University of Pretoria, Prof. M. Haigh, said that "creation of a black middle class would play an important role in reducing conflict."[67] The accuracy of that statement became tested much sooner than the professor expected.

Crisis and Conflict Among the Whites

As awareness of crisis in the apartheid system caused the white minority regime to search for allies and for ways of dividing the black majority, the impact of crisis conditions produced serious divisions and problems among the whites themselves. The South African whites had never been a monolithic group. Besides the differences between the Afrikaaner and English sections of the population, the class interests of the rising industrial, financial and commercial bourgeoisie tended to separate from those of the traditional rural Boers. A white working class, although heavily tainted with racism in the job reservation areas, had growing numbers who found common ground in the trade unions with nonwhites against white employers. Finally there was a sector of anti-apartheid whites who for left-wing, humanitarian or bourgeois democratic reasons was prepared to work for a multiracial society.

The two-fold nature of apartheid's crisis—the rise of militant Black struggle against the racist system, and the spread of economic recession—had begun to tear away at the privileges and master-class way of life of most whites. An erosion of the sense of security and of living off the fat of the land, which had been felt by all of the colonial rulers in the African countries that had now won their liberation, was now occurring in South Africa. The Black townships that had once been looked upon as segregated reservoirs of servants and menial laborers now took on the aspect of seething cauldrons that could boil over into the white suburbs of the cities. A feature of this development were the new demands placed upon the white citizens, for the defense of the laager.

Fear of the future, of Black revolt specifically, began to permeate white society in the 1970s, especially after the upheaval in Soweto and other townships in 1976. By 1980 over 750,000 whites had small arms in their possesssion, for "protection,"[68] and by 1984 it was reported that 150,000 whites were applying for permits to hold arms each year.[69] The spectacle of white wives and daughters attending target practice sessions and classes on care and use of the side-arm and shotgun, instead of afternoon teas, had become common.

From the mid-1970s onward South Africa became increasingly an armed camp. The growing role of the military in the state became acutely noticeable, particularly in the top-level State Security Council and in the ordering of daily life of the white population. Communities, industries, farms and schools came under a "total strategy" of defense, affecting the lives of all whites.

The South African Defense Force and its general staff had itself undergone a significant transformation since 1948. Whereas the top echelons of the army had formerly been dominated by "the English," the posts of command were now filled by Afrikaaners.[70]

An observer pointed to the implications of this: "What we are seeing in South Africa today is the displacement of the old British ethic where the soldier was the subject of the state. It is replaced by the commando ethic where the soldier and civilian are interchangeable."[71]

An areas defense system, for example, amounting to war preparations, was mapped out for the whole country. Each area was to have its commando unit of civilians with military training, to be backed up by a regular army "reaction force."[72] In each white community, Civil Defense Organizations were set up to serve as a vigilante-style second line of defense to assist the army in the case of "military emergency," to maintain essential services, maintain law and order, and suppress popular dissent.[73]

Influencing the the sense of emergency that began to grip both military and civilian Afrikaaners were the diehard racists who had fled from Zimbabwe to South Africa after white-ruled Rhodesia had crumbled from the guerrilla war of the liberation movements. Saying that "We are very bitter about what happened in Zimbabwe and we will go all-out to prevent the same from happening here," Rhodesians from the counter-insurgency Selous Scouts of Ian Smith set up Citizens Anti-Terrorist Units in the Kreugersdorp area. A former Rhodesian cabinet minister, Rowan Cronje, speaking in a seminar on what South Africa could learn from the Rhodesian experience, warned of the costs facing South Africans as the guerrilla war developed. "In 1974 we had just 16 guerrillas in a small northeast territory. In 1979 not a square kilometer of territory was without an enemy presence."[74]

To the SADF the reality of such a situation was already developing in Transvaal and Natal, in the areas bordering Botswana, Zimbabwe and Mozambique. Six months after the transfer of independence to the Mugabe government in Zimbabwe, the alarm was raised over the fact that 4,000 white farms had been evacuated from the Transvaal bushveld border areas alone.[75] In some districts of northern Transvaal over 80% of farms were abandoned or no longer held by whites, some being occupied in defiance of law by Blacks who had illegally "overflowed" from Bantustans.[76] As liberated Africa moved to the South African borders, the borders were being literally depopulated by fearful white farmers. Along the Transvaal borders, the population had dropped from 100,000 in 1965 to 60,000 in 1982.[77]

These bushveld districts had been regarded as a buffer zone between regions of guerrilla activity and the urban-industrial complex of Pretoria-Witwatersrand-Vereeneging. Now, according to a Botha cabinet minister, Hendrick Shoeman, "A terrorist can walk from the Limpopo River right through to Pietersberg without having set foot on a farm occupied by whites. That is an unhealthy situation."[78]

The Botha government took two main emergency steps. It gave generous support loans to white farmers to discourage evacuation and to persuade those who had left to return. Loans totalled 2 million rands in 1981-1982. "Although there have been no incidents with insurgents," said government spokesmen, "this is the front line and at some stage in the future there will be a security threat." Despite the loans and the pleas, the white farmers continued to leave.[79]

At this point the army stepped in with the other emergency arrangement, imposing conscription into commando units in border districts, requiring the registration of all white men to the age of 55 for commando duty.[80] Major General Hans Paetzhold declared: "Rural areas form an important part of counter-insurgency against the enemy. The farmer in his capacity as manager, planner, specialist and economist, must now also become a leader and a soldier. Farmers notice suspicious changes in the behavior of staff [i.e., Black workers] and can be the first to give the warning." Said the SADF general, it is a fight "against the insurgent, the terrorist and the enemy in our midst. Their object is to break down the resistance of the people and enable a communist revolutionary government to take control."[81]

This attention to the border areas was based on the theory that the guerrilla threat came from the neighboring liberated countries, from which the ANC's Umkhonto we Sizwe was presumed to strike into South Africa from bases outside the country. U.S. policy supporting South African aggression into neighboring countries and forcing such arrangements as the Nkomati Accord on them had the snuffing out of anti-apartheid guerrilla struggle as one of its main aims. The policy, however, proved to be ill-founded: guerrilla acts within South Africa continued at an undiminished, if not increased, rate after Nkomati, indicating that bases had been established inside the country.

By the latter part of 1985, every white farmer in the border districts was reported to be enrolled in the commando units and each farmer was supplied with two-way radios for close communication with army units. Nevertheless, in the latter part of November 1985 a series of land-mine explosions near the border with Zimbabwe caused army and farmworker casualties. Although the Botha government was quick to charge Zimbabwe with harboring guerrillas who were responsible for the attacks, and to threaten a punitive attack on Zimbabwe, the African National Congress announced that its Umkhonto we Sizwe had laid the mines in an operation carried out from bases within South Africa.

For the apartheid regime, however, "total strategy" meant the turning of the whole country into a defended laager. The planning for war against "the enemy in our midst" embraced all districts and the whole economy. A Key Points Act was adopted in 1980 which defined and listed the key or vital industries and other sites in the country. The listing was kept secret, and one provision of the Act banned press coverage of any incident of unrest or sabotage at "vital centers."[82] Dams, picnic spots and vantage points were fenced off "to preclude sabotage."[83]

At the beginning of 1981 the SADF began setting up "industrial commandos" to guard key plants and installations. The proliferation of Umkhonto we Sizwe attacks on a wide variety of targets soon impressed on the SADF the enormity its task.

Minister of Defense General Malan, therefore, called on South African industrialists in June of 1983 to "provide their own first line of defense" against "terrorist attacks." There are such a multitude of possible targets, he said, that government security organizations cannot provide protection. Industrial Commandos had to be organized and paid for by employers themselves.[84]

An outcry of resistance came from industrialists and businessmen who were called upon to establish costly armed units and arsenals. At the end of 1984 the SADF and the government were still insisting that "The army and other services cannot cope with guarding all national key points, it is becoming too expensive." a compromise was the creation of a private commando "rapid deployment force," armed with shotguns, semi-automatic rifles and side-arms. It was on a 24-hour standby "to react to an attack on a national key point or to assist a client faced with industrial trouble."[85]

In spite all all the official efforts to generate a war situation psychosis in the white population, resistance occurred to the confrontational measures for maintaining white power. Whites failed to volunteer in sufficient numbers to meet the mounting military demands, either for the regular army or for commando units. By early 1982 the SADF claimed that it was 37% undermanned.[86] Recruitment of a proportion of Blacks partially filled the gap, but this was not a policy that could be carried too far. Conscription of whites finally had to be resorted to, with all white males from 15 to 60 years of age made liable for call-up. Such a step was felt by many to be a depressing admission of failure in defense policy. Some recruitment of white women was subsequently added. The extension of separate parliamentary chambers to Colored and Indian sectors of the population had, in part, a solution of the military manpower problem in aim, because voting rights included the right to be conscripted. However, mass resistance to the parliamentary reform among both sectors made conscription in these cases a dubious proposition. Basically, the white laager had to be defended by whites.

To make up for the manpower shortage, military service periods were extended in 1982 from an initial 240 days to 720 days. This brought protest from businessmen. The president of the Associated Chambers of Commerce, G. Stuart Reckling, opposed the extended call-up because it pulled skilled workers out of industry. He complained that productivity and the trend of inflation were likely to be affected.[87]

Another proposal made in 1982 was for the conscription of immigrants, who could not be drafted unless they had acquired South African citizenship. There were 388,986 immigrant whites in 1983, out of whom an estimated 100,000 in the younger age brackets could be conscripted.[88] Legislation was introduced to make all white male immigrants of 15 to 25 years of age automatically citizens after 5 years' residence, and liable to the draft. Anyone rejecting citizenship would lose residence rights and work permit.[89] The new Act came into effect in October 1984. This step also drew strong protest from businessmen. The Federated Chamber of Industries argued that it would restrict immigration and simultaneously cause an exodus of non-citizens, both of which would deprive the economy of much-needed manpower. "There are a lot of people thinking seriously about their future," was an ominous statement by a spokesman of the British Embassy in Pretoria.[90]

Conscription had a graver consequence that went beyond mere objection. It was estimated early in 1984 that 40,000 whites, both citizens and non-citizens, had left South Africa to escape military service.[91] At least 5,000 of those drafted each year did not show up for induction;[92] in the single month of January 1985, over 7,000 failed to report when drafted. Many left the country solely to evade the draft and formed anti-conscription committees in Britain, the U.S., the Scandinavian countries and elsewhere. Of more serious significance was the setting up of a broad End Conscription Campaign in South Africa itself in 1984. The committee set up for this in Johannesburg had 11 organizations behind it: in the Cape Town area 40 organizations participated—students, religious organizations, civic groups, anti-apartheid groups. The leading opposition white political party, the Progressive Federal Party, came out against compulsory conscription at the end of 1984.[93]

Opposition in the white community itself to the repressive military trends of the government was only one facet of the divisions opening up within the white population. As the crisis of the system grew, a graver, more basic and far-reaching rift developed out of the intense debate over how to cope with the crisis and to preserve white dominance.

The debate took place from the early 1970s onward within the ruling National Party. In this thoroughly right-wing party of white domination, there was a more extreme wing of rigid dogmatists who favored the carrying of apartheid to the furthest lengths of racial separation and exploitation, the advocates of "pure apartheid" and of its enforcement through the most ruthless means. These were known as the "verkrampt" (conservative) wing of the National Party; the others, considered to be not so extreme, were known as the "verligte" (liberal) wing.

Differences within the National Party have not been a question of pro-apartheid vs. anti-apartheid attitudes. The conflict arose over how best to preserve apartheid, how to cope with the growing crisis, to deal with the threat of revolutionary upheaval, and to maintain capitalist economic development in South Africa. (Similar differences are involved, chiefly on the level of Afrikaaner-British interests, in the political party rivalry of the National and the opposition Progressive Federal Party.)

Verligte-verkrampt struggles reached the point of an open breach in the 1970s, when first the Vorster regime and then the successor Botha government, pressed by their western partners, proposed "reform" steps to ease the emerging crisis and to strengthen the regime: constitutional changes to create the Colored and Indian chambers of parliament, labor changes extending trade union rights and improved wages to Blacks, changes in the Black townships to encourage growth of a Black middle class and to draw it into forms of collaboration, modification of "petty apartheid" conditions, and other alternatives. None of these basically changed the apartheid system. They have indeed been aimed at perpetuating it and at depriving anti-apartheid forces of struggle issues, but to the rigid racists any concession to the Black or other nonwhite people is tantamount to dismantling apartheid and weakening white rule.

The first break occurred in the early 1970s with the setting up of the Herstigte (Reformed) National Party. Led by Jaap Marais, it had its base of support in Transvaal and Orange Free State provinces that were the traditional heartland of the Afrikaaners. In 1972 the split in the National Party was carried into the Broederbond with the expulsion of the HNP supporters from the Afrikaaner core body.

In 1982, as the Constitutional "reform" was set on its legislative course, its introduction in parliament produced a more serious split in the ruling party: 18 of the 143 NP members of parliament broke away to establish the Conservative Party, led by Andries Treurnicht, who had been a member of the Botha cabinet. For the National Party, the possibility of a merger or of unity between the DP and HNP was a looming threat, and tended to act as a retarding check on modifications of apartheid.[94]

The divisions in the National Party were one facet of a conflict over policies of maintaining white minority domination that spread through the whole structure of Afrikaanerdom. One of the main battlegrounds was in the 12,000-member Broederbond. As the original secret society vanguard of racist rule, organized in 1918, the Broederbond had rapidly seized the top posts for its members in every

Afrikaaner institution—in the banks, industrial concerns, building societies, the Dutch Reformed Church, and elsewhere. In the NP governments it held most of the cabinet positions and the top civil service posts.

As the Botha government took its "reform" stance at the opening of the 1980s, the Broederbond was controlled by verkrampt elements. Its chairman, Prof. Carel Boshoff, was close to Andries Treurnicht, and was a vocal opponent of "reform." He sought to bring the Broederbond into play aginst the "reform" grouping. In the latter part of 1981 the Broederbond, under his direction, rescinded the 1972 act of expelling the HNP members. It was then proclaimed that membership in the organization would henceforth depend on "support for the Afrikaaner cause."[95]

The verligte wing that backed Botha policies fought back, however, with government support. In mid-1983 it finally succeeded in winning leadership control in the organization, and in forcing the resignation of Boshoff. The Broederbond was then mobilized to back the Botha constitutional change of creating a three-tier parliament.[96] A confidential Broederbond document was circulated in the organization and among its associated bodies, arguing that the Coloreds and Indians would inexorably make common cause with the Blacks if their existing exclusion from representation was left unaltered. The Broederbond executive council, by a majority decision overriding Boshoff and his group, came out for a "yes" vote in the referendum among whites on the government's constitutional proposal.[97]

Verligte control of the Broederbond was then extended to its "front" organizations. In July 1984 Botha supporters won control of the major Afrikaaner cultural movement, the Federasie van Afrikaanse Kultuurverenigings (FAK), which has over 4,000 national, provincial and local cultural and language organizations affiliated to it.[98]

Voting in the referendum of November 1983 indicated the proportions of alignment in the white population. The result—1,360,233 "yes" votes to 691,577 "no"—was about 2 to 1 in favor of the Botha position. Nevertheless, the verkrampts who called for a "no" vote had a major base of support that could be enlarged as the crisis situation became aggravated.

Early in 1984 they counterattacked, setting up a new Afrikaaner cultural movement, the Afrikaaner Volkswag, with Carel Boshoff in a leading role. It aimed itself particularly at whites in the rural areas and at those blue and white collar workers concerned with job reservation.[99] Although the Afrikaaner Volkswag failed to win out in the fight for control of the FAK, they retained a following of importance.

In reaction to the verligte drive against them, 200 verkrampt whites resigned from the Broederbond in August 1984. Their tendency, along with others in the AV and elsewhere, was to move toward association with Andries Treurnicht and Jaap Marais, with the aim of forming a new united right-wing party merging the CP and HNP. One of the polemical arguments used against the Botha government was to claim that it was making moves "to break South West Africa from South Africa." Afrikaaners in Namibia were called upon "to fight against a repetition of Rhodesia and a diplomatic, military and psychological defeat for South Africa and a humiliation for Afrikaaners."[100]

One of the main program calls by Prof. Carel Boshoff has been for a separate white homeland. After his removal from the Broederbond chairmanship, Boshoff has used the white supremacy South African Bureau of Racial Affairs (SABRA), of which he is the head, to promote this concept. In January 1985 the SABRA sponsored a gathering of leading Afrikaaners at which commitment was affirmed for separate development, separate freedoms, and separate homelands for all ethnic groups. Priority was proclaimed for the creation of a sovereign white state where the "Afrikaaner nation" could run its own affairs, keep its traditions, and share power with no one. The greatest possible geographical separation of the races was called for, with each group having effective control over its own area. It was vital, it was said, to remove all Blacks to the homelands for their development.[101]

The sharpening of the crisis in South Africa in 1984-1985 and the consequent rise of Black and Colored militancy was seized upon by the verkrampts to try to spur a white "backlash," blaming the violent clashes in the townships on Botha's alleged tampering with the apartheid system. In a set of parliamentary by-elections in October 1985, a major increase in the votes of both the Conservative Party and the Herstigte National Party occurred; the CP and HNP for the first time supported each other's candidates, and the HNP elected its first member of parliament, in an Orange Free state constituency. It was estimated that such a trend carried into the next national election could increase the verkrampt members of parliament to 40 or more.

While it seems unlikely that the ultra-racist Afrikaaner right wing could be capable of gaining governmental power, it constitutes a strong pressure force against even the type of reform advocated by the Urban Foundation and other worried capitalist groupings in South Africa. The possibilities of rule being assumed by the military in alliance with the verkrampts are, however, more real.

The activity and agitation by verkrampt groups have undoubtedly blocked or impeded the "reform" moves. One of the steps attributed to the Botha government, to present it in a positive light internationally, has been a reported elimination of "petty apartheid," including the supposed removal of segregationist signs and the desegregation of some hotels, transportation waiting rooms, and public facilities. In actuality, white racist resistance to such a policy has caused an even harsher drawing of the color line in some cases.

Thus, in April 1983 the city council of Pretoria, the central government seat, adopted new rules on public recreation facilities in which Blacks were excluded from 17 city parks, were permitted to be in fenced-off sections in only 3 parks, while uniformed guards with guard dogs were employed to enforce the regulations. The vote in the Pretoria council was 23 to 7 for this policy.[102] Another case was the reported decision by the Botha government to desegregate trains. After verkrampt-type racist pressure, the Minister of Transport, Hendrik Shoeman, announced in March 1985 that apartheid trains would stay. Said Shoeman: "The separate equivalent accommodation which is provided for passengers is essential to prevent friction and to maintain harmonious relations among the different population groups."[103]

For both anti-apartheid and verligte elements serious concern arose in the 1980s over the activity of white fascist organizations, a number of which have sprung up as the struggle has sharpened. These take the most extreme of racist positions and of action to preserve and extend apartheid. The Afrikaaner Weetstandsbeweging, Kappie Kommando, Wit Kommando, Aksie Eie Toekoms, National Conservative Party, Christian League, and the umbrella Action: Save White South Africa are among the more active of these groups.[104] Kappie Kommando, a women's organization, said it is prepared to use violence against Afrikaaners who have "forsaken national and religious traditions." A member, Mrs. Marie van Zyl, wife of a Pretoria dentist, said the organization was based on secret cells, forming a countrywide "beehive" that was growing fast.[105] In February 1981, four members of the Wit Kommando were arrested for bombing and intimidating verligte academics, non-racial institutions, Black leaders, and Blacks living in white areas.[106] During 1985 the murder of many leaders of the United Democratic Front and other anti-apartheid organizations and trade unions was believed to have been perpetrated by fascist gunmen.

The splits and divisions in the white community as the crisis of apartheid has grown have produced instability and confusion in the ruling sectors of South Africa. It is a situation that could enable further advances by the anti-apartheid forces against a weakened racist enemy, but it also contains serious dangers of a last-ditch racist assault that could be carried to murderous extremes before the democratic forces win ascendency.

The Crisis and Foreign Investment

The crisis of the apartheid system, which can be indicated in innumerable signs of disruption, decline and conflict in the South African society, can also be seen acutely in the behavior of foreign investment interests. As economic and social problems have grown and intensified due to the nature of apartheid, the euphoria with which U.S., Western European, Japanese and other foreign companies poured investment and loan capital into South Africa in the 1960s and early 1970s has tended to dissipate, turning to caution, concern and even reversal.

Apartheid South Africa had been attractive to foreign capital for the plain reason of offering extremely cheap Black labor in a setting of harsh police-state controls. Once that system of low pay and denial of rights began to crumble under the upheaving pressure from the oppressed, while the cost of trying to maintain apartheid became an unbalancing weight on the unequal economy, the attractions of South Africa began to fade.

The trend took shape in the 1970s, having its origin in the huge Black worker strike wave of 1973-1976, which was climaxed by the Soweto revolt of the latter year. These events showed that the control apparatus could no longer hold a massively exploited Black working class fully in check, and the forced yielding of somewhat higher wages signaled the coming reduction of abnormally great profits. The first U.S. corporation of prominence to withdraw from South Africa, Polaroid, did so significantly in 1977, the year after Soweto. In part this was due to disinvestment pressure from anti-apartheid groups in the U.S., but Polaroid's assessment of future prospects in the apartheid state had an equal effect on the decision.

One of the major considerations in the Wiehahn Report of 1979, which studied the strikes and township rebellions of the period and recommended the granting of trade union rights to Black workers, was the need to adopt stabilizing measures to assure the continued influx of foreign capital and the retention of existing foreign investment. This was obviously a reaction to the fears and uncertainties being expressed by apartheid's foreign partners.

A shifting attitude by foreign capital toward the character of its links with the apartheid system could be traced in the relative decline in direct investment. A study of the trend between 1962 and 1982 has shown an upward swing taking place in the ratio of total foreign liabilities to domestic fixed capital stock in the decade from 1962 to 1973. The ratio was 31.5% in 1962, and it rose to 40% in 1973, the highest point reached. However, by the end of 1982 the ratio had fallen back to 35.9%. Within the total of foreign liabilities, direct investment had accounted for 17.2% in 1962 and indirect investment 14.3%. By 1982 these proportions were reversed: direct investment having dropped to 15.6% and indirect rising to 20.3%. The increase in indirect investment had occurred by way of stock exchange share-buying participation in domestic capital formation.[107]

Behind this shift is the practical outlook of the foreign investor who would find it easier to dispose of stock shares in an emergency than the fixed capital of plant and equipment. Another phase of the trend was a move from a long-term to a short-term outlook, as exhibited in an emphasis on loan capital instead of investment capital. Within loan capital, too, the greater stress was on the provision of the shorter term commercial bank loan than the longer term government agency loan.

All told, these trends showed a growing sensitivity and a dwindling confidence regarding the apartheid economy, particularly due to the growth of mass struggle against apartheid, but also, as the Wiehahn Report pointed out, due to the limitations of the system that were causing a declining growth rate, low productivity, and an increasingly acute lack of skilled labor desired by high technology foreign companies.

The uncertainties for foreign investment were voiced early in 1981 by Syd Newman, chairman of the British corporation, Lonrho, which had a $250 million subsidiary in South Africa:

> From an economic point of view, South Africa is a very good place for investment, even fantastically good. Politically, however, South Africa is in a very sad situation. I wish I knew what was going to happen . . . Revolution? We have very draconian laws and security police roaming all over the country. But I would hate to think of how many unemployed, hungry, frustrated youngsters are wandering in the streets of Soweto. If we don't give them a chance to earn a living there must be trouble.[108]

One of the effects on foreign companies that underscored the handwriting on the wall for the apartheid of the 1960s was the adoption of the U.S. Sullivan Code and the EEC Code of company behavior toward Black workers. The codes, conceived in 1979, came about from the combination of rising mass anti-apartheid struggle, including by trade unions, in South Africa and international campaigns for foreign companies that were profiting from apartheid to disinvest and withdraw from South Africa.

In the U.S., the code was named after a Black director of General Motors Corporation who participated in drawing it up, the Rev. Leon Sullivan. It put forward six principles for U.S. companies in South Africa to follow:

- Equal and fair employment practice for all employees;
- Equal pay for all employees doing equal or comparable work for the same period of time;
- Initiation and development of training programs that would prepare blacks and other non-whites in substantial numbers for supervisory, administrative, clerical and technical jobs;
- Increasing the number of blacks and other non-whites in management supervisory jobs;
- Non-segregation of the races in all eating, comfort and work facilities;
- Improving the quality of employees' lives outside the work environment, such as housing, transportation, schooling, recreation and health facilities.[109]

A full implementation of such principles would inevitably mean a curtailment of the rate of profit that U.S. and other foreign companies were obtaining. Consequently less than half of U.S. companies operating in South Africa had signed the Code over a year after its introduction—140 out of more than 350.[110] By the end of 1985 the number had risen to only 186.[111] Of these less than 75% claimed in reports that their facilities were now "common." As pointed out by a U.S. researcher and critic of the Sullivan Code, Elizabeth Schmidt, the principles were "intended not to eliminate apartheid but to modernize it and ensure its perpetuation." Researcher Schmidt found that the reports claiming "common" facilities were misleading if not untrue. Companies were merely removing racist signposts, but facilities remained segregated. Black workers remained segregated in workplaces and in jobs where no white worker was employed. "Equal pay for equal work is simply an empty slogan," said Ms. Schmidt.[112]

When the Rev. Leon Sullivan visited South Africa in August 1980, he spoke to U.S. businessmen but Black trade unionists refused to meet him. Although a director of General Motors, he evaded a visit to the General Motors or Ford plants in Port Elizabeth, the auto industry center, where the two companies were in dispute with Black trade unionists over union recognition. At a mass meeting of 10,000 Black auto workers, disappointment was expressed over the failure of Sullivan to visit them and to look into their conditions. "As a director of General Motors he could at least have paid a visit to know what is taking place there," said one worker. At the meeting the Sullivan Principles were called "An extension of oppression by American firms operating in South Africa and a complete fake."[113]

Black leaders in South Africa charged that the Codes were actually perpetuating apartheid by slightly improving, not changing, conditions.

It was said that they "lack teeth," a charge that was accurate: there was no legislative way to enforce them, and no effective monitoring machinery existed not in company control.

Nevertheless, the Codes were a harbinger of the anti-apartheid pressures that were building up within and outside South Africa. In the early 1980s some of the changes called for in the Sullivan Code were put into effect not because of voluntary steps by foreign companies but because they were forced on both foreign and South African companies by militant Black trade unions. Also, the crisis factors in the economy were becoming increasingly intolerable. In December 1985 the inadequacies of the apartheid system to produce skilled Black workers led 186 U.S. companies in South Africa to submit a memorandum to the Minister of National Education. F. W. De Klerk, calling for abolition of racially divided education and the upgrading of under-qualified Black teachers.[114]

The Sullivan and EEC Codes were an attempt to forestall the gathering storm in South Africa. Events, however, overrode such efforts. At the end of 1980 a special report on prospects in South Africa, commissioned by Business International Corp. of New York, estimated that South Africa would remain "in a state of more or less stable violent equilibrium" for the next ten years. Transnational corporations, it said, faced numerous serious challenges, including from Black trade unions and from rising Black resistance to apartheid, and from anti-apartheid pressures at home. The South African government may not be "seriously challenged," it said, but "neither will the authorities succeed in meeting Black demands or in suppressing militant expression."[115]

A year later a study funded by the Rockefeller Foundation, on *U.S. Policy Toward Southern Africa,* appeared with a sub-heading, "South Africa: Time is Running Out." It urged the U.S. to meet the deteriorating situation by advocating policies for genuine power sharing in South Africa, for assisting the economic development of other states in the region, and for taking steps to reduce the impact of a stoppage of key minerals presently obtained from South Africa. The report recommended a broadening of the arms and nuclear embargoes on South Africa, called on U.S. companies not to expand operations there and for new investment to stay out, and urged U.S. aid to other countries in southern Africa to reduce the imbalances in their relations with the apartheid state. It was recommended that the U.S. stockpile key minerals, such as ferrochrome and ferromanganese, to offset the impact of possible stoppages as the situation worsened.[116]

At the beginning of 1982 a French trade guide published one of the first official, public warnings of what was developing in South Africa. It warned French bankers, financiers and businessmen that they had only another five good years to invest in South Africa. From 1986 on, it declared, there could be major financial losses for foreign investors due to Pretoria's apartheid policies.[117]

In April 1982 came a further assessment of South Africa as a business risk, by the Business Environment Risk Information service. It called South Africa "prohibitive" in terms of political risk and said that it did not recommend long-term investment. "Risk levels are increasing and profit potentials diminishing," it warned, pointing to an increase in labor militancy, a shortage of managers and technicians, and the adverse effect of bureaucratic interference and restrictions on labor by the apartheid government.[118]

These themes were carried further in a major speech delivered at the University of Witwatersrand, Johannesburg, on October 21, 1982 by Robert McNamara, former U.S. Secretary of Defense (1961-1968) and President of the World Bank (1968-1981). Asserting that "if South Africa fails to deal effectively with its internal racial problem, that failure will impose heavy economic, military and political penalties on other societies in the western world as well, and particularly on the U.S.," McNamara painted this picture:

> What should U.S. policy be? It should be based on the recognition that black nationalism in South Africa is a struggle whose eventual success can at most only be delayed—and at immense cost—but not permanently denied . . . Opposition in the U.S. to the South African government's racial policies has been increasing throughout the last decade. The U.S. will not support the South African government if it is confronted by militant opposition from those who condemn apartheid—even if the withholding of U.S. support carries with it the risk that South Africa will fall within the Soviet sphere of influence.
>
> I recognize that South Africa's official reaction to such a U.S. position might well be to terminate its exports of the four key minerals it now supplies the West: chromium, manganese, vanadium and okatinum, which are essential to western industry and defense. In anticipation of such retaliatory action by South Africa, the U.S. and the other western nations should begin to increase their stockpiles, to develop alternative sources of supply, and to prepare contingency plans to share such limited supplies as would be available.[119]

Arguments of this kind, warning of crisis and discounting the strategic importance of South Africa to the U.S. became prevalent in the latter stage of the Carter administration, with which the Rockefeller interests and their Trilateral Commission were linked, and onward. It moved the South African government to conduct a big advertising campaign in the U.S. press to arouse fears of the loss of essential minerals. "Who needs South Africa anyway? You do, we all do," proclaimed one. Others said: "Does American prosperity depend on South Africa?" (asserting that it did) and "Without South Africa Americans may have to eat pickles from wooden barrels." It was claimed that the U.S. would have to rely—horror of horrors—on the Soviet Union for minerals if South Africa was lost.[120]

The campaign was answered by a spokesman for the U.S. metals industry, E. F. Andrews, vice-president of Allegheny Ludlum Industries. After admitting that the loss of South African minerals would be very grave, he pointed to a Congressional report that denied that the U.S. would have to rely on the Soviet Union. Andrews contended that the means were available for dealing with any eventuality, listing "stockpiling, conservation, process changes, alternative technology, use of functionally acceptable substitutes, providing incentives to encourage design changes, recycling, exploiting untapped reserves."[121]

One of the purposes of the Reagan administration's "constructive engagement" policy was to reverse this line of thinking and to try to assure a prolonged survival of apartheid and of the profitable western relationship with it. However, despite all the U.S. efforts to bolster South Africa, and perhaps because of them in some respects, the crisis of apartheid continued to worsen. Furthermore, "constructive engagement" was paralled by, and contributed to, a growing international campaign by anti-apartheid movements to isolate South Africa and for disinvestment or withdrawal by western corporations.

The early 1980s were marked by a disinvestment surge by U.S. and British companies in particular. Some of the major British corporations with a long-standing presence in South Africa began to pull out in 1982. Three of them—Associated British Foods (which sold its interests in nearly 100 subsidiaries), Metal Box (which cut its stake in tin and plastics subsidiaries from 52% to 25%) and Jardine Matheson (which sold its whole stake)—sold shares worth 604 million rands to South African interests. Foreign stock shares worth 1.3 billion rands were sold on the Johannesburg Stock Exchange between February and August 1983; mining shares alone accounted for 723 million rands of this.

Foreign ownership of South African mining shares that stood at 33.7% of the total in December 1982 dropped to 31.9% by June 1983; the proportion held by U.S. investors fell from 19.5% to 18.3%.[122]

Between 1981 and 1985 at least 41 U.S. companies withdrew their operations from South Africa or sharply reduced the size of their interests. Among these: Chrysler Corp. sold its 25% holding in Sigma Motors Co. (worth $32.5 million in 1981) to its partner, the Anglo-American Corp., in 1983; Amerifin consumer finance of Chicago sold its two subsidiaries in 1983 and 1984; Blue Bell textiles sold its interest in South Africa's largest jeans manufacturer to the South African-owned SA Clothing; Coca-Cola reduced its 55% stake in the subsidiary Amalgamated Beverages Industry to a minority 30%, selling to the big South African Breweries; International Harvester sold its truck subsidiary in 1985; Pepsi-Cola sold its two bottling plants in January 1985; Phibro-Salomon sold its commodities trading arm in August 1985; City Investing of New York divested itself of its South African financial services in December 1984.[123]

Coincident with this trend, and with share-selling by investors, was the cessation of loan activities by many U.S. banks. By the first quarter of 1985 these included Morgan Guaranty Trust, Manufacturers Hanover Trust, Wells Fargo, Cigna, Phibro-Salomon Inc., North Carolina National Bank, First National Bank of Boston and others. They had stopped making loans or extending lines of credit to the South African government, government corporations, and even to private banks.[124]

Internationally, anti-apartheid movements had initially campaigned for western companies to withdraw from South Africa on moral grounds. When disinvestment did set in, however, it was chiefly because of hard capitalist considerations. David Hough, head of Investor Responsibility Research, a non-political organization financed by 160 U.S. banks, insurance companies, pension funds, university and other institutions, said in October 1983: "Internal political risk studies rather than protests of pressure groups have influenced bank decisions about loans to South Africa."[125]

During the 1980s the anti-apartheid forces focused increasingly on the economic interests of the corporations operating in South Africa. Disinvestment campaigns took the form of persauding withdrawal or selling of shares in such corporations, through demands on politically sensitive state legislatures, city councils, student-pressurable university boards, and trade union pension funds. The result was a drying up of investment capital and a decline of share prices in affected companies.

The effect of such campaigns could be seen in the case of the British Barclays Bank, the biggest foreign bank in South Africa with assets of nearly $15 billion in South Africa and Namibia. A campaign in Britain to remove deposits from Barclays branches as a form of anti-apartheid protest had, between 1980 and March 1985, caused Barclays the loss of accounts worth more than $8 billion.[126] In November 1985 Barclays cut its shareholding in its main South African subsidiary from 50% to 40%, and at the end of that month the Barclays Bank chairman in Britain, Sir Timothy Bevan, delivered a speech to the bank's branch managers in which he made a startling reversal of the Barclays' policy of defending its presence in South Africa and of rejecting the anti-apartheid arguments. Bevan attacked the South African government for being "woefully slow" in dismantling apartheid, which he called "repugnant, wrong, unchristian and unworkable."[127]

By the latter part of 1984 both the South African government and business circles were deeply worried by the disinvestment trend. U.S. state and municipal legislatures had divested themselves of over $500 million worth of shares of companies with South African investments and another $750 million had been pledged to be sold off. There was fear that about $5 billion to $7 billion in union pension funds might be similarly withdrawn.[128] The South African government created a special section in its Department of Foreign Affairs in February 1985 to deal with this problem.

The greatest concern was exhibited by the American Chamber of Commerce in South Africa, which had 300 members affiliated to it in the middle of 1984. It reported then that despite disinvestment there were still between 350 and 450 U.S. companies with a total investment of $2.5 billion in South Africa. However, by the end of 1984 AMCHAM felt compelled to set up 15 industry sector sub-committees to work for the encouragement of U.S. investment and trade, to offset the disinvestment pressure. Finally, in March 1985 the AMCHAM executive director, Stephen Bisenius, (a former director of Business and Government Relations for the Reagan administration in the U.S. Mid-Atlantic region), resigned his post in order to head a new organization, the American Association for Trade and Investment, to fight disinvestment. One of the greatest worries expressed by Bisenius and AMCHAM was over "secondary boycotts" in the U.S.—withdrawal of funds from companies *trading* with South Africa, of which there were 8,000 engaging in a $5 billion trade.[129]

Gravity of the disinvestment issue brought about a major conference held in wholly secret circumstances in Leeds Castle, England in March 1985. The only information given was that it dealt with "disinvestment and investment" in South Africa.

Present from South Africa were: Basil Herson, executive director of Anglo-Vaal mining interests; Mike Resholt, chairman of Barlow Rand; Tony Bloom, executive chairman of Premier Milling; T. R.

Hofmeyer, executive director of Anglo-American; and Jan Steyn, executive director of the Urban Foundation. From the U.S.: Robert Mercer, chief executive of Goodyear International; William Norris, chief executive of Control Data Corp.; John Reed, chairman of Citibank; Roger Smith, chief executive of General Motors; David Tappan, chief executive of Fluor Corp.; Peter Walters, chairman of Mobil Oil; and Howard Yergin, chief executive of Caltex. From Britain: Sir Peter Baxendall of Shell UK; Sir Peter Bevan, chairman of Barclays Bank; Sir Alistair Frame, chairman of Rio Tinto Zinc; Rawleigh Warner, chairman of British Petroleum; from Sweden: Henry Faulkner, chairman of Alfa-Laval; Dr. Leonard Johansson of SKF; Bengt Kvarnback of Fogersta-Seco; Aake Magnusson, chairman of the Council of Swedish Industries. Also present was the Rev. Leon Sullivan of General Motors. The meeting was chaired by the former British prime minister, Edward Heath.[130]

It was reported that one of the main matters discussed at this cross-sectional conference was how to encourage the South African government to adopt the "reform" steps advocated by business circles to aid capitalist development as well as to reduce conflict in the apartheid society. However far this objective was pressed, the worsening of the economic and political crisis throughout 1985 indicated the failure of such encouragement.

In September 1985, in a climate of emergency, a U.S. Corporate Council on South Africa, consisting of the executives of 70 top companies with interests in South Africa was set up, to concern itself with a "contribution to solving South African problems." It organized another top-level meeting in London in November 1985, this time of top U.S. and South African businessmen. The participants refused to reveal the substance of the discussion, except to let it be known that the aim was "to continue efforts to draw up an alternative strategy to economic sanctions and disinvestment and to discuss a greater business role in efforts to bring about change in South Africa."[131]*

* See also p. 233

VI THE ANTI-APARTHEID LIBERATION STRUGGLE

The circumstances at the heart of the apartheid system that have made it non-viable in the long run even for those economic interests, South African and foreign, that profit from institutionalized racism, cannot of themselves lead to the destruction or dismantling of that system and its replacement by a democratic society of equality and national freedom.

In all modern cases of genuine social change the transformation has been brought about by organized forces or movements that are equipped to overcome the defenses and repressive agencies of the existing order, that are able to mobilize decisive numbers of the population to struggle for the change, and that have an alternative program and the administrative capacity to put it into effect.

The imperialist partners of apartheid—the U.S., Britain, West Germany, France and others—have cooperated to the utmost with the racist rulers of South Africa to impede, to disrupt and to smother such a movement. Although compelled by their own concerns for profit to agree to or even to encourage some modifications or "reform" of apartheid as originally set up, the imperialists have had the aim of outflanking and pre-empting the anti-apartheid movement. Pretending to favor change in the system, they talk of the need for change to occur through evolution, and not revolution, through peaceful processes and not violent means. The fact that apartheid *is* violence, and that the oppressed majority have been denied the exercise of peaceful processes in the most brutal way, is ignored or covered over by those who maintain ties and "constructive engagement" with apartheid. The prescriptions they lay down for the anti-apartheid struggle are intended to disarm the people's movement, to lead it into hopeless avenues of futile gestures, and to cause the people to turn away from it in disillusionment, leaving racist rule unchallenged.

However, the anti-apartheid movement in South Africa is mature, highly sophisticated, of great integrity, headed by extremely able and experienced leaders with immense political acumen. They have recognized that apartheid can only be destroyed by a revolutionary struggle that must bring about a revolutionary change in the society that has bred it and has maintained it. Just as in many countries where the most reactionary capitalist ruling sectors turned to fascism to maintain their rule and to deny democratic opposition and where the destruction of fascism meant the downfall of capitalism itself, so in South Africa those who have erected apartheid and who cling to it with savagery may find the entire social system that bred it collapsing as they fall.

The revolutionary struggle against apartheid has been maturing in South Africa for over a quarter of a century. Its climax is nearing.

A Record of Resistance

For the oppressed majority in South Africa, anti-apartheid struggle is but the latest stage in a long history of resistance and liberation warfare against encroaching white imperialist rule, extending over nearly 350 years. The liberation movement of the present time holds up numerous fighting African leaders of the past as national heroes to be emulated, tribal chiefs who fought both Boer and British invaders as they moved inland to seize land, cattle and mineral wealth.

Among them were:

• Ndlambe, Hintsa and Makana, chiefs of the Xhosa tribes in what is now the Eastern Cape, in the 18th and early 19th centuries. Makana in December 1818 drove out an invasion by the British and mercenary troops and counterattacked deep into the British Cape Colony: his forces, armed only with assegais (spears), heroically charged the British riflemen, in disregard of enormous casualties. In two major resistance wars in the mid-19th century, in 1847 and 1850-1853, the Xhosa armies were commanded by a prince named Maqoma and by chiefs like Sandile. Maqoma and Sandile were taken captive and confined by the British on Robben Island, off Cape Town, used then, as it is today by the Afrikaaner government, as a penal colony island for political prisoners.

• Shaka ka Senzangakhona, founder and king of the Zulu nation (1787-1828), a military genius who created the Zulu impi, a highly trained and disciplined fighting formation which he armed with a short thrusting type of assegai for hand-to-hand battle. Shaka died in an intertribal dispute before he could employ his army against the Boers or British, but his son, Dingane, led the impis in resistance to the great trek inland by the Boers in the 1830s.

• Mzilikazi, chief of the Nguni people (later to be known as the Ndebele) who fought and defeated the voortrekker Boers at the Battle of Vegkop in what is now Transvaal. When the Boers returned with reinforcements, Mzilikazi waged an epic nine-day battle before having to retreat across the Limpopo River, to establish a Kingdom of Matabeleland in what is now the Southwestern part of Zimbabwe.

• Mosheshwe, king of the Sotho, who founded Lesotho, one of the strongest and most stable of the African nations, which in 1966 was able to preserve its identity and emerge from British rule as an independent state. Mosheshwe, a very able general, inflicted several crushing defeats on British forces as large as 2,500 men and fought off constant attacks by the Boers. A political leader as well, he was unique at the time, between 1840 and 1870, in trying to build a united resistance to imperialism among the African tribes.

• Sekhukhuni, king of the Bapedi in the eastern Transvaal, who held off Boer Conquest from 1850 to well into the 1870s.

• Cetshwayo, ruler of the Zulus who led a revival of the Zulu nationhood and of resistance spirit in the 1870s. His impis inflicted one of the worst defeats ever suffered by a British army, at Isandhlwana, where a fortified camp of 1,800 British troops was destroyed with only 400 survivors. Frederick Engels wrote of this battle that Cetshwayo's impis "did what no European army can do. Armed only with pikes and spears, and without firearms, they advanced under a hail of bullets from breech-loaders, right up to the bayonets—acknowledged as the best in the world for fighting in close formation—throwing them back in disorder and beating them back more than once; and this despite the colossal disparity in arms."

Great military leaders of the African tribes in South Africa continued to emerge and to conduct important struggles against colonial rule until 1906. In 1905-1906 the political leader of the Zondi clan, Bambatha, led a rebellion against the poll tax imposed by the British colonial regime. It did not subside until Bambatha was killed in a battle at Mome Gorge in June 1906.[1]

The Bambatha revolt was the last major episode of armed resistance by the Africans to colonial conquest prior to the consolidation of white minority rule with the establishment of the Union of South Africa in 1910. By that act, the white settlers, British and Boers, achieved a unitary state to serve their interests. It was a development that had a parallel, however, in the process gradually taking place among the African tribal groupings.

Armed struggle had had the serious shortcoming of being waged on a tribal basis. The wars and revolts of the 18th and 19th centuries were each confined to single tribes and isolated to the lands they occupied and sought to retain. Concepts of nationhood embracing all Africans in South Africa had not evolved and occasional efforts to create unity of two or more tribes to oppose the colonizing whites brought little response. As in other colonial situations, national consciousness was slow to grow and was kept retarded by colonial power policies of dealing separately with each African entity. It grew, as elsewhere, as education, printed expression, religious organization and other factors of broadening consciousness developed. The first organization of a political tendency emerged from such strata in the Eastern Cape in the 1880s, Imbumba Yama Afrika. Similar organizations began to appear in each of the four South African states or provinces just after the turn of the century.[2]

The British parliament's South Africa Act, adopted in 1909 as the constituting measure for the Union of South Africa and containing color-bar provisions for white minority rule, stimulated the holding of a national convention of these bodies at Bloemfontein in March of that year, at which objections were formulated and sent with a delegation to Britain. Britain ignored the protest and proceeded with the Union, the white government of which then passed the Native Land Act of 1913, virtually erasing African land rights. This drove home the need for an African national unity to oppose white minority oppression. One of those calling for unity, Dr. P.I. Seme, of Transvaal, said:

"The demon of racialism, the aberrations of the Xhosa-Fingo raids [intertribal conflicts], the animosity that exists between Zulus and the Tsongas, the Basotho and every other Native, must be buried and forgotten . . . We are one people."[3]

The African National Congress

On January 8, 1912 the historic unity convention was held that created the African National Congress, dedicated to fighting for the rights of the African majority. Founded as a "National Society or Union for all Natives of South Africa," the African National Congress (ANC) has had for three-quarters of a century the central aim of attaining national liberation for the African or Black majority in South Africa. That objective has been indisputably and unalterably the cornerstone of a free and democratic South

Africa, although the means, the tactics and the alliances for achieving it have changed and developed as the conditions and the social forces in the country have altered and matured.

The ANC set out to remove the partitions of tribalism that had segmented the African people. In its first constitution, two "houses" of leadership were provided for, one of them being a "House of Chiefs" made up of the existing kings of the Sotho, Lozi, Zulu, Pondo, Tembu, Rolong, Kgatla and Ngwato peoples, a unity device that underlined nationhood.[4] In the subsequent 1919 constitution the aim was precisely stated: "Congress would encourage mutual understanding and bring together into common action and as one political people all tribes and clans of various tribes or races, and by means of combined effort a united political organization to defend their freedom, rights and privileges."[5]

Although the essential revolutionary element of striving for national freedom was embodied in the ANC from its beginning, it took many years for it to develop as a movement of mass struggle and to acquire the full-fledged liberation movement character that it has today. Like a number of other liberation movements in other countries, national consciousness and aspirations came initially from an emerging educated stratum as well as from tribal leaders with a recollection of resistance to colonial conquest. This came before an African working class had taken mature shape. While tribal heads comprised the "upper house" of the early ANC, leaders and activists in the "lower house" were from the small educated strata, mainly teachers, lawyers, writers and small property owners. Activities and campaigns for the removal of the color bar and for abolishing racially discriminatory laws and practices were confined to petitions, resolutions and deputations to the Union government and to London. Not until the annual conference of 1943 was the constitution amended to democratize and update the ANC.[6]

Above all, the ANC was not founded as nor did it develop the characteristics of a racially exclusive or ultra-nationalist organization. Its assertion of itself as an African movement for achieving African or Black liberation was a statement of the cardinal aim of any revolutionary movement in South Africa, which was recognized and asserted by all other revolutionary and freedom organizations which subsequently arose in that country. It took some time for the concept of alliances and broad forms of unity for basic aims to be brought forward by the ANC, but this was related to the fact that other such movements did not appear until a later date than the ANC. Significantly, in the 1943 conference an amendment was introduced in the constitution to broaden the concept of membership: "*Any person* over 17 years of age who is willing to subscribe to the aims of Congress and to abide by its constitution and rules may become an individual member upon application to the nearest branch."[7]

This spirit of the ANC came to its fullest fruition in the historic Congress of the People, held in 1955 mainly at its initiative, which adopted the Freedom Charter, the preamble of which proclaims that "South Africa belongs to all who live in it, black and white," and asserts that "we the people of South Africa, black and white together—equals, countrymen and brothers—adopt this Freedom Charter. And we pledge ourselves to strive together, sparing neither strength nor courage, until the democratic changes set out here have been won."

The Congress Alliance

The transformation of the ANC, from a relatively loose-knit organization that concerned itself mainly with the holding of annual national and provincial conferences as the means of expressing African demands, to a mass organization of an increasingly radical character that undertook to mobilize the people as a whole around its program, was closely linked with the development of workingclass movements in South Africa. In particular the emergence of the Communist Party of South Africa and its efforts to achieve a correct line of organization and struggle around the national question had a deep impact on the ANC.

In the period immediately after its founding in 1921, the Communist Party of South Africa (CPSA), which had a precursor in the International Socialist League that had come into being in 1915, gave emphasis to organization and education among the white workers, especially the white miners, who were still engaged in class battles against the white owners. Both the ISL and the fledgling CPSA campaigned against racism and projected the necessity for white and black unity, but complex problems arose as the white mine owners and others moved to replace higher-paid white workers with very low-paid black labor. In 1922 the white miners struck in protest, and a three-month armed conflict with the state ensued which employed the full weight of its armed forces to crush the strike. Most Communist Party members were in the ranks of the white workers and perforce had to fight along with them, striving in the midst of the confused struggle to point out that the government was a class enemy, not the African workers (who took no part in the strike). However, the consequence was that the white workers in defeat were swung to the racist demagogy of the Nationalist Party, not to the principled position of the CPSA—i.e., to job reservation for white mine workers, not black and white unity. Following the 1922 events the CPSA increasingly put its concentration on organizing and working among the African workers, a process formalized in a decision at the Party's third congress in 1924.

A tendency for the activity of the ANC and the CPSA to converge had already occurred, and this now increased. One of the main areas of cooperation was in the building of a remarkable and fast-growing labor movement, the Industrial and Commercial Workers' Union (ICU). Started in 1919, the ICU, composed of African and Colored Workers, grew to a membership of hundreds of thousands, including tens of thousands of peasants in the rural areas and some of their chiefs. A moving spirit in the ICU was an ANC leader who was committed to working class organization, Selby Msimang.[8]

Many ANC leaders were impressed by the dedicated and principled work of the CPSA which, from an initial membership mainly of whites, had become predominantly African in composition (by 1928 African members numbered 1,600 out of a total of 1,750). The ANC president elected in 1924, J.J. Gumede, visited Moscow to attend the 10th anniversary of the October Revolution, as well as representing the ANC at the February 1927 International Congress of the League Against Imperialism. In Brussels, at that Congress, Gumede told the delegates: "I am happy to say that there are Communists in South Africa. I myself am not one, but it is my experience that the Communist Party is the only party that stands behind us and from which we can expect something."[9]

Gumede was elected to a second three-year term as ANC president, running until 1930, sharing leadership with a Communist, E.J. Kaille, who became secretary-general. In 1930, however, the unity trend was interrupted when conservatives in the ANC combined to remove Gumede and Kaille, installing leaders who steered the organization away from mass action for the next decade. This coincided with a switch to the right by some ICU leaders who forced the Communists out of the union, a retrograde step resulting in the swift disintegration of the ICU. It was a period that provided important lessons for the young Africans who came into the ANC later.[10]

The years of struggle against fascism prior to and during World War II revived both unity and the trend to mass action. Between 1941 and 1943 alone membership of the CPSA quadrupled, the result not only of militant campaigns against the home-grown fascists in the

Nationalist Party like Vorster, Verwoerd and Malan who formed the pro-Nazi Ossewa Brandweg, but more importantly those for African rights and equality. The CPSA called on the ANC to turn to the masses and to acquire leaders with a revolutionary outlook.

Such a process, in fact, was occurring. In 1943 the annual ANC conference did away with the lower and upper house divisions and shifted emphasis from the almost exclusive role of the annual conference for taking action, to the building up of local branches rooted in agitational and organizing activity among the people, especially the working people. April 1944 saw the formation of the ANC Youth League, a dynamic organization that had Nelson Mandela as its first secretary and Oliver Tambo and Walter Sisulu among its leaders. The Youth League was a major factor in pressing the ANC to adopt new forms of struggle involving the people.[11]

One of the first outcomes was the anti-pass campaign of 1944-1945, in which there was close cooperation between the ANC and CPSA. It was welcomed with great popular enthusiasm. At the broadly representative conference in May 1945, presided over by ANC president Dr. A.B. Xuma, the National Anti-Pass Council that was elected, headed by Xuma and the Transvaal ANC secretary David Bopape, included such leading Communists as Yusuf Dadoo, Moses Kotane, J.B. Marks, E. T. Mofutsanyana and A. Maliba.

It was followed in the immediate postwar years by a rapid development toward mass struggle. A powerful impetus was given by a massive strike of Black miners in August 1946. Called by the African Mine Workers' Union (which had Communists in its leadership), the strike was supported by 100,000 miners, a third of the total African working force at the time, and had widespread public backing. Although crushed by armed police who killed and wounded hundreds of workers, the strike aroused a militant spirit.[12]

Before the election of the Nationalist government and the installing of its apartheid program in 1948, therefore, the unity and cooperation of the ANC and CPSA had had a long development and had been tested in major struggles against the racist oppression of the African majority. The coming to power of the most extreme racist and fascist-minded sectors of the white minority had a galvanizing effect on the already unifying movement.

At its annual conference in 1949, a milestone in its history, the ANC adopted a Program of Action that completed its thorough transformation into a revolutionary mass organization. It put into implementation concepts of struggle that had only been discussed previously, having to do with the boycott of apartheid institutions. It called for "immediate and active boycott, strike, civil disobedience, non-cooperation" and other actions, including a political strike—"preparations and making of plans for a national stoppage of work for one day as a mark of protest against the reactionary policy of the Government."[13]

Nelson Mandela, who had by this time been elevated from the Youth League to the National Executive Council of the ANC, said later of this conference:

> Up to 1949 the leaders of the ANC had always acted in the hope that by merely pleading their cause, placing it before the authorities, they—the authorities—would change their hearts and extend to them all the rights they were demanding. But the forms of political action which are set out in Program of Action meant that the ANC was not going to rely on a change of heart. It was going to exert pressure to compel the authorities to grant its demands.[14]

The first action flowing from this decision was undertaken by the Transvaal ANC organization in coordination with the Transvaal Indian Congress, the African People's Organization, and the Johannesburg District Communist Party—the holding of a huge Defend Free Speech Convention which called for a general strike on May 1st. The strike was massively successful, shutting down almost every industry on the Witwatersrand. Black workers gave overwhelming support.

As the Program of Action thus began, the apartheid government reacted with its first major step designed to smash opposition to its racist policies: the adoption in 1950 of an Unlawful Organization Act (later renamed as the Suppression of Communism Act), outlawing the CPSA. The ANC promptly responded in a manner vividly demonstrating its broad and mature character as a national liberation movement. It called an emergency conference that decided on mass action against the suppressive act. In a speech to the conference Oliver Tambo reflected its tone, saying that if the ANC sat by while the Communist Party was attacked, the blow would fall on all other democratic organizations as well: "Today it is the Communist Party. Tomorrow it will be our trade unions, our Indian Congress, our African People's Organization, our African National Congress."[15]

The protest campaign that followed was taken up all over South Africa, an outstanding example of the unity that had been developed.

Adoption of the measure outlawing the CPSA resulted in a temporary dislocation in the anti-apartheid campaigns, however. In a hasty and confused move, the CPSA Central Committee met and decided to dissolve the party, underestimating the readiness of its members to go underground and to carry on the anti-apartheid struggle in a vanguard manner illegally. There was no intention to dissuade Communists as individuals from continuing the struggle. Party members continued to work as usual in other democratic organizations. Almost as soon as dissolution occurred, leading cadres moved to set up a provisional center and began to reestablish party committees and cells. By the beginning of 1953 an illegal national conference had been held, adopting a program and a new name, the South African Communist Party (SACP). Declaring itself to be "the heir to the tradition created by the CPSA . . . of unflinching struggle against oppression and exploitation, for unity of the workers and freedom-loving people of our country, irrespective of race and color," the SACP set forth its task of "combining legal mass work with the illegal work of building the Marxist-Leninist Party."[16]

In the meantime the ANC, joining forces with the South African Indian Congress, launched in 1952 a Campaign of Defiance of Unjust Laws. Superbly disciplined, it was sustained for six months and was unprecedented in its scope and its militance, holding up firmly despite the arrest of more than 8,000 of its voluntary participants. The Campaign had a great impact in South Africa and abroad, awakening anti-apartheid steps at the United Nations and in Western European countries.

Among the repercussions of the Defiance Campaign was the creation in 1953 of the South African Colored People's Organization (SACPO) and the South African Congress of Democrats, an organization of white opponents of apartheid. In 1955 the South African Congress of Trade Unions (SACTU) was formed, at the urging of the ANC and with the active coordination of the underground SACP.[17] The ANC and the South African Indian Congress joined with these three new organizations to form the Congress Alliance (with the SACP giving all-out unity assistance), comprising a powerful and growing liberation movement that increasingly challenged the apartheid regime.

An outstanding feature of the ANC in this struggle period was the unwavering leadership given by Chief Albert John Lutuli, a Zulu who became president of the ANC in 1954 and held that post until his death in 1967. Chief Lutuli was awarded the Nobel Peace Prize in 1960, an honor that reflected upon the ANC as well as its president. Another impressive feature of the period was the contribution of African women to the anti-apartheid movement, especially in the stirring march against the pass laws by 20,000 African women in Johannesburg in 1956 led by the ANC women's section headed by Florence Mophosho.

The spreading network of apartheid, added to in each session of the white minority parliament, creating a vast structure of racist and extremely undemocratic laws, led to a momentous step by the ANC to set forth the features of an alternative democratic society that would replace the apartheid system. Such a step was proposed at the 1953 annual conference of the ANC, in a resolution moved by Professor Z.K. Matthews that called for the holding of a national conference to work out the details.

Such a conference met in March 1954, attended by the executives of the organizations comprising the Congress Alliance. They set up a National Action Committee which circularized all the branches of the member organizations as well as communities where no branches existed, asking them to submit suggestions for a democratic charter. The result was an extensive nationwide discussion at meetings to formulate proposals, to elect delegates to a special congress, and to raise money for the occasion. During this period the intensity of interest was heightened by the constant campaigning by the ANC against apartheid measures.

The Freedom Charter

On June 6, 1955 a Congress of the People assembled in the township of Kliptown, near Johannesburg. In spite of the presence of an army of police who surrounded the meeting area, setting up roadblocks that prevented hundreds of delegates from reaching the congress, a total of 2,888 elected delegates were present. It was the largest, most representative democratic conference ever held in South Africa. Ignoring the police who penetrated the assemblage searching people and demanding names, the delegates thundered approval of each section of a Charter that was put to them.

The Freedom Charter is the foremost document of African liberation. From the time of its adoption it has guided and set the goals for the freedom movement in South Africa, and, although other organizations of the Congress Alliance participated in its shaping, it has been identified with the African National Congress and as its program.

Says the Charter preamble:*

We, the People of South Africa, declare for all our country and the world to know:
—that South Africa belongs to all who live in it, black and white, and that no government can justly claim authority unless it is based on the will of all the people;
—that our people have been robbed of their birthright to land, liberty and peace by a form of government founded on injustice and inequality;
—that our country will never be prosperous or free until all our people live in brotherhood enjoying equal rights and opportunities;
—that only a democratic state, based on the will of all the people, can secure to all their birthrights without distinction or color, race, sex or belief;
And therefore, we the people of South Africa, black and white together—equals, countrymen and brothers—adopt this Freedom Charter. And we pledge ourselves to strive together, sparing neither strength nor courage, until the democratic changes set out here have been won.

Besides the preamble, the Freedom Charter has ten sections with the following headings: "The people shall govern!", "All national groups shall have equal rights!", "The people shall share in the country's wealth!", "The land shall be shared among those who work it!", "All shall be equal before the law!", "All shall enjoy equal human rights!", "There shall be work and security!", "The doors of learning and of culture shall be opened!", "There shall be houses, security and comfort!", "There shall be peace and friendship!"[18]

The apartheid regime attacked the Freedom Charter as "high treason," chiefly for what are referred to as its "economic clauses"—those dealing with sharing the country's wealth and sharing the land. Accusations that the Charter is a program for socialism or communism have accompanied the attacks. There is no such intent or content in the document.

On sharing the country's wealth, it is stated:

The national wealth of our country, the heritage of all South Africans, shall be restored to the people; the mineral wealth beneath the soil, the banks and monopoly industry shall be transferred to the people as a whole; all other industry and trade shall be controlled to assist the well-being of the people.

*Full text in Appendix, p. 237.

This is certainly a form of nationalization, but Nelson Mandela, in an article in the South African journal *Liberation* in 1956, explained the nature of it:

> It is true that in demanding the nationalization of the banks, the gold mines, and the land the Charter strikes a fatal blow at the financial and gold-mining monopolies and farming interests that have for centuries plundered the country . . . But such a step is absolutely imperative and necessary because the realization of the Charter is inconceivable, in fact impossible, unless and until these monopolies are first smashed up and the national wealth of the country turned over to the people . . .

> Under socialism the workers hold state power. They and the peasants own the means of production, the land, the factories and the mills. All production is for use and not for profit. The Charter does not contemplate such profound economic and political changes. Its declaration "The people shall govern" visualizes the transfer of power not to any single social class but to all the people of the country, be they workers, peasants, professionals, or petty bourgeoisie.

In view of the extensive ownership of the national wealth and land by foreign corporations and banks, these aims of the Freedom Charter have an anti-imperialist essence as well, being directed equally against the Afrikaaner, British, U.S. and other large owning interests that have underpinned the racist state. For this reason, U.S., British, West German and other imperialist sharers in the apartheid economy have regarded the Freedom Charter as subversive.

Pursuing its charge that the Freedom Charter and the Congress of the People were "high treason," the apartheid government set out to remove the leading participants from the scene. After attempting to build up a case through months of raids and searches of homes and offices, the government finally arrested 156 people, including the principal leaders of the ANC and the other Alliance groups, and tried them for treason and Communism. The trial stretched over four and a half years, until March 1961, until all 156 were acquitted. In the course of that shared experience, ANC leaders, Communists and others attained a deeper and more profound unity than ever.

The trial of leaders, far from intimidating the anti-apartheid movement, intensified the defiance campaign. In the latter 1960s the popular resistance, in the form of boycotts, burning of passes (especially by women, thousands of whom were arrrested) and political strikes, reached a peak. One national general strike after another occurred in the country's main industrial areas in response to ANC calls.

Resistance to apartheid had one of its most militant manifestations in the rural areas of the bantustans being set up by the racist regime. Patriotic chiefs and those tribal leaders opposed to the apartheid plans were arbitrarily removed and even deported by the government to other regions, to be replaced by collaborating elements. The people in several areas rebelled against these acts.

A large-scale revolt occurred in early 1958 in Zeerust, a region in Transvaal, where women destroyed their pass books and the masses set up their own courts which tried and executed four of the government collaborators. The reprisals were ruthless, but in Sekhukhuniland, in Transvaal, in May 1958 another revolt occurred in which some peasants took up arms in addition to setting up courts to try those appointed officials whom they called traitors. In Sekhukhuniland government forces executed 16 peasants, including a woman. Biggest of the revolts took place in Pondoland in the Transkei where an enormous resistance movement with thousands of members, calling itself Intaba (The Mountain), took control of a large area, set up people's courts, levied taxes on both Black and white, and held out until well into 1960. Intaba finally adopted the ANC program. In the military suppression by the government 5,000 peasants were arrested, 32 sentenced to death, and many hundreds sent to prison. A state of emergency that was declared in Transkei at the time has never been lifted.[19]

In this setting of intensified anti-apartheid action, the South African government, then headed by Hendrik Verwoerd, turned to more ruthless means of eliminating opposition to the racist system. Early in 1960 the ANC prepared the launching of a national campaign against the pass laws, and the government moved to smash it.

On March 21, 1960 the police opened fire upon a peaceful anti-pass law gathering in the township of Sharpeville in the Transvaal. They shot people in the back as they ran from the scene, killing 69.

The slaughter at Sharpeville was a turning point in the struggle between the racist government and the great majority of the people in South Africa. For the government it marked a declaration of war against all who resisted its policies. Proclaiming a state of emergency, it began mass arrests of up to 20,000 Africans besides about 2,000 national and local leaders of the ANC and other Congress Alliance organizations. A particular target were the trade union leaders and activists of SACTU.

Under a new Unlawful Organizations Act, the ANC was banned and declared an illegal organization. With all legal and peaceful channels now blocked, the outlawed ANC and SACP had no alternative but to accept that for the oppressed majority in South Africa nonviolent forms of struggle alone were not sufficient to contend with the violent and all-encompassing suppression of the racist state. In such circumstances, revolutionary including armed means had become essential.

Umkhonto we Sizwe

In the months following the outlawing of the ANC, crucial decisions were made by the liberation movement. These culminated in the formal launching of an armed fighting force on December 16, 1961—Umkhonto we Sizwe (Spear of the Nation). On that day its first operation was carried out, the blowing up of electric pylons, beginning a program of acts of sabotage that dramatically demonstrated the arrival of a new, militant form of resistance struggle.

The initial manifesto of Umkhonto we Sizwe declared:

The people prefer peaceful methods of change to achieve their aspirations without the suffering and bitterness of civil war . . . The government has interpreted the peacefulness of the movement as weakness. We are striking out along a new road for the liberation of the people of this country. The Government policy of force, repression and violence will no longer be met with non-violent resistance only! The choice is not ours; it has been made by the Nationalist Government which has rejected every peaceable demand of the people for rights and freedom and answered every such demand with force and yet more force.[20]

Said the manifesto:

Umkhonto we Sizwe will be at the front line of the people's defense. It will be the fighting arm of the people against the Government and its policies of race oppression. It will be the fighting force of the people for liberty, for rights, and for their final liberation.[21]

From the outset it was plain that the struggle would be prolonged and difficult. Anti-apartheid organizations had been driven underground and many of their leaders and effective members had been arrested, placed under ban conditions, or exiled internally. Others, including

Oliver Tambo, Moses Kotane, Yusuf Dadoo, Moses Mabhida, J.B. Marks, were sent out of the country by their organizations to develop the struggle from abroad.

In July 1963 the underground suffered a heavy blow when government agents raided a clandestine headquarters in Rivonia near Johannesburg and arrested a number of leading figures of the ANC and SACP in the midst of a meeting. Of those arrested and tried for attempting armed overthrow of the state, eight of top stature in the liberation struggle were sentenced to life imprisonment and confined on Robben Island: Nelson Mandela, Walter Sisulu, Govan Mbeki, Dennis Goldberg, Raymond Mhlaba, Ahmed Kathrada, Elias Motsoaledi, and A. Mlangeni. Among them were some who were guiding the development of the armed struggle. Only one of the leading figures arrested, Lionel "Rusty" Bernstein, was able to evade conviction and gain acquittal due to faulty introduction of evidence.[22]

Besides these setbacks and disasters, a number of other factors made necessary a considerable period of low-level activity by Umkhonto we Sizwe. The movement required time to recruit, to train, and to produce the military leadership for an armed force. In the conditions of South Africa few Black people had experience with arms, being excluded from the country's armed forces and military training (until the shortage of white recruits led to the lowering of that color bar in the latter 1970s). For Umkhonto we Sizwe, recruits or volunteers had to be sent abroad where training could be carried on without interruption.

Not until August 1967 did reports of major action by Umkhonto we Sizwe (or MK, as it is commonly known) appear. They were of fighting on a sizeable scale against the South African army. It occurred not in South Africa itself but in Rhodesia (Zimbabwe), where South African troops had been sent in 1966 to aid the Ian Smith regime in contending with Zimbabwe liberation forces. The action involved an alliance between the guerrilla force of the ANC and that of the Zimbabwe African People's Union (ZAPU), and it took place at Wankie in the Zambezi River Valley, and in the districts of Bulawayo, Urungwe and Siplilo. In fighting which lasted for many days, South African casualties were heavy, more than 40 dead and a larger number wounded. SADF units were bested in the use of weapons and were compelled to withdraw from the battle area. It was a shock to the apartheid government.[23]

Oliver Tambo, then deputy president-general of the ANC, made the dramatic announcement of the engagement on August 19, 1967:

We wish to declare that the fighting that is presently going on in the Wankie area is indeed being carried out by a Combined Force of ZAPU and ANC which marched into the country as comrades-in-arms on a common route, each bound to its destination. It is the determination of these Combined Forces to fight the common settler enemy to the finish, at any point of encounter as they make their way to their respective fighting zones.[24]

For the ANC the fighting zone was in South Africa. In this particular case, MK units were literally fighting their way back to their home territory after receiving arms and training abroad. The fact that the initial major action was in Rhodesia, together with ZAPU, demonstrated the unity of liberation forces in southern Africa as a whole. In a later interview in October 1967 Oliver Tambo asserted: "It can be said that for the ANC this is the beginning of the armed struggle for which we have been preparing since the early '60s."[25]

The return of trained fighters to South Africa did not mean that armed struggle on a confrontational scale, even of the kind that had occurred at Wankie, could now begin on apartheid's home grounds. It was not the intention of the ANC and its allies that armed struggle would be made the main form of struggle on an ascending, open scale as in other countries where liberation wars had occurred.

In its program, "The Road to South African Freedom," adopted at its Fifth National Conference in 1962, soon after the launching of Umkhonto we Sizwe, the SACP put the question of armed struggle in this way:

> The Communist Party considers that the slogan of "non-violence" is harmful to the cause of the democratic national revolution in the new phase of the struggle, disarming the people in the face of the savage assaults of the oppressor, dampening their militancy, undermining their confidence in their leaders. At the same time, the Party opposes undisciplined acts of individual terror. It rejects theories that all non-violent methods of struggle are useless or impossible, and will continue to advocate and work for the use of all forms of struggle by the people, including non-collaboration, strikes, boycotts and demonstrations.
>
> The Party does not dismiss all prospects of non-violent transition to the democratic revolution. This prospect will be enhanced by the development of revolutionary and militant people's forces. The illusion that the white minority can rule forever over a disarmed majority will crumble before the reality of an armed and determined people. The crisis in the country, and the contradictions in the ranks of the ruling class will deepen. The possibility would be opened of a peaceful and negotiated transfer of power to the representatives of the oppressed majority of the people.[26]

This has continued to be the position of the SACP, as Umkhonto we Sizwe and its armed actions have shown. In a statement by its augmented Central Committee meeting in November 1979 the SACP said:

> The policy of armed struggle, the armed blows being delivered against the enemy and the steps being taken to create conditions for the entrenchment of a national liberation army in both urban and rural areas, constitute a vital part of the liberation movement's strategy. But, as we have always stressed, it is a strategy which can only take effective shape if it is rooted in the broadest possible mobilization and organization of our people in mass legal and semi-legal struggles. It is politics which is in command and it is politics which determines the nature and level of armed activity at every stage.[27]

For its part, the ANC, in its important 1969 program document, "Strategy and Tactics of the African National Congress," made this formulation of the use of armed struggle:

> When we talk of revolutionary armed struggle, we are talking of political struggle by means which include the use of military force even though once force as a tactic is introduced it has the most far-reaching consequences on every aspect of our activities. It is important to emphasize this because our movement must reject all manifestations of militarism which separates armed people's struggle from its political context.
>
> Reference has already been made to the danger of the thesis which regards the creation of military areas as the generator of mass resistance. But even more is involved in this concept. One of the vital problems connected with this bears on the important question of the relationship between the political and the military. From the very beginning our movement has brooked no ambiguity concerning this. The primacy of the political leadership is unchallenged and supreme and all revolutionary formations and levels (whether armed or not) are subordinate to this leadership. To say this is not just to invoke tradition. This approach is rooted in the very nature of this type of revolutionary struggle and is borne out by the experience of the overwhelming majority of revolutionary movements which have engaged in such struggles. Except in very rare instances, the people's armed challenge against a foe with formidable material strength does not achieve dramatic and swift success. The path is filled with obstacles and we harbor no illusions on this score, in the case of South Africa. In the long run it can only succeed if it attracts the active support of the mass of the people. Without this life-blood it is doomed. Even in our country with the historical backgrounds and traditions of armed resistance still within the memory of many people and the special developments of the immediate past, the involvement of

the masses is unlikely to be the result of a sudden natural and automatic consequence of military clashes. It has to be won in all-round political mobilization which must accompany military activities. This includes educational and agitational work throughout the country to cope with the sophisticated torrent of misleading propaganda and "information" of the enemy which will become more intense as the struggle sharpens. When armed clashes begin they seldom involve more than a comparative handful of combatants whose very conditions of fighting-existence make them incapable of exercising the functions of all-round political leadership. The masses of the peasants, workers and youth, beleaguered for a long time by the enemy's military occupation, have to be activated in a multitude of ways not only to ensure a growing stream of recruits for the fighting units but to harass the enemy politically so that his forces are dispersed, and therefore weakened. This calls for the exercise of all-round political leadership.[28]

Questions were raised about reliance by the liberation forces on armed struggle, considering that South Africa is a highly developed capitalist country with an extensive infrastructure of modern roads, railways, airways, its own arms industry and other industrial power, and a large white population on which to draw for military manpower. In addition, the terrain is lacking in mountain ranges of large extent, in wide forested areas, and in swamps of appreciable size, all geographical features favoring guerrillas in other countries.

These questions were dealt with early in the MK armed struggle by one of the liberation movement leaders, the South African Communist Joe Slovo:

We must not overlook the fact that over a period of time many of these very same unfavorable factors will begin to operate in favor of the liberation forces:

a) The ready-to-hand resources including food production depend overwhelmingly upon non-white labor which, with the growing intensity of the struggle, will not remain docile and cooperative.

b) The white manpower resources may seem adequate initially but must become dangerously stretched as guerrilla warfare develops. Already extremely short of skilled labor—the monopoly of the elite—the mobilization of a large force for a protracted struggle would place a further burden on the working of the economy.

c) In contrast to many other major guerrilla struggles (Cuba is one of the exceptions) the enemy's economic and manpower resources are all situated within the theater of war and there is no secure external pool (other than direct intervention of a foreign state) safe from sabotage, mass action and guerrilla action on which the enemy can draw.

d) The very sophisticated character of the economy with its well-developed system of communications makes it a much more vulnerable target. In an underdeveloped country the interruption of supplies to any given region may be no more than a local setback. In a highly sensitive modern economic structure of the South African type, the successful harassment of transport to any major industrial complex would inevitably inflict immense damage to the economy as a whole and to the morale of the enemy. (The South African forces would have the task of keeping intact about 30,000 miles of railway lines spread over an area of over 400,000 square miles . . .)

. . . guerrilla warfare can be, and has been, waged in every conceivable type of terrain, in deserts, in swamps, in farm fields, in built-up areas, in plains, in the bush and in countries without friendly borders. The sole question is one of adjusting survival tactics to the sort of terrain in which operations have to be carried out.[29]

MK units, whether organized within South Africa or returning over long land routes through neighboring countries, did not rush into armed clashes with the SADF. From the latter 1960s a gradual development of small-scale guerrilla actions occurred. The South African Commissioner of Police, General Johan Coetzee, admitted in March 1985 that 275 acts of "terrorism" by ANC guerrillas had been carried out from 1976 to 1985, and broke these down to: 61 attacks on the police, 125 attacks against the economy (acts of sabotage), 56 attacks on state or public buildings (bombings of military, police or apartheid agency offices), and 35 attacks on "private citizens" (liquidation of informers or collaborators).[30] General Coetzee, by all indications, was understating MK activity, the Botha government having by that time forbidden mention of guerrilla actions of many types.

In the 1960s and early 1970s a prime concern was the building of underground routes in and out of the country, the establishing of arms storage sites, and the creation of secure bases for MK units. The pattern of bombing of industrial and other installations and of raid attacks indicated that bases or safe places had been developed amidst the urban population.

A constant effort by the government to claim that MK bases were in neighboring countries from which attacks were allegedly being made (an excuse for the invasions and destabilizing raids made by South Africa on neighboring states in order to dominate them and reverse the liberation process) could not explain the MK operations carried out hundreds of miles from borders. Said Oliver Tambo early in 1985: "We planned our military activities in the knowledge that the Frontline States were vulnerable. We never believed that the Frontline States would offer their countries as rear guard bases."[31]

Decisions at Morogoro

Understandably, it took time for the ANC and the other members of the Congress Alliance that had put forward the Freedom Charter to recover from the setbacks and dislocations of the liberation movement caused by the government offensive of the 1960s. The arrests, trials and imprisonments of ANC and SACP leaders had temporarily decapitated and disrupted the underground apparatus that had been set up within South Africa. As a consequence, the group of leaders who had been sent out of the country to build an external apparatus for organizing international support for the anti-apartheid struggle was compelled to assume the additional task of reforming and directing the building of the internal underground movement.

The Zambezi Valley campaign in Rhodesia in 1967 and the sharp blows it struck at the South African army that had been played up as invincible were given maximum publicity by the ANC to demonstrate that the movement was indestructible and able to confront the armed power of the racist state. Even more impressive were the political successes of the ANC in the same period, in winning support internationally and in reconstructing the underground structure.

This was clearly shown in the holding of the First Consultative Conference of the ANC at Morogoro, in Tanzania, on April 25-May 1, 1969. Attended by over 70 delegates, from both the internal and external wings of the ANC, and from the Umkhonto we Sizwe commands established in South Africa, the Conference was the most stirring and decisive ever held to that time by the ANC. Having the aim of "Total Mobilization for the National Democratic Revolution in South Africa," it made changes in the ANC's structures and administrative organs designed for the vigorous implementation of such a program.

A new, smaller and more tightly-knit National Executive Committee was elected, and a Revolutionary Council was created and given the task of stepping up the armed struggle and mobilizing the people in support of the revolutionary struggle. The Revolutionary Council had representatives from all the national groups and revolutionary forces in South Africa, including the SACP, the Indian and Colored People's Congresses, SACTU and of course MK (all of which were represented at Morogoro and placed themselves under the banner of the ANC).

The Morogoro Conference was a milestone event in its adoption of a highly significant document, "Strategy and Tactics of the African National Congress," that carried further some of basic precepts of the

1955 Freedom Charter. One of its features was an elaboration of the Charters' reference to "we the people of South Africa, black and white together—equals, countrymen and brothers," in the context of the national liberation struggle.

In approaching this as a fundamental aspect of the circumstances molding ANC revolutionary strategy and tactics, the document firmly stressed:

> The main content of the present stage of the South African revolution is the national liberation of the largest and most oppressed group—the African people. This strategic aim must govern every aspect of the conduct of our struggle whether it be the formulation of policy or the creation of structures. Amongst other things, it demands in the first place the maximum mobilization of the African people as a dispossessed and racially oppressed nation. This is the mainspring and it must not be weakened. It involves a stimulation and a deepening of national confidence, national pride and national assertiveness. Properly channelled and properly led, these qualities do not stand in conflict with the principles of internationalism. Indeed, they become the basis of more lasting and more meaningful cooperation, a cooperation which is self-imposed, equal and one which is neither based on dependence nor gives the appearance of being so.

It was pointed out that while "The national character of the struggle must therefore dominate our approach," the South African struggle was occurring in a different era and context from earlier anti-colonial struggles for national liberation, in a world with a powerful socialist system and liberated areas altering the world balance of forces, and with wider horizons that embrace not just the gaining of political liberation but also of social emancipation, shaped in South Africa by the existence of a large and well-developed working class. Therefore the ANC's nationalism "must not be confused with the classical drive by an elitist group among the oppressed people to gain ascendency so that they can replace the oppressor in the exploitation of the masses."

Having emphasized these essential features of its stand, the ANC document continued:

> The African, although subjected to the worst intense racial oppression and exploitation, is not the only oppressed national group in South Africa. The two million strong Colored Community and the three-quarter million Indians suffer varying forms of national humiliation, discrimination and oppression. They are part of the non-white base upon which rests white privilege. As such they constitute an integral part of the social forces ranged against white supremacy. Despite deceptive and,

often, meaningless concessions they share a common fate with their African brothers and their own liberation is inextricably bound up with the liberation of the African people."

Delineating the record of militant struggle by both groups ("The jails in South Africa are a witness to the large-scale participation by Indian and Colored comrades at every level of our revolutionary struggle"), the ANC document underscored the need to "integrate committed revolutionaries irrespective of their racial background." It declared:

Whatever instruments are created to give expression to the unity of the liberation drive, they must accommodate two fundamental propositions:
  Firstly, they must not be ambiguous on the question of the primary role of the most oppressed African mass and,   Secondly, those belonging to the other oppressed groups and those few white revolutionaries who show themselves ready to make common cause with our aspirations, must be fully integrated on the basis of individual equality. Approached in the right spirit these two propositions do not stand in conflict but reinforce one another.

Mere awareness of oppression, it was pointed out, would not push the Colored and Indian peoples into opposing the enemy and aligning themselves with the liberation movement.

Active support and participation must be fought for and won. Otherwise the enemy will succeed in its never-ending attempt to create a gap between these groups and the Africans and even recruit substantial numbers of them to actively collaborate with it.

It concluded on the key point, "that the Colored and Indian people should see themselves as an integral part of the liberation movement and not as mere auxiliaries."

That integration was exemplified in the composition of the Revolutionary Council chosen at Morogoro.

Along with formulating this approach to the national question and its aspects, the Morogoro strategy and tactics decision gave special attention also to the role of the working class in the national struggle. Victory, it said, must include more than just "formal political democracy." It had to remove the "root of racial supremacy" by assuring that basic wealth and basic resources are put at the disposal of the people as a whole "and are not manipulated by sections or individuals be they white or black."

Such a "genuine and lasting emancipation" was linked with "the existence in our country of a large and growing working class whose class consciousness complements national consciousness. Its political organizations and the trade unions have played a fundamental role in shaping and advancing our revolutionary cause. It is historically understandable that the doubly-oppressed and doubly-exploited working class constitutes a distinct and reinforcing layer of our liberation and Socialism and do not stand in conflict with the national interest. Its militancy and political consciousness will play no small part in our victory and in the construction of a real people's South Africa."[32]

The ANC-SACP Alliance

Although not specifically referred to in the decisions and resolutions of the Consultative Conference, except perhaps indirectly in mentioning the fundamental role of the "political organizations" of the working class, the Morogoro gathering was notable also for the visible unity of the ANC and the SACP. This had already reached a new stage in the formation and development of Umkhonto we Sizwe, which had a leading member and later general-secretary of the SACP, Moses Mabhida,* as its political commissar in the early period including the Wankie battle. At Morogoro the delegates included such leading South African Communists as J.B. Marks, Moses Kotane, Moses Mabhida, Dr. Yusuf Dadoo, Joe Slovo and others, the last named a white South African. Several of them were selected as members of the new Revolutionary Council.

The close relations of the ANC and the SACP were made possible by two factors: the unique character of the ANC as developed in the long South African liberation struggle, and the revolutionary position of the SACP toward it. In its program, the SACP stated: "The Communist Party unreservedly supports and participates in the struggle for national liberation headed by the African National Congress, in alliance with the South African Indian Congress, the Congress of Trade Unions, the Colored People's Congress and other patriotic groups of democrats, women, peasants and youth." The SACP's recognition of the ANC as the leader of the national liberation struggle was based on its assessment of the ANC's character:

> As a national liberation organization, the ANC does not represent any single class, or any single ideology. It is representative of all the classes and strata which make up African society in this country. With the advance of members of the working class, together with revolutionary young intellectuals, to leading positions in the ANC, the organization

*As this manuscript was being written, Moses Mabhida died in March 1986 at the age of 63.

steadily developed and went forward in its policy and methods of struggle. Congress has steadfastly rejected narrow nationalism, black chauvinism, anti-Communism and other outlooks which are harmful to the people's cause.[33]

Perhaps the clearest statement of the ANC's attitude toward alliance with the SACP was made by President Oliver Tambo at a meeting celebrating the 60th anniversary of the founding of the SACP, held in London on July 30, 1981. He said:

The ANC speaks here today, not so much as a guest invited to address a foreign organization. Rather we speak *of* and *to* our own. For it is a matter of record that for much of its history, the SACP has been an integral part of the struggle of the African people against oppression and exploitation in South Africa. We can all bear witness that in the context of the struggle against colonial structures, racism and the struggle for power by the people, the SACP has been fighting with the oppressed and exploited.

Notwithstanding that it has had to concentrate on thwarting the efforts to destroy it, cadres of the SACP have always been ready to face the enemy in the field. Because they have stood and fought in the front ranks, they have been amongst those who have suffered the worst brutalities of the enemy, and some of the best cadres have sacrificed their lives.

And so, your achievements are the achievement of the liberation struggle. Your heroes are ours. Your victories, those of all the oppressed.

The relationship between the ANC and the SACP is not an accident of history, nor is it a natural and inevitable development. For, as we can see, similar relationships have not emerged in the course of liberation struggles in other parts of Africa.

To be true to history, we must concede that there have been many difficulties as well as triumphs along our path, as, traversing many decades, our two organizations have converged towards a shared strategy of struggle. Ours is not merely a paper alliance, created at conference tables and formalized through the signing of documents and representing only an agreement by leaders. Our alliance is a living organism that has grown out of struggle. We have built it out of our separate and common experiences. It has been nurtured by our endeavors to counter the total offense mounted by the National Party in particular against all opposition and against the very concept of democracy. It has been strengthened through resistance to the vicious onslaught against both the ANC and the SACP by the Pretoria regime; it has been fertilized by the blood of countless heroes, many of them unnamed and unsung. It has been reinforced by a common determination to destroy the enemy and by our shared belief in the certainty of victory.

Saying that "Our history has shown that we are a powerful force because our organizations are mutually reinforcing," Oliver Tambo went on:

> It is often claimed by our detractors that the ANC's association with the SACP means that the ANC is being influenced by the SACP. That is not our experience. Our experience is that the two influence each other. The ANC is quite capable of influencing, and is liable to be influenced by others. There has been the evolution of strategy which reflects this two-way process . . .
>   This kind of relationship constitutes a feature of the South African Liberation movement, a revolutionary movement, a feature of the SACP which helps to reinforce the alliance and make it work as it is working. It is a tribute to the leadership of the SACP.   We are therefore talking of an alliance from which, in the final analysis, the struggle of the people of South Africa for a new society and a new social system has benefited greatly.[34]

Soweto: The Beginning of Revolt

The ANC's 1969 Consultative Conference, through no coincidence, took place on the eve of vast stirrings of struggle among the nonwhite majority in South Africa. Awareness of the maturing of circumstances for a renewed upsurge of resistance permeated the discussion at Morogoro. Its projections in strategy and tactics—in regard to the role of armed struggle, and to the "all-round political mobilization" of the people that is its indispensable concomitant—proved to be wholly in keeping with the events that transpired in the decade of the 1970s.

After the repressions of the 1960s and the reinforcement of the racist system in that decade by the massive injections of foreign capital, the anti-apartheid struggle developed as several threads that gradually came together. Undoubtedly these were due to a considerable extent to ANC and SACP underground activity. Educational and agitational literature was distributed increasingly—a favorite device for this was the leaflet bomb exploded in busy or crowded places, scattering large numbers of leaflets widely—and recruiting to the liberation organizations went on steadily. Although struggle movements that arose were often a spontaneous boiling over of popular demands, inevitably these turned to or were influenced by the ANC-led alliance.

The growth of worker militancy that led to the unprecedented strike wave in the early 1970s was one such trend. It was paralleled by another significant thread that emerged from among the Black student youth, a harbinger of one of the most powerful factors in the development of the liberation struggle: the winning of the Black youth to the revolution.

Limitations of the curriculum and of an inhibiting learning-by-rote under the Bantu Education system, the segregation of Black universities and schools even from Colored and Indian institutions, the imposition of severe discipline, and the white control of university councils and of teaching or lecturing staffs caused simmering unrest in the higher schools. This became extended to the African secondary schools in the early 1970s when demands made by industry on the government for a better-trained labor force to solve the skilled labor shortage resulted in the lowering of relatively high entrance exam pass levels. Between 1970 and 1975 a near trebling of African students in secondary schools occurred (from 122,489 in 1970 to 318,568 in 1975), a trend that raised hopes at first but the lack of accompanying classrooms meant severe overcrowding, a shortage of teachers and the frustration of inadequate instruction.[35]

As resentment built up over this apartheid situation, the government's Ministry of Bantu Education threw its match into the powder keg: it issued a directive that beginning in 1976 half of all school subjects would henceforth be taught in the Afrikaans language, in particular arithmetic, mathematics, history and geography. The reaction to this was fueled not only by the fact that Afrikaans was the language of the oppressor group but by the need for English in most areas of employment after leaving school.

Student protest that had begun to burst forth in sporadic school disturbances from 1972 onward was nurtured by the Bantu Education system that trained Africans for inferiority. The Black student organizations that sprang up in this period, however, had wider causes. A South African Students Organization (SASO), formed in 1968, was a part of the Black Consciousness Movement which aimed at making the Black community aware of its own identity, power, and need for separate organizational forms. An African Students Movement (ASM), set up in three secondary schools in Soweto in 1970, developed into the enlarged South African Students Movement (SASM) in 1972 when links were established with schools in the Eastern Cape and Eastern Transvaal. A Black publication said at the time:

The main aim of SASM is to coordinate activities of high school students. Their other main areas of operation are their informative programs concerning injustice in society and in schools and their campaign to preach Black Consciousness.[36]

SASM, however, did not tie itself closely to the Black Consciousness groups. Its links, through many of its leaders and members, were with the ANC; in some places it followed ANC clandestine methods and organized underground cells for protection of its members. In 1974 and 1975 some SASM members were arrested and tried under the Suppression of Communism and the Terrorism Acts, charges usually made on suspicion of ANC or SACP connections.[37]

It was the SASM organization in the Johannesburg township of Soweto that initiated the actions that led in June 1976 to the earth-shaking events known as the Soweto Revolt. The move to introduce Afrikaans as the language of instruction was the precipitating factor. The secretary-general of the SASM, Tebello Motopanyane, a student at the Naledi High School in Soweto and the head of the SASM Action Committee that directed the events, has told of the beginnings:

As early as March 1976, Thomas Mofolo was the first school to have Afrikaans imposed on it, and immediately there was student protest. In March 1976, the principal called in the police to cool the students and force them to accept Afrikaans. Some students from my school, Naledi High School, went there to investigate their problems. We also visited schools in Meadowlands. We found that these students also felt bitter about what the government was doing. They immediately stopped attending classes because they felt as we did that what was needed was a positive reaction.

The Naledi High SASM branch also went to Orlando West Junior Secondary . . . The students there agreed with us and started destroying their books and refused to attend classes. And this was the first effective protest started in Soweto because the students there were quite clear about what they wanted. Despite the threat by the Bantu Education inspector that the schools would be closed . . . they remained very firm . . . We went on to other schools . . . By May 1976, the protest actions were quite general in many schools.[38]

On June 16, 1976 the Action Committee called for a mass protest demonstration against the Afrikaans directive. Fifteen thousand students aged 10 to 20 turned out to march to the Orlando stadium for a meeting, carrying makeshift banners with slogans like "Afrikaans is oppressors' language," "Abolish Afrikaans," and "Blacks are not dustbins—Afrikaans stinks." It was a peaceful march.

They were met on the way by massed white police who, without giving any order to disperse, fired tear gas canisters into the ranks of youth and attacked them with batons. As the young people scattered, the police opened fire with guns, killing many. The students fought back, advancing to throw stones, regardless of bullets and casualties.

Total deaths of African youth on June 16 have never been accurately reported. Estimates of 100 or more have been made, with many more wounded. The Soweto Massacre, as it became known, exceeded Sharpeville in slaughter, and in the consequences.

The reaction by the Soweto youth was immediate. In large groups they swarmed through the township, setting up barricades, burning down government buildings especially of the Bantu Administration Board, stoning passing white-driven vehicles and halting traffic. Among the main targets of destruction were the beerhalls and bottle stores that were symbols to the youth of the degrading living conditions produced by apartheid. The rebellious outburst was in general a near-revolutionary assault on the symbols and structures of the racist state.

For days Soweto was in a state of revolt against the apartheid regime. Its youth fought the police with stones and bottles in guerrilla-type actions, and the police roamed the township in armored cars indiscriminately shooting to kill at any young people they saw. A tendency to spontaneous actions of violence by the youth in various sections of Soweto (a huge sprawling area) was soon brought under central disciplined control by student leaders. The Action Committee was transformed into the Soweto Students Representative Council (SSRC); like the Action Committee it was composed of two representatives from each Soweto school. In a few days the SSRC had assumed full leadership over not only the students of primary and secondary schools but also the large numbers of unemployed youth who joined in the struggle.

These June days were the beginning of an extended period of the greatest upsurge that had yet occurred against the apartheid system. It lasted for about a year, to the middle of 1977. Solidarity protests against the Soweto Massacre and in support of the Soweto students began within a few days in the Black and Colored townships of the Cape Province, particularly around Cape Town and Port Elizabeth. Marches and demonstrations of from 300 to 4,000 students, in some cases together with parents, also took place during July and August in Transvaal, Orange Free State and the bantustans of Ciskei and Transkei—in Brakpan, Dobsonville, Kagiso, Mhluzi, Mdantsane, Uitenhage, Zwelitsha (King Williamstown), Lady Frere, Genadendal, Graaf Reinet, Idutywa, Stutterheim, Kimberley, Upington, Bloemfontein, Kroonstad. In many of these places schools and school libraries were burned down. The demonstration march of 500 in Lady Frere, in the Transkei, turned into a protest against the proposed "independence" of that bantustan to occur in October.[39]

The biggest revolt outside of Soweto came in the Cape Town area. Colored and Black students demonstrated in the townships of Langa, Nyanga and Guguletu and classes were boycotted. An echo of the Soweto Massacre occurred on August 16 when 33 were killed by police gunfire in Langa. After repeated shootings, both Black and Colored students organized unprecedented marches into the city center of white Cape Town, demanding equal education and an end to police violence. On September 1, 3, 4 and 5 Cape Town was entered. On the first occasions the youth did not resist, chanting "No violence, no violence," as police attacked them with tear gas and birdshot, but on September 4-5 Colored and Black youth fought back in the Cape Town suburbs and in nearby Stellenbosch and Somerset West, destroying white shops and vehicles.

Cape Province struggles were marked by the participation of adults as well as youth, including workers who joined in clashes with the police on returning home from work. In general, in all the areas of disturbance from June onwards the arrest and "preventive detention" of adult Black leaders occurred, precisely to bar such association.

In Soweto strong links of the students with the rest of the population existed from the outset. Within a few days a Black Parents Association was set up (Winnie Mandela was one of its members) backed by many Black organizations. It took care of injured students but it also served unofficially as intermediary with the government.

From Soweto, on August 4, up to 30,000 Black youth marched on Johannesburg, seeking to penetrate to police headquarters in John Vorster Square in the city center to demand the release of hundreds of arrested and tortured students. They were blocked by cordons of police who opened fire, killing 3 and wounding 12.

August 4, however, had a far more significant aspect than the well-organized march by youth. The SSRC had called upon the Soweto workers who commuted to Johannesburg to support them by staying at home. About 60% did so.

This first sign of student-worker unity startled the government: the police crackdown was intensified and the policy of "indefinite preventive detention" was introduced. The greatest shock of all then came on August 23. A call for a three-day sympathy strike by workers was responded to by over 80% of the workers of Soweto. For three days the industries of Johannesburg were shut down or reduced to a barely operable state. The workers held firm despite police intimidation, employer threats of dismissal, and attempts to divide them from the students.

On September 13-15 the Soweto workers again responded to a student call for a three-day strike. (The appeal leaflet was headed "The black students' message to their beloved parents.") In the call was this politically-advanced statement:

> The students believe that South Africa is what it is, and has been built by the blood, sweat and broken bodies of the oppressed and exploited black workers. It is a well-known fact that the blacks carry the economy of this country on their shoulders. All the sky-scrapers, super-highways, etc. are built on our undistributed wages.
>
> It is because of these facts that the students realize that in any liberation struggle, the power for change lies with the workers.[40]

The September strike was much more effective than the stayaway in August. It affected not merely Soweto but the whole Witwatersrand industrial region, embracing half a million workers, and, impressively, was joined in a two-day stayaway by 200,000 Colored workers in the Cape Town area.

The SACP made this assessment of the strike action:

> "The disturbances at Soweto and elsewhere throughout South Africa have not only shown the growth of black determination and capacity to fight. They have also revealed the class content of national resistance. The initiative was taken by the youth, but became a formidable force when allied with the power of the urban African working class which rallied to its call. The white establishment, racists and liberals alike, reacted either not at all or with only mild deprecation when schoolchildren were being shot down in cold blood in the townships. But when their workforce was removed during the two successive three-day strikes in Soweto which brought commerce and industry in Johannesburg to a halt, the shouts of alarm rose on all sides.
>
> Consider well the implication of those strikes. After 13 years of detention without trial, 13 years of unrestrained police terror in which the organizations of the people and their leaders were harassed and hounded; after the mass arrests from June 16 onwards of practically every black leader able to give advice to anybody about anything; with the townships and the streets under police siege—despite these massive counter-pressures, the strikes succeeded on a scale never before seen in South Africa, showing not only political consciousness but also capacity to organize of a very high order. The worker-student alliance was able to rally the forces of the entire community in disciplined mass action.[41]

Matching the significance of the worker-student unity in the Soweto Revolt was the role of the ANC. The students may have taken the initiative in the struggle, but the presence of the ANC and its underground cells largely determined its course. Tebello Motoponyane, the secretary-general of the SASM and the head of the Soweto Action Committee, was a member of the ANC, and others in the SASM and SSRC leaderships were certainly either in or close to it.

ANC publications and leaflets were widely circulated and well known in Soweto. Immediately after June 16 they appeared, to call for broad unity and the extending of the struggle to wider issues, especially into the factories and mines. The leaflet passed by the SSRC to virtually every Soweto home calling for the three-day strike in August was signed by the ANC. The presence of Winnie Mandela on the executive of the Black Parents Association indicated the ANC influence there. Consultation with the internal ANC underground undoubtedly occurred at every stage of the Soweto Revolt period, and some SSRC members were reported to have gone clandestinely to a neighboring country to meet leaders of the external ANC. The Cape Town area had been a center of ANC and SACP activity for decades.

The best sign of its leading role was the growth of the ANC's prestige in the wake of the Soweto Revolt. From that time onward the ANC, the MK and the SACP were all seen in enhanced perspective, as the leaders of the national liberation struggle. The most impressive indication of this was the outflux of Black youth from South Africa following the Revolt. Many of them were on the police wanted lists in Soweto and elsewhere, but many also were stirred militantly to greater participation in the anti-apartheid struggle. The vast majority left to join Umkhonto we Sizwe in its training camps abroad or the external ANC for cadre training and return to work in the underground. The South African police estimated that 4,000 had left for this purpose between 1976 and 1980.[42]

Growth of MK

The Soweto Revolt and the upheavals it touched off in Cape Town and other places marked a point of qualitative change for the anti-apartheid struggles in South Africa. A readiness to confront the racist government and a boldness in standing up to its repressive agencies became much more evident from that time, and Umkhonto we Sizwe quickened the trend by increasing the number and daring of its attacks as the temper among Blacks, Coloreds and Indians mounted.

A specialist in politics at the University of Witwatersrand, Tom Lodge, detailed 150 major MK attacks between 1976 and 1982. He concluded that these were intended to "build up popular support among Blacks rather than to terrorize whites." He listed 33 bombing or other sabotage operations on railroads, 25 on industrial establishments, 15 on banks and other "public places," and 14 on administrative buildings (mainly military centers and apartheid departments), besides 19 "shoot-outs" with the police and army, 13 assaults on police stations, 3 assaults on "military targets," and 35 assassination attacks on individuals.[43]

An MK attack of the type that aroused confidence and militance was the assault on the police station in the white suburb of Booysens in Johannesburg on April 4, 1980. Eleven armed men in two cars carried out the swift and efficient assault, employing rockets, hand grenades and automatic rifles. They scattered leaflets in addition before getting away cleanly.[44]

Respect for the MK and its members was heightened by the behavior of the few who were captured in battle by the police or army. The most outstanding of these, who stirred the admiration of the townships, was Solomon Mahlangu, a former Mamelodi High School student who left South Africa in June 1976, in the wake of the Soweto battles with the police, to receive ANC training. He returned as an MK soldier but was captured in a fire-fight with the police soon afterward, in 1977. After torture and trial he received a death sentence and was 25 months in a death cell, maintaining unflinching defiance. Despite an international campaign in his behalf, he was executed on April 6, 1979. His last words, to his mother, have echoed in South Africa ever since:

> Do not worry about me but worry about those who are suffering. I have done my bit of contribution and may God spare you. My blood will nourish the tree which will bear the fruits of freedom. Tell my people that I loved them and that they must continue the struggle. A luta continua.[45]

In South African conditions, guerrilla warfare and bases for the MK were developed in and around the Black townships, and to a lesser extent in the countryside. MK targets were mostly urban. Its attacks listed as directed against individuals were, from the latter 1970s, aimed at eliminating informers from amidst the people, their presence having had an intimidating effect after the banning of the ANC and the SACP. As a result of such steps and as a result of mass struggles, control in the townships gradually passed from the central government to the people and their spokespersons, and bases for the MK became more secure.

Boycott!

From the latter 1970s a proliferating and reinvigorating of community-based organizations occurred, through which opposition to apartheid was expressed—civic organizations, welfare associations, the churches, student organizations and the trade unions. Committees for the release of Nelson Mandela and other political prisoners, and committees for the protection of political prisoners from abuse and torture sprang up. Committees to resist the forced removals of people from townships to the bantustans, or to resist the demolition and removal of entire districts, were formed.

One of the most effective and significant forms of struggle to acquire new force was the boycott. In the 1950s this had been employed on a number of occasions, one of the most outstanding being the boycott of the Putco Bus Company and its fare increases; after losing nearly $500,000 Putco gave in. The boycott against Putco ws repeated in 1975, for the same reason, and was again won, the Johannesburg Chamber of Commerce finally stepping in with an annual subsidy to the bus company in place of fare increases. The bus boycott was essentially a reaction to the apartheid circumstances of locating townships miles from places of employment in the "white areas" and compelling Black workers to commute for hours to and from work on transportation systems that put them at the mercy of price-rising white-owned buses.[46] In 1980 a boycott of City Tramways in Cape Town was won, and 1982 a prolonged boycott occurred in Pinetown, Natal, where hundreds of workers walked 4 to 5 miles to take other, Indian-run buses.[47]

Consumer boycotts took place against price rises for food and other commodities. This became an extensive movement in the early 1980s, against chain stores and wholesale firms, Fattis and Monis, O.K.Bazaars, the South African Bottling Co., and a particularly long, nearly two-year boycott of the British company, Wilson-Rowntree.[48]

The boycott was a potent weapon because of the heavy reliance by white-owned stores on Black consumers. It became really effective from the latter 1970s onward because it depended on strong unity of the Black communities which had to overcome the relative demoralization of the 1960s before such unity could be possible.

By the beginning of the 1980s, as struggle and unity reached a high point, the nature of the boycott underwent a change, from economic to political purposes. One of the first major political boycotts came in

1981, in regard to the apartheid regime's celebration of Republic Day, the 20th anniversary of the proclamation of the white republic. Over 100 nonwhite political, civic, educational and student organizations declared opposition to "Republic Day." A mass African boycott of celebrations occurred, and the slogan "People's Republic, not White Republic" was projected.[49]

1980 saw the application of the political boycott to the regime's attempt to establish new government-controlled administrative bodies or local councils in the townships as adjuncts of the apartheid government. This was presented as a "reform" move to replace the old Bantu Administrative Boards that had collapsed or had been burned and driven out by the Soweto Revolt and its echoing upheavals in other townshps. Elections for a Soweto council were called for 1980. The move meant the replacing of white officials with collaborating Blacks who would carry out apartheid policies.

Countering the government move, the Committee of 10 in Soweto backed the setting up of a Soweto Civic Association, an independent Black organization that served as a counterweight to the collaborationist council. The Association boycotted the council election. As a result, so few candidates for councillor came forward that only two wards in the Township were contested and the total poll was only 5.6% of eligible voters.[50] In a special by-election two months later, strenuous efforts to overcome the boycott brought out only 6%.[51] The council chairman, David Thebahali, received only 97 votes to elect him as councillor. In a subsequent popularity poll in Soweto, Dr. Nthato Motlana of the Committee of 10 and the Civic Association received 73% of the votes and Thebahali 7%.[52]

The Botha apartheid government pressed ahead setting up local councils; by 1985 a total of 134 had been installed or planned. Boycotts, however, reduced the electoral turnouts to negligible numbers. The 1983 council election in Soweto was a less than 10% affair. In the Cape Town area the poll was 11.6%, but in Nyanga township a mere 130 out of a possible 10,464 voted.[53] In 1984, in Lenasia, an intensifying boycott trend caused all but a tiny 0.28% of more than 45,000 eligible voters to ignore the ballot; on the local management committee only two seats out of seven could be contested for lack of candidates and of the two who "won" one had 34 votes, the other 87.[54]

Boycott of council elections, which were rejected as part of the apartheid system, was carried a step further in the opposition that developed to measures that the councils sought to implement for raising revenue. This was seen as part of the central government's policy of passing the costs of apartheid on to its victims, of making them pay for their segregated conditions. In the white communities revenues were drawn chiefly from property taxes, but in the Black townships the denial or severe restriction of freehold rights on property made this tax source virtually nonexistent. Revenues were therefore based on house rents and charges for electricity, water and other services.

In implementation of this policy in Soweto in 1980, the council chairman who bore the title of mayor, David Thebahali, announced a 75.2% boost in house rents to be spread in three phases over six months. The outcry of protest, taken up by the Committee of 10 and the Soweto Civic Association, was tremendous. A boycott of rent payments began.[55]

By 1984 the boycott movement against increases in rents and service charges was widespread and extended over periods of many months, particularly in the townships of Transvaal. An increase of only 5.90 rands in rents in the Vaal Triangle area produced not only a refusal to pay but demonstrations and protest meetings.[56]

Over 350,000 resident households in the Vaal townships were engaged in the boycotts at the end of 1984, refusing to pay the tariffs on rents, water and electricity.[57]

The growing use of the boycott tactic by the Black communities had a powerful echo in the Colored and Indian peoples' response to the Botha Government's strategy of trying to draw them into an alliance with the white minority by granting them parliamentary representation in segregated assembly chambers. Botha's "reform" Constitution embodying this gesture had its answer in the elections staged for the two new chambers in August 1984. In that election only 18% of the Colored and 15.5% of the Indian voters went to the polls. The boycott was massive, rendering the government's scheme effectively unworkable.

Community boycotts were enriched and broadened with the resurgence of student struggles from 1980 onwards. Colored and Indian students were involved in these as well as Blacks. The establishment and growth of the Congress of South African Students (COSAS) was the key organizing factor in the trend.

At the beginning of 1982 COSAS put forward a framework of demands on education: free, compulsory and equal education for all South Africans; education that liberates and instills a creative, critical ability; education replacing competitiveness with cooperation and comradeship; and education directed at creating a democratic South Africa.[58] Refusal by school authorities to heed the demands, which were concretized in specific demands in various schools, especially for democratic student representative councils, led to a wave of classroom boycotts by 1983. Mass school boycotts developed through 1984. In October 1984 over 110,000 students were boycotting classes in the Vaal Triangle alone,[59] while in the great November 1984 stayaway action in the townships over 400,000 students participated.[60]

In the latter 1970s the students had taken the lead to serve as the spearhead of opposition to apartheid features in the townshps. In the 1980s they were only one of a wide range of forces that were actively in struggle against the racist system—trade unions, community organizations, religious groups and others. The boycott weapon used by these unified groups combined economic and political demands with powerful effect.

Typical of the Boycott Committees that were set up in Pretoria, Johannesburg, Port Elizabeth, Adelaide, East London, Fort Beaufort, and numerous other urban areas in 1985 was the Western Cape boycott movement. It embraced 14 organizations: the United Democratic Front, Sacos, Western Province Council of Churches, Muslim Judicial Council, Western Province Council of Sport, AME Ministers' Alliance, Western Cape Youth League, Call of Islam, Al-Jihaad, Thornhill Residents' Association, Plastic and Allied Workers' Union, Sarepta Youth and Workers' Organization, Thornhill Youth, and District Six Interim Youth Movement.[61]

The boycotts by these committees were directed at all shops owned by whites or by government collaborators from all racial groups. In the case of the Western Cape Committee, the demands were for the lifting of the state of emergency declared by the Botha government in 38 districts in July 1985, for the release of all political detainees, and for the removal of police and army troops from the townships.[62] The Adelaide Boycott Committee had a list of 22 demands, ranging from the removal of police and army to the repair of township roads.[63] The Consumer Boycott Committee of the Duncan Village and Mdantsane townships of East London had these demands: lift the state of emergency, release the persons or the bodies of three Port Elizabeth Civic Organization officials who had disappeared (they were later found dead), withdraw the South African Defence Force from townships, end forced removals, recognize the democratically elected Student Representative Councils, dismantle the homelands, remove community councils and management committees, recognize trade unions, and end worker layoffs.[64]

Such mass boycotts (in the Port Elizabeth-East London-Uitenhage area alone an estimated 600,000 Black residents participated), which remained firm despite attempts by police to drive the people to the white shops and despite arrests and detentions of committee leaders, had a shattering effect on white-owned businesses.[65] Within a few weeks these suffered a 32% decline in business in Port Elizabeth.[66] Turnover for shopkeepers was down 50% in Uitenhage and Grahamstown.[67] In Adelaide, in Cape Province, the township participation was nearly 100% and there was a 90% fall in shop business.[68] After a three-month boycott in Fort Beaufort the local white Chamber of Commerce complained that white shopkeepers faced bankruptcy unless it was ended.[69] Chambers of Commerce in several cities sent delegations to the Botha government urging concessions to African demands. The Port Elizabeth Chamber issued a manifesto in October 1985 calling for Blacks to be fully involved in decision-making, for removal of discriminatory legislation, for common citizenship, and end to forced removals, the phasing out of influx control and pass laws, full participation by Blacks in private enterprise, and a single education system.[70]

In the Barberton township of Eastern Transvaal the boycott of rent increases turned into a general drive against the local council. The mayor's house was burned down. A meeting of 2,000 people decided on a wholesale stayaway from work, from school and from council-run facilities until the council backed down. The councillors fled from the township.[71]

Inclusion in the boycotts of "collaborationist" Black businessmen, whose premises in many cases became targets of physical attacks as well, had a salutory effect on those members of the National African Federated Chambers of Commerce (NAFCOC) who had become involved in the government's schemes to tie African entrepreneurs into the white-dominated capitalist structure. NAFCOC officials lamented that they were "disturbed and alarmed by the destruction of Black businesses in our townships for reasons absolutely questionable, self-defeating and counter-productive," and set up a special commission to look into what kind of image Black businessmen had acquired that would cause such a reaction. The NAFCOC president, Sam Motsu-enyane, hastily came out with a comprehensive call for the government to release Nelson Mandela, lift the ban on the ANC, grant full citizenship to all Africans, scrap all discriminatory legislation against Blacks (including the Urban Areas Act, the Land Acts of 1913 and 1936, and the Population Registration Act of 1950), open all public schools to all races, open business opportunities to all races in all areas, abolish social and residential segregation, and announce an intention to dismantle apartheid.[72]

The United Democratic Front

The anti-apartheid struggles that developed in the townships from the beginning of the 1980s had at first a spontaneous character, springing up sporadically in one locality and another. Underground activities by the ANC and SACP undoubtedly figured in these, but it was inevitable that such extensive mass anti-apartheid expressions should acquire an organized, open nature.

Among the numerous new committees and action groups was the Transvaal Anti-South African Indian Council Committee, formed in June 1981. This had been set up to oppose the puppet SAIC that had become a collaborating body in the Indian community. At the annual congress of the Transvaal Anti-SAIC in January 1983, Dr. Allan Boesak, a leading spokesman of the Colored people and the president of the World Alliance of Reformed Churches, delivered an address in which he called for the formation of a United Democratic Front of anti-apartheid forces.[73]

His proposal immediately took hold and was acted upon. On August 20, 1983 a founding conference launched the United Democratic Front (UDF).[74] The requirements for membership that were adopted had this key provision: "An unshakeable conviction in the creation of a non-racial, unitary state in South Africa, undiluted by racial or ethnic considerations as formulated in bantustan policy."[75]

Initially, Dr.Boesak's proposal was inspired by the need to campaign against the Botha "reform" Constitution and its three-chamber parliament that excluded Blacks and aimed at drawing Indians and Coloreds into a kind of alliance with the white minority. The idea immediately took hold. On January 26 an Eastern Cape Coordinating Committee was set up to work for a United Democratic Front. Among its members were the Port Elizabeth Black Civic Organization, the Port Elizabeth Council of Sport, the KwaZakhele Rugby Union, the Eastern Cape Council of Churches, the Motor Assembly and Component Workers' Union of South Africa, and the Congress of South African Students.[76]

A Natal Committee was formed on May 14, headed by the chairman of the Release Mandela Committee and having as affiliates the Natal Indian Congress, the Democratic Lawyers Association, the Islamic Council of South Africa, Azaso, and the Durban Housing Action Committee. It was followed on May 21 by a Transvaal committee that had 32 organizations represented on it, including the

Soweto Civic Association, the Municipal and General Workers' Union, the Detainees Aid Movement, the Black Students' Society, the Vryburg Civic Association, the Council of Unions of South Africa, the National Education Union of South Africa, the Transvaal Anti-President's Council Committee, the Transvaal Indian Congress, the Federation of South African Women, and the Young Christian Students.[77]

The Western Cape branch, when formed, had more than 20 organizations but these in turn had extensive ramifications: the United Women's organization with 19 branches in the region, the Western Cape Civic Association with branches in all 13 townships of the region, the Inter-Church Youth Organization with over 200 affiliated clubs in the Western Cape alone, the multiracial Cape Youth Congress with 38 affiliates, the Moslem Judicial Council with over 60 mosques, the Western Cape Council of Churches with scores of linked bodies, the Western Cape Trades' Association with 2,000 members, the Cape Area Housing Action Committee, the Council of Union of South Africa, and others.[78]

By the time the founding conference of a national United Democratic Front was held, on August 20, 1983, the UDF had an affiliated membership of 1 to 1.5 million.[79] It continued to grow and by the latter part of 1985 there were over 700 organizations affiliated to it, cutting across racial and class distinctions, young and old, worker and professional. A first national UDF convention was held in December 1983 in Port Elizabeth to solidify the rapidly growing movement.[80]

At the outset the UDF concentrated on resistance to the Botha new constitution and its discriminatory parliament, conducting a campaign for one million signatures on a petition against the constitutional proposals.[81] The massive boycott by Colored and Indian people of elections to the segregated parliament in August 1984 was due to great extent to the effective UDF campaign.

However, the issue of a unitary state was only the starting point for the UDF. Along with the signature campaign decided upon by the first national convention went campaigns for resistance to military conscription and to forced population removals.[82] Eventually the UDF, through its general council and its regional and local branches, assumed the calling and direction of boycotts, stayaways and demonstrations all over South Africa, giving increased coordination to anti-apartheid struggle. A number of factors prevented this from being fully unified, but the UDF was a major step toward that possibility.

The growth and scope of the UDF was indicated at the annual general council meeting, attended by 400 delegates, held at Azaadville near Randfontein in March 1985. Popo Molefe, the UDF general secretary, set out these goals: to isolate the state increasingly from the people, to isolate South Africa from the international community, and to deepen the schism between the junior and senior partners in the Botha parliament so that the tricameral system might collapse. The meeting set forth these wide-ranging demands:

Immediate scrapping of the 1913 and 1936 Land Acts and all Group Areas laws, and ending of all forced removals; dissolving of the bantustans and ending of the migratory labor system; scrapping of the tricameral parliament and all other puppet authorities; a unified and democratic system of education; repeal of the pass laws and all restrictions on freedom of movement; the right of free organization of trade unions and of collective bargaining, the right to strike, security of employment, housing, social welfare, pensions, and maternity leave in accordance with United Nations Human Rights Covenants and charters of the International Labor Organization; release of all political prisoners, unbanning of the banned, the return of exiles, lifting of all restrictions on free speech and assembly; disbanding of the South African Defense Force, Koevaat, South African Police, and other repressive apparatus; the scrapping of all barbaric security laws which violate fundamental freedoms of the Universal Declaration of Human Rights.[83]

UDF demands extended beyond the apartheid system at home. In the launching period a trade union leader, Samson Ndou, told a rally of 12,000 people in Cape Town: "We demand an immediate end to the U.S. and British governments' support for the South African government and we reject the policy of constructive engagement."[84] In March 1985 a UDF demonstration occurred at the Citibank offices in Johannesburg, and a statement wss handed in to Citibank officials, condemning the collaboration of the U.S. and South Africa under the guise of constructive engagement, the providing of a financial backbone to South Africa by foreign companies, the silence of foreign companies when South Africa violates the rights and humanities of the people, and the pretension of concern for the people in claims that foreign investment benefits the oppressed.[85]

A UDF memorandum was delivered in August 1985 to seven western powers. It declared that the South African government would not be able to subjugate the majority of the people and defy world opinion "without the active assistance and connivance of certain governments and local and foreign business in particular." It charged that foreign governments lent the South African government diplomatic support, encouraged investment in South Africa, actively collaborated with the

SADF and police through supply of intelligence and resources, and promoted "cosmetic changes" of the alleged Botha reform as fundamental attacks on apartheid. The memorandum accused foreign businessmen of pouring "billions of rands" into the South African government, the homelands and the white private sector. "The effect is to strengthen apartheid."[86]

The remarkable growth and national spread of the UDF brought inevitable suppressive steps by the Botha government. Botha himself in April 1985 accused the UDF of becoming "the internal extension of the banned ANC and South African Communist Party." He said: "The process of politicization and mobilization, in which the UDF has an especially important role and which takes place in a still deteriorating economic situation has attained such proportions that the potential for extreme countrywide violent disturbances has increased markedly."[87]

Arrest and detention of UDF executive committee members and of leaders of affiliated organizations began in September 1984 and was stepped up following the stunningly effective two-day "stay-away" backed by the UDF in November of that year in theVaal Triangle. A group of 22 leaders was finally selected for trial, under the main charge of high treason and alternative charges of subversion, murder and terrorism. It was the allegation of the state that the UDF was actively involved in and responsible for the death of five township residents including community councillors, the destruction of homes and shops, the November massive stayaway in which up to 800,000 workers did not report for work, school boycotts, intimidating of Black community councillors to resign, and indoctrination of youth and women. Among the 22 charged were UDF general secretary Popo Simon Molefe, UDF publicity secretary Patrick Terror Lekota and UDF Secretary for the Transvaal Moses Chikane. Their trial began in the Delmas Circuit Court on January 20, 1986.[88]

The apartheid government, however, has found it difficult to behead the movement in this way. Acting leaders have stepped immediately into the posts of those arrested and when they have been detained in turn have been replaced by others. There has been no repetition of the 1960s when mass arrests and bannings caused a subsiding of the anti-apartheid struggle. In the 1980s, repressive acts, however violent, have led to greater and more militant reactions among the people. When arrest and jailing had no effect, the undercover police and ultra-racist gangs began the murder of local and regional UDF officials, either through kidnapping and killing or through fire-bombing and shooting-up of homes.[89] This, too, has failed to retard the growth and activity of the UDF.

Contrary to government propaganda, the UDF is not the "internal extension" of the ANC. While it is true that many of those who have emerged as UDF officials were actively associated with the ANC in the 1950s and early 1960s, and while it is no doubt true that many leading participants in the UDF are members of the underground ANC in the present period, this does not indicate that the UDF is the ANC in another form. As the recognized leader of the liberation struggle in South Africa, the ANC certainly encourages and assists that struggle wherever it develops, but the spontaneity and broad character of the UDF are marks of the open mass movement, not of the tightly organized underground vanguard.

Trade Unions and Apartheid

Significant as the development of the United Democratic Front has been, a trend of more basic importance has been the growth and militant activity of the Black trade union movement.

The UDF acquired its main strength and impact from the affiliation of the new trade unions, whose participation in the anti-apartheid struggles is the decisive factor in crippling and disrupting the apartheid system.

The upsurge of Black trade unionism had received its impetus in the strike struggles of the early 1970s which had compelled white employers to acknowledge the need to deal with Black worker organization and its representatives. When this was legalized in the legislation that flowed from the recommendations of the Wiehahn Commission, a proliferation of new trade unions occurred, pouring through the door that had been forced open.

Many problems had to be confronted, however, before the trade union movement could grow into its key place in the present-day national liberation struggle. First of all was the need to break through the impediments to the organization itself of African trade unions. This had had a long forward and backward history, with successes attained from the 1920s onward through Communist and ANC leadership, and with setbacks due to the disruptive influence of racism engendered principally among sectors of the white workers. Even before the Nationalist Party won white power in 1948, the all-white unions linked with the Nationalists—miners, iron and steel workers, some of the construction trades—had erected color bars. As the apartheid system was built, the racist, right-wing trade union leaders set up the Trade Union Council of South Africa (TUCSA) which had a constitution barring affiliation of African unions, although Colored and Indian workers' organizations or membership were accepted. Another all-white union federation, the South African Confederation of Labor (SACOL), added to the predominantly racist character of most of the labor movement. On top of this structure, the 1950 Suppression of Communism Act was employed to purge existing African or multiracial unions of their militant anti-apartheid leaders. African trade unions were to have no place in the apartheid state.[90]

Nonracial and internationalist principles, however, could not be purged from the labor movement. Militant unionists formed the South African Congress of Trade Unions (SACTU), which was formally launched on March 5, 1955 as the first nonracial trade union movement in South Africa. SACTU had 50,000 or more members in its multiracial or wholly African trade unions. Furthermore, SACTU did not confine itself to economic issues. It participated in the formulation of the Freedom Charter and was a prominent part of the Congress Alliance along with the ANC, the SAIC, the SACD and the underground SACP.

SACTU was affiliated to the World Federation of Trade Unions, was a member of the Organization of African Unity, and was represented in the International Labor Organization (ILO) and in the United Nations. The emergence of such a principled trade union movement disturbed the western partners of apartheid. In 1958 a delegation of the International Confederation of Free Trade Unions (ICFTU), especially its U.S. and West European adherents, visited South Africa and made an effort to lever SACTU away from its progressive associations and anti-apartheid activities. SACTU was advised by the ICFTU to cease cooperation with the ANC, not to engage in political action, and to break ties with the WFTU. When SACTU refused to do any of these, the ICFTU backed the separation of a few dissident unions from SACTU and heavily financed them in the setting up of another federation, the Federation of Free African Trade Unions (FOFATUSA).

The banning of the ANC and the general suppression of anti-apartheid organizations in the 1960s struck at SACTU as well. Although SACTU was never formally banned, its leaders and most active members were severely persecuted. Between 1962 and 1965 hundreds of its officials and activists were put under banning conditions, were arrested, tortured and killed in detention (Lawrence Ndzanga, Luke Maswembe and Elijah Loza among the latter), or were exiled to bantustans or forced to go abroad. TUCSA, which received funds for the purpose from the West German National Trade Union Center and from foundations like the Deutsche Gewerkschaft Bund, set up rival unions in opposition to those of SACTU, such as an Engineering and Allied Workers' Union to counter SACTU's Iron and Steel Workers' Union. SACTU, however, refused to be suppressed or smothered. While maintaining an organization in exile abroad that kept alive the international associations, SACTU never ceased to function as an organizing force within South Africa and as an undeviating force for unity of the trade union movement, using every possible means, legal and illegal, open and underground.[91]

When the upsurge of strikes and of African worker organization began in the early 1970s, the established unions and their federations were white-dominated or controlled and were linked with the government and its policies. SACOL, which has included the 17,000-member white Mine Workers Union and the 36,000 member white South African Iron and Steel and Allied Workers' Union, has been linked with the far-right Herstigte National Party and the Conservative party and has fought for job reservation and retention of wage differentials. TUCSA has adhered to its constitution preamble which committed it to "oppose communism in all its forms, to resist actively all attempts by any political parties to exploit the trade union movement for political ends" (i.e., anti-apartheid ends).

As the 1973 strike wave brought the spontaneous formation of Black unions, TUCSA moved to amend its constitution to permit the affiliation of "bona fide" African unions, so as to assert control over them. At the same time TUCSA endeavored to counter anti-apartheid tendencies in the new unions by coming out against international boycotts and sanctions in the field of the economy, labor, culture, sports, science, diplomacy and other areas. TUCSA leaders like general secretary Arthur Grobbelaar and Black collaborationist Lucy Mvubelo of the clothing workers were brought to the U.S. to speak to conventions of industrialists and bankers who were urged to step up investment and trade with South Africa, a TUCSA role designed to offset reports of anti-apartheid worker struggles. By 1980 TUCSA had 7 African unions with 21,122 members among its 59 affiliated unions and 252,734 members (of which the majority were Colored and Indian workers in 17 Colored or Asian unions and 23 mixed-race unions). An indication of white control is that while there were only 10 white unions with 59,865 members in TUCSA, the federations's executive committee of 30 had 21 whites, 4 Colored, 3 Indians and 2 Africans. (By 1983 the pressure on TUCSA to take part in the rapid growth of union membership, or to find itself with a diminishing role, had swelled membership in the federation to 478,400, comprised of 215,280 Colored and Indians, 138,726 Africans and 124,384 whites.)[92]

White control of organized labor was overwhelmed and essentially demolished in the strikes and organizational drives in the 1970s and the early 1980s. In 1971 there had been only 10 weak Black parallel unions. By 1974 the strikes of the preceding year had given birth to 17 new unions with 66,000 members. Total trade union membership, of all races, was 713,134 in 1975; it rose to 974,970 in 1980, and to 1,545,824 in 1983. The increase was almost wholly accounted for by Black workers, in a democratic union movement committed to one degree or another to ending apartheid.[93]

The greatest burst of unionization took place in the 1980-1983 period, especially following the adoption of the legislation recommended by the Wiehahn Commission, the Labor Relations Act of 1981. This had the positive features of legitimizing African trade unions, removing racial and sex discrimination in collective bargaining, and ending statutory job reservation in all industries except mining. The Act, however, also laid down a number of major restrictions on union activity: the Department of Manpower had powers of control over union finances and affairs; association with any political party or political group was banned, which meant a ban on political activity; and severe limitations on the right to strike were enacted, such as long cooling off periods and the prohibition of political strikes. Nevertheless, in the three years following the Act, African union membership jumped by 58%, making Blacks the largest single group of organized workers, comprising 43.5% of the overall total.[94]

In the huge upsurge of Black trade unionism there was a considerable amount of confusion and chaos until the mandates of unity and of the ideology of struggle asserted themselves. A number of new federations and centers of African unions soon formed. Among these the most prominent were the Federation of South African Trade Unions (FOSATU), established by 12 unions on April 14-15, 1979, in Durban; the Council of Unions of South Africa (CUSA), set up with 11 unions around the same time; the South African Allied Workers' Union (SAAWU), formed in March 1979 and soon drawing in 20 affiliated unions; and the General Workers' Union (GWU).

Several important issues caused divisions and contradictory trends in the early stages of the trade union growth. One of these was whether to join federations or to remain independent. In 1983 over two-thirds of Black unionists were in independent unions, and in some industries a number of unions were competing (such as the motor industry). Another issue was whether to register with the Department of Manpower or to remain unregistered: actually the 1981 Labor Relations Act provided for government controls to be applied to both, but non-registered unions were able to evade controls to a great extent. In 1984 there were 272,000 in unregistered unions.[95]

SACTU, working from underground as a major influence on the emerging unions, urged non-registration and freedom from any restraining force that would impede a political role for the trade unions. In this respect a struggle was waged over tendencies in FOSATU which fluctuated between non-involvement and involvement in anti-apartheid political battles. Although FOSATU was aggressive in negotiating collective bargaining agreements (in 1984 it had or was negotiating 285 such agreements and had representation in 490 factories),[96] it was prone to take an apolitical stance in the first few years and to evade confrontation with the government, belying its own initially proclaimed intention to fight not only for trade union rights but against racial oppression and to "secure social justice for all workers."[97]

CUSA posed a problem issue of a more divisive kind: it pursued the Black Consciousness line of including only all-Black unions in its federation and of opposing the multiracial or non-racial approach of the ANC, of SACTU and of most of the new trade union movement. It was significant that CUSA received most attention from right-wing Western agencies and trade union centers. It became affiliated to the ICFTU, and was heavily funded by the U.S. Afro-American Labor Center, the ICFTU and the Friedrich Ebert Foundation of West Germany.[98] In the momentous strike years of 1981-1984 CUSA unions had only minor involvement, while its president, Phiroshaw Camay, whose labor training was financed by the AALC, was a popular speaker at employers' and corporation conferences. CUSA claimed in 1984 to have 120,000 affiliated members in 11 unions, nearly half of whom were in the newly formed National Union of Mineworkers which initially aligned itself with the Black Consciousness tendency.

Another form taken by the new trade unions was that of the South African Allied Workers' Union (SAAWU), which came on the scene in March 1979. This was a union center of a general type, which organized all workers without regard for industry, its members including everyone from steel workers to domestics. A number of similar unions sprang up, in particular the General Allied Workers' Union (GAWU) in theTransvaal and the General Workers' Union of South Africa (GWUSA) in the Port Elizabeth area. These unions were democratic and politically oriented, rejected registration, and had strong support at a community level and from SACTU, although the SACTU position was for the general unions to be transformed into industrial unions. The president of SAAWU, Thozamile Gqwetha, one of the most respected of the trade union leaders, put his union's outlook in this way: "Exploitation doesn't end in the factory. We believe trade unionism should extend beyond the shop floor to the squalid conditions we live under in the locations or villages."[99] SAAWU was opposed to the Blacks-only concept, favoring non-racial unions. Said Thozamile Gqwetha: "There can be no other solution for the problems of this country than one based on the Freedom Charter."[100]

As Black trade unionism began to exhibit its power and its potential for growth, the most active attention by those western owners with a major stake in the South African economy came from the United States. There the main U.S. government and corporation policies toward overseas labor questions were channeled through the Afro-American Labor Center linked with the AFL-CIO. Over 90% of the AFL-CIO's "foreign aid" funds came from the U.S. government.[101] On February 16-27, 1981, the AFL-CIO executive met in Bal Harbor, Florida to draw up a "Program of Action in Support of Black Trade Unions in South Africa." Declaring that its aim was for "non-violent solutions" in South Africa, the program outlined steps for providing "study programs" for Black trade unionists to be held in the U.S., for sending U.S. trade union representatives to South Africa to conduct programs there, and for assigning an AALC representative and office to work in South Africa. At this the AALC director, Irving Brown, announced opposition to campaigns for boycotts of South Africa and for withdrawing foreign investment from the apartheid state.[102]

An AALC office was set up in South Africa in 1981, with Norma Mahomo as its director. According to a one-time South African intelligence agent, Gordon Winter, who later wrote exposures of the BOSS agency and its western connections, Norma Mahomo had worked with the CIA since the early 1960s, including in a well-known CIA front organization, the Center for International Studies.[103] The numerous accusations about the AALC being a CIA channel caused an AALC director, Pat O'Farrel, to issue an ambiguous denial: "We are not a CIA front. I don't suppose we would acknowledge it if we were."[104]

Through the AALC, which was reported to have a cash budget of millions of dollars for the purpose,[105] a long list of Black trade union leaders in South Africa were invited to the U.S. for "labor study programs." In 1985 the U.S. operation to control and influence the new trade unions was expanded under the "U.S.-South Africa Leader Exchange Program" of the Reagan administration, which included trade union leaders among a wide range of those Blacks selected for studies "to develop skills necessary for exercising leadership in effective running of community organizations."[106]

These U.S. attempts to influence the course of the African trade unions in South Africa failed to deflect the great majority from an anti-apartheid, pro-ANC position, but some of those given particular attention by the AALC, such as the CUSA group, have noticeably been disruptive of broad unity in the organized labor movement.

The differences and divergences of the many-featured trade union movement began to be resolved with the broad upsurge of anti-apartheid struggle in the 1980s. An early episode of this was the reaction to the death of Neil Aggett, the white Transvaal secretary of the African Food and Canning Workers' Union, whose death by hanging in a cell of police headquarters at John Voerster Square in Johannesburg on April 2, 1982 was attributed by workers to police torture.[107] The Aggett funeral was attended by 15,000 multiracial mourners bearing the black, green and gold banner of the ANC,[108] but a national day of mourning for Neil Aggett was proclaimed by trade unions for February 11, 1983 and was supported by numerous trade union centers—FOSATU, SAAWU, CUSA, MACWUSA, GWU, GAWU, MWASA. All told, over 100,000 participated in what constituted a political strike. Only TUCSA and SACLA of the union federations refused to participate.[109] TUCSA's failure to do so resulted in the disaffiliation from that federation of the National Union of Distributive Workers and the Commercial and Allied Workers' Union.[110]

Between 1979 and 1982 a number of instances had occurred in the Cape Town and Port Elizabeth areas in which striking workers had been backed by strong effective Black community boycotts of products from the struck companies. The strike and boycott against Wilson-Rowntree (a British subsidiary) lasted for nearly two years, 1981-1982, with the community supporting the strikers through boycott. Other cases were the strike-boycotts against the South African Bottling Co. and the Fattis-Monis chain (also a long strike).[111] The community-worker unity in these cases had a national impact.

In the 1976 Soweto revolt the workers had responded to a stayaway call by the Soweto Students Representative Council, but this had not been at either the initiative or decision of trade unions, of which there was as yet little presence. In 1984, however, the call by the UDF for a large-scale stayaway in the industrial areas of the Vaal Triangle not only had official backing from a broad spectrum of the new trade unions but they took part in its organization and constituted the key factor in the stayaway's powerful impact.

This was an outright political strike directed against the apartheid state and its policies, for such demands as the removal of police and troops from the townships, the cancelling of service charge increases (rents, electricity, bus fares) and of taxes, the release of political prisoners, the resignation of collaborationist community councillors, and the right of election of student representative councils in Black schools.[112]

Supporting the stayaway were FOSATU, CUSA, SAAWU, GAWU, the Commercial, Catering and Allied Workers' Union, the United Mining, Metal and Allied Workers' Union, and the Municipal and General Workers' Union. In the Vaal Triangle as a whole up to 90% of workers stayed away, at the very least 300,000 but probably nearer 800,000.[113] It was a stunning warning to the apartheid rulers of the power of the new trade unions.

The November 1984 stayaway was of major importance as a sign of the growing unity of action between trade unions and the broad community-based anti-apartheid movement represented by the UDF. Up to that time, most trade unions had refrained from actual affiliation to the UDF, still affected by the largely unresolved debate over the alleged contradiction between workplace interests and political action. FOSATU had said it would not join the UDF on grounds that "the unity of purpose created within worker-controlled organizations, whose class base and purpose are clear, would be lost within such an organization as the UDF. The UDF represents a wide variety of class interests with no clear constitutional structure within which the majority of citizens can control the organization."[114] Similar views were expressed by the general secretary of GWU. Some union leaders expressed the critical view that the UDF was dominated by "middle class" people which was said to make it difficult for workers to participate. However, FOSATU and other unions pledged that they would give support to progressive organizations opposed to apartheid and the racist regime.[115]

Such arguments were answered in December 1984 by the UDF's publicity secretary, Mosioua Terror Lekota, who said: "We see the participation of workers in the UDF as important. The more workers that come in, the closer we are to gaining a truly national character. South Africa is still under colonial conditions and the struggle against imperialism is a struggle against capitalism. For this reason the working class must provide the backbone of the struggle."

Lekota thought that the unions' attitude was affected by the lack of unity among the trade unions themselves. The UDF sent a letter to the unions urging the reaching of unity: "It will thus be easier to take actions and to take decisions if the trade unions have already formed themselves into a single federation." Lekota saw the UDF as a vehicle for assisting the attainment of that kind of unity.[116]

At the beginning of 1985 eighteen African trade unions accepted the logic of this and joined the UDF as affiliates "as a means of attaining the unity of workers throughout the country." They included SAAWU, MWASA, GAWU, GWUSA, MACWUSA, the South African Scooter Drivers' Union, the South African Domestic Workers' Union, the Retail and Allied Workers' Union, the South African Laundry, Dry Cleaning and Dying Workers' Union, and others. A GAWU spokesman said they had joined the UDF because it was "a wider field through which we can fight for workers with bosses."[117] Undoubtedly the mounting broad anti-apartheid struggles by the UDF and its affiliates had an impact on the unity trends in the trade union movement. The first unity step had been taken as early as August 8, 1981, when delegates from 29 unions representing over 150,000 workers met in the Langa township of Cape Town. Some limited agreements were reached on supporting each other in strike actions, in defiance of anti-labor legislation, and in opposing registration insofar as it meant control and interference in the internal affairs of unions, but a federated unity was not agreed.[118] A second unity conference was held in the latter part of April 1982 in Welgespruit, Johannesburg. Attended by 200 delegates from FOSATU, GWU, SAAWU and other general and independent unions, it could not reach agreement on the basis for unity and was marred by disputes between registered and unregistered unions that culminated in a walkout by the Motor Assembly and Components Workers' Union of South Africa (MACWUSA). CUSA stayed away from the conference entirely, without stating why.[119] A third conference, in Port Elizabeth in the first week of July 1982 made no headway on the differences.[120]

At the fourth unity effort, however, on April 9-10, 1983, in Athlone, near Johannesburg, most of the differences were ironed out. This, the largest of the conferences to that time, drew several hundred delegates representing over 200,000 workers from the main trade union groupings. FOSATU, GWU, GAWU, Cape Town Municipal Workers' Union, the Food and Canning Workers' Union, the African Food and Canning Workers' Union, and the Commercial, Catering and Allied Workers' Union all voted in favor of a new large-scale federation. CUSA and MACWUSA eventually agreed to consider it.[121] The Athlone conference was an important milestone for its decision to set up a feasibility committee to work out the formation of the proposed federation.

The tasks of the feasibility committee occupied a lengthy period. It was not until November 1985 that the unity efforts had fruition in a momentous conference in Durban. In the interim the African trade union movement was given a powerful impetus with the establishment of a new National Union of Mineworkers, aimed at the organizing of all 484,000 Black miners. Launched on July 31, 1982, at Hammanskraal, the NUM was initially affiliated to CUSA and through CUSA linked with the ICFTU, which made efforts to influence the direction it took. The larger the NUM grew, however, the more independent and militant it became. Its membership reached 55,000 in its first two years, but in the next two years, by March 1986, it had accelerated to 250,000. As CUSA vacillated over participating in trade union unity steps, taking the extreme Black Consciousness position of insisting on Black leadership of unions and the rejection of any white leadership, the NUM withdrew from CUSA in September 1985, hitting at CUSA's "lack of seriousness" on the unity issue.[122]

On November 30, 1985, the huge Durban conference, with 871 delegates representing 450,250 paid up members of 37 trade unions, formally launched the Congress of South African Trade Unions or COSATU. The keynote speech was delivered by the general secretary of the National Union of Mineworkers, Cyril Ramaphosa, who set the tone of the launching by calling on the united workers to recognize that "struggle on the shop floor cannot be separated from the wider political issues." He said the aim was not just to change the government of South Africa but to restructure the economy so the wealth of the country could be "democratically controlled and shared by all its people." Along with the redistribution of wealth must go the elimination of unemployment and poverty. The elected president of COSATU, Elijah Barayi, called for nationalization of the mines and major industries and told an interviewer: "Ultimately there will be a socialist state in South Africa."

COSATU founding conference resolutions covered a wide range of political as well as industrial issues, urging greater political involvement by unions, participation in community issues, the withdrawal of security forces from townships, the release of political prisoners, the scrapping of pass laws and influx controls, and others. Support was proclaimed for all forms of international pressure against apartheid, including disinvestment by foreign companies. In general, it was an overwhelming victory in the trade union movement for the policies advocated by the underground SACTU.

Within the trade union movement COSATU won acceptance for and immediately began the process of creating single industrial unions in place of the general unions and the prevalent multiple unions that weakened bargaining power and gave employers a disunifying lever. The 37 affiliated unions agreed to establish single unions in the following ten industrial sectors: food and drink; textile, clothing and leather; paper, wood and printing; mining and electrical; metal, motor assembly and components; chemical and petroleum; commercial and catering; transport, SA Transport Services and cleaning and security; local government, public administration, including health, education, post and telecommunication and domestic workers; all to be set in motion within six months. As part of the reorganization, and the unification in COSATU, FOSATU agreed to dissolve itself as a federation. The outcome of these steps could only be a increase of Black worker strength in contending with apartheid labor relations.[123]

The qualitative leap in the Black working class role in the anti-apartheid struggle, signified in the achievement of broad federation unity, became even more accentuated in the step that followed. On March 6-7, 1986, a delegation of COSATU leaders jorneyed to Lusaka, Zambia and met with leaders of the ANC and SACTU. Out of this meeting came a declaration of shared revolutionary aims, signed by COSATU's general secretary Jay Naidoo, ANC president Oliver Tambo, and SACTU's general secretary John Nkadimeng.

In the joint declaration it was stated that "lasting solutions [of the South African general crisis] can only emerge from the national liberation movement, headed by the ANC, and the entire democratic forces of our country, of which COSATU is an important and integral part." Said the declaration:

After extensive discussions on the current internal and international situation, characterized by a warm spirit of comradeship, the three delegations agreed on a number of important issues. They agreed that the solution to the problems facing our country lie in the establishment of a system of majority rule in a united, democratic and non-racial South Africa. Further, that in the specific conditions of our country it is inconceivable that such a system can be separated from economic emancipation . . . The meeting reiterated the commitment of the three organizations to fight for a society free from the chains of poverty, racism and exploitation which would require the restructuring of the present economy.[124]

By April 1986 the number of organized workers, mainly Black, embraced by COSATU had risen to 650,000.[125] The Federation's leaders forecast a membership of one million by the end of 1986.

The Fallacy of a "Third Force"

As the anti-apartheid struggle has developed in South Africa, confronting the minority ruling group and its foreign partners with the prospect of overwhelming mass opposition, the alliance led by the ANC has had to contend with and to counter a number of divisive movements among the African majority. These have had the covert encouragement and support of U.S. and other foreign interests.

A tendency of this kind which has had to be dealt with sharply at times within the liberation movement has been that of Black ultra-nationalism. The Pan-Africanist Congress (PAC) has been the ideological spearhead of the trend, setting itself up as a movement rival to the ANC both in South Africa and externally.

The PAC was founded in April 1959. Significance has been attached by the ANC to the fact that it was formed at that time in the library of the U.S. Information Service in Johannesburg; it was reported that the U.S. Embassy's labor attache was involved in the organization's establishment.[126]

It came into being after the proclamation of the Freedom Charter, and for its principal stance the PAC chose to assail the miltiracial character of the Charter. Robert Sobukwe, the PAC's first president, had originally been associated with the ANC; the small group around him which left the ANC with him took the ultra-nationalist line.

African members of the ANC, said the PAC, are "self-confessed lackeys and flunkeys of the white ruling class and the Indian merchant class." It was charged that the ANC was led by a "white pseudo-leftist directorate." After making this attack, the PAC proceeded to call for mass actions at the same time as those held by the ANC and in disruption of them.

Indeed, the massacre at Sharpeville in March 1960 was a consequence of the PAC policies. As the ANC was preparing for its national anti-pass law campaign of that year, the PAC jumped the gun by issuing a call for people to stand outside police stations as an anti-pass demonstration, a provocative action that gave the police an excuse for the savage order to open fire.[127]

Along with the banning of the ANC, the PAC was also banned; its leader, Robert Sobukwe, confined on Robben Island. When the Umkhonto we Sizwe was established by the ANC, the PAC took the step of setting up its own armed unit, called Poqo. This, however, was destroyed by the apartheid intelligence agencies in the same police operations that led to the arrest of Nelson Mandela and other ANC-SACP underground leaders in 1963. The difference in the capability of the two movements was that the ANC was able to build the MK and to recruit extensively for it, while the PAC was never able to field an armed force for liberation.

Although the PAC succeeded in obtaining recognition, along with the ANC, by the OAU, it did not develop to any significant extent either inside South Africa or as an external force. A crippling factor was that it followed the course of most sectarian organizations and divided into warring factions. There were at least two of these that split in the early part of 1979. One of them, calling itself the Azanian People's Revolutionary Party, charged that the leader of the other faction, Potlako Leballo, who had been the PAC leader for 20 years, had been receiving money from "a well-known western intelligence agency for nearly two decades."[128]

Factional warfare continued to disrupt the PAC exile camps in Tanzania. In March 1982 the deposed faction of Potlako Leballo attacked the new dominant PAC leader, John Pokela, in his office in Dar es Salaam.[129] A few weeks later, the new leadership was split, with the PAC foreign director, Henry Isaacs, resigning in discontent with Pokela.[130]

As Umkhonto we Sizwe launched its accelerated armed struggle from the latter 1970s onward, the PAC endeavored to project itself also as capable of armed action. In October 1981 PAC sources put out the claim that it would be one to two years before its own military program would be ready to get going.[131] An Azanian People's Liberation Army was mentioned. South African police published an estimate that the PAC had "an operational force of 300."[132] (This was at a time when the ANC was estimated to have an armed force of 8,000, while thousands of youth were reported to be leaving South Africa for training in MK camps abroad.)[133]

Although the PAC has continued to exist as an organization and to project itself internationally as an important part of the national liberation struggle, it has been unable to win African masses to the position of African exclusivism that it advocates.

Ideologically, however, the PAC has represented a trend that has had several strands in the anti-apartheid movements, basically having to do with the approach to the national and racial factors in the South African revolution. The PAC has remained an influence on this trend, which has been given careful nurturing attention by the apartheid regime and its imperialist partners, particularly the USA.

The most publicized of these tendencies was the Black Consciousness movement which took shape in the early 1970s. One of its own main organizational forms, the South African Students Organization (SASO), had its inception in 1968, and the other, the Black People's Convention (BPC), was conceived in 1971 and formally launched in 1972, as a national political organization.

Involved in the formation of the BPC were SASO, the Association for Educational and Cultural Advancement of Africans, the Inter-Denominational African Ministers Association of South Africa, the African Independent Churches'Association, and the Young Women's Christian Association. The latter three were religious bodies, while many of the SASO members had been influenced by the University Christian Movement. Black Consciousness, therefore, had a strong religious impulse, urging a spiritual liberation to recover a black identity.[134]

BPC aims were stated to be:

> To help the black community become aware of its identity.
> To help the black community create a sense of its own power.
> To enable the black community to organize itself, analyse its needs and problems and also mobilize its resources to meet those needs.
> To develop black leadership capable of guiding the development of the black community.[135]

These aims were viewed by the ANC and the SACP as positive as far as they went, but when tied to certain SASO declarations such as "whites must be excluded in all matters relating to the struggle towards realizing our aspirations," Black Consciousness was made by some into a divisive tendency.[136] There was also a tendency not to direct the movement in the direction of struggle. As the BPC's first secretary-general, Drake Kota, said, "we are not a movement of confrontation, but a movement of introspection."[137]

In truth, the Black Consciousness movement looked in varying directions. Contradictorily, the BPC accepted the essence of the Freedom Charter up to 1975, but it had no program of struggle to remove apartheid or to win power for the oppressed, and it tended to reject alliances with whites and Indians, although it did link itself with Coloreds.

Dr. Yusuf Dadoo, national chairman of the SACP, stated the view of the SACP central committee in 1974:

> Paying lip service to Black Nationalism is not the same as advancing the true national cause and can, in some cases, become a camouflage for

harmful approaches in the actual struggle. No doubt many who have stated their adherence to Black Consciousness . . . do so as a counter to the Government-inspired efforts to divide the black people, as an honest reaction to the diluting influence of white Liberal 'do-gooders,' and also as part of a search for additional organizational forms to advance the cause of the oppressed people. Such elements can and must be won over to the common program of the liberation alliance. But at the same time where these organizations act against the policies and programs of our liberation alliance, or project themselves as alternatives . . . they must be opposed and, if possible, diverted from such a path.[138]

Neither the ANC nor the SACP dismissed or opposed the Black Consciousness phenomenon, but, as the SACP's journal put it, called organizations of the movement "important tributaries of the Great River of the liberation movement headed by the ANC, tributaries which will tap new sources and add new strength to the main stream."[139] The ANC, for its part, noted in 1973 that: "In the last few years . . . there has come into being a number of black organizations whose programs, by espousing the democratic anti-racist positions that the ANC fights for, identify themselves as part of the genuine forces of the revolution," but the ANC pointed out that "The assertion of the national identity of the oppressed black people is . . . not an end in itself." However, instead of aligning itself against the black Consciousness movement, the ANC established close fraternal relations with the movement and won many of the movement's leaders and members to the struggle for the Freedom Charter.[140]

An aspect of Black Consciousness that did have to be countered was the way in which the phenomenon was seized upon by apartheid ruling sectors and by U.S. imperialism to try to confuse and divide the liberation movement.

This was done by playing up such organizations as the Black People's Convention as the political leaders of the South African liberation struggle, although it had no program or strategy and tactics for overthrowing apartheid rule and winning power. By trying to make it appear that Black Consciousness constituted the ideology of the liberation movement as a whole, it was hoped to split the black majority from its allies, to give Black Consciousness the semblance of a "Third Force," and to misdirect the anti-apartheid struggle into blind channels. U.S. propaganda in particular played up Steve Biko, who had been president of SASO and had become a prominent spokesman of the Black Consciousness trend, as allegedly the foremost liberation leader. The intention was to overshadow and displace such ANC leaders as Nelson Mandela and Oliver Tambo in the regard of the people.

In 1985 ANC president Oliver Tambo, addressing the second Consultative Conference of the ANC, swept away the persistent efforts to project Steve Biko as a "Third Force" symbol:

This is the appropriate occasion to disclose that in the course of our work we had, by 1976, arrived at a point where the time had come for us to meet that leading representative of the Black Consciousness Movement, the late Steve Biko. By this time Steve and his colleagues had arrived at the following positions:

a) That the ANC is the leader of our revolution;
b) That the Black People's Convention should concentrate on mass mobilization;
c) That the BPC should function within the broad strategy of our movement; and
d) That a meeting between the leadership of the BPC and ourselves was necessary.

Arrangements were made for us to meet Steve Biko in 1976. Unfortunately, it proved impossible to bring Steve out of the country for this meeting. Another attempt was made in 1977 but this also did not succeed. Subsequent arrangements also failed as, for instance, Barney Pityana was arrested when he was due to lead another delegation. Steve Biko was, of course, subsequently murdered.[141]

It can be validly suspected that the murder of Steve Biko while in police custody on September 12, 1977, was an act of reaction by the repressive apartheid authorities to a Biko inclination to move toward the ANC.

In general, it could be said that Black Consciousness emerged and occupied the stage in South Africa at a time when the ANC-led alliance had been driven underground and was unable openly to rally people around the Freedom Charter. Despite the diversionary uses to which U.S. interests were inclined to put the BPC/SASO, the Botha regime was much less able to countenance the movement.

In 1975-1976 it tried and sentenced nine Black Consciousness leaders under the Terrorism Act, and in 1977 it banned at one stroke 17 Black Consciousness organizations. The movement had no structure either internally or externally for mounting a counterstruggle to survive; organizationally, it subsided.

Those Black Consciousness leaders who succeeded in going into exile were quickly recruited into the ANC. Among them were key figures in the movement like Barney Pityana, the one-time general secretary of SASO, and Miss Tenjiwe Mtintso.[142] Another Black Consciousness leader, Mosiuoa Terror Lekota, subsequently became publicity director of the United Democratic Front and a firm advocate of the Freedom Charter. Terror Lekota said later that it was the slow death in prison of the white Communist, Abram "Bram" Fischer, of cancer as he steadfastly upheld his principled opposition to apartheid, that jolted him away from his exclusively Black politics to a non-racial position.[143]

Black Consciousness as an organized movement may have been banned, but another form of its ideology and of that of the PAC soon reappeared with the setting up of the Azanian People's Organization (AZAPO) in 1978. Black exclusiveness is still at the center of AZAPO's outlook, but it has been transformed from a simple racial stance to one of "class." The concept of "racial capitalism" is projected, with the strategic line not one of national liberation and of passing through a national democratic stage of the revolution in South Africa, but of direct procedure to socialism, the goal being "the establishment of a democratic anti-racist workers republic in Azania" under Black working class leadership.[144]

AZAPO, confusing race and class and projecting national and class concepts as identical, set itself against the Freedom Charter, against the ANC-SACP-SACTU alliance, and subsequently against the United Democratic Front. As the UDF was being organized and was preparing for its formal national launching, AZAPO moved to convene a separate organization, the National Forum. This was established at Hammanskraal, near Pretoria, on June 11-12, 1983.

Nearly 600 delegates from about 100 organizations reportedly attended the launching conference. Eventually the National Forum claimed the affiliation of about 200 organizations representing 200,000 members (compared with 700 organizations and 1-1/2 million or more members of the UDF).[145]

A manifesto adopted by the National Forum, proclaimed as expressing "socialist democracy" in contrast to what it alleged to be the Freedom Charter's "liberal democracy," termed "racial capitalism" as the real enemy in South Africa. It said:

> Our struggle for national liberation is directed against the system of racial capitalism, which holds the people of Azania in bondage for the benefit of a small minority of white capitalists and their allies, the white workers and reactionary sections of the black middle class. The struggle against apartheid is no more than the point of departure for our liberation effort. Apartheid will be eradicated with the system of racial capitalism.[146]

The AZAPO-National Forum grouping failed to develop as more than a minority tendency. A public opinion poll in Durban in May 1985 resulted in a 57% vote for the UDF and a mere 5% for AZAPO.[147] However, AZAPO has had some influence in the trade union movement, preventing full unity around COSATU, for example. CUSA and a new federation called AZATU rejected the non-racial COSATU position and stayed out of COSATU, mainly influenced by AZAPO and its version of Black Consciousness.

AZAPO's divisive stance and activities have been very evident as the anti-apartheid struggle has accelerated. When U.S. Senator Edward Kennedy visited South Africa at the end of 1984, a visit that was welcomed and made the occasion of anti-apartheid publicity by the UDF and that served to help build anti-apartheid sentiment and organization in the U.S., he was met by hostile demonstrations by AZAPO. "We don't need no Yankee saviour!" and "Kennedy, imperialist American," were slogans used. "Tell Jesse Jackson to stay home," was another.[148]

Very noticeable was the leniency displayed by South African police toward the anti-Kennedy AZAPO demonstrators, who at most mustered about 120 out of crowds of thousands. The police protected the AZAPO members from the anger of the rest of the assemblage.[149]

The apartheid regime took advantage of the AZAPO opposition to the UDF and ANC to provoke clashes between their members. A blatant example of this occurred in May 1985 when government provocateurs sprayed fake slogans on the walls of the Regina Mundi Catholic Cathedral in the Rockville area of Soweto, reading: "UDF hates AZAPO," "Up UDF—Down AZAPO," "AZAPO Support Botha and UDF Kill AZAPO." On this occasion both UDF and AZAPO leaders quickly took steps to make public statements condemning the crude splitting attempt, but in other townships bitter fighting was precipitated between UDF and AZAPO adherents.[150]

As the prestige of the ANC and of the UDF soared through 1985 and into 1986, as the people of the townships openly followed their leadership in mass revolt against the apartheid system, AZAPO and its National Forum (the president of AZAPO, Saths Cooper, is also the convenor of the NF) increasingly took up a divisive role. In April 1986 the National Forum suddenly launched vehement attacks on non-racial organization, which was denounced as a device to "smuggle whites into the black national liberation struggle." The NF proclaimed that it was "claiming sole rights to the liberation struggle," and announced a campaign to "internationalize its socialist position in Southern Africa, Africa and the rest of the world." This, it said, would be done by approaching the Organization of African Unity for recognition, by opening an overseas office in London, and by a recruiting drive among "Azanian exiles" abroad. The aim of competing with the ANC for international support was clear.[151]

Inkatha

Of all the divisions that the apartheid regime and its western partners have sought to drive between the multiracial people of South Africa, however, the most openly destructive is the movement called Inkatha, headed by the leader of the KwaZulu bantustan, Chief Mangosuthu Gatsha Buthelezi.

An organization called Inkatha was originally founded in 1928 by King Solomon Ka Dinizulu, as a cultural movement to preserve the Zulu heritage. Dinizulu had been a participant in the 19th century Zulu resistance wars, and when the ANC was founded in 1912 he had been invited to be an honorary vice-president. His Inkatha was a genuine cultural movement but it did not last long, becoming dormant in a few years.

On March 22, 1975 Chief Buthelezi undertook to revive Inkatha as a "National Cultural Liberation Movement," establishing it as an act of his KwaZulu legislative assembly. Inkatha, in other words, is a bantustan organization, set up by an organ composed of tribal chiefs and created by the apartheid regime. The Inkatha constitution states that no one can be eligible for election as president or council member unless he is a KwaZulu citizen, is literate and is conversant with the language of KwaZulu. It is an elitist organization for Zulus that is not only not a national movement but is designed to prevent Zulus from being involved in a national movement, like the ANC or the UDF.

As a young man, prior to assuming his chieftan role, Buthelezi had been a member of the ANC Youth League. The ANC, in fact, had kept a line of contact open with him until 1979. ANC president Oliver Tambo has related the nature of that contact and why it broke down:

> . . . after the Morogoro Conference . . . we maintained regular contact with Chief Gatsha Buthelezi of the KwaZulu bantustan. We sought that this former member of the ANC Youth League who had taken up his position in the KwaZulu bantustan after consultations with our leadership, should use the legal opportunities provided by the bantustan program to participate in the mass mobilization of our people on the correct basis of the orientation of the masses to focus on the struggle for a united and non-racial South Africa. In the course of our discussions with him, we agreed that this would also necessitate the formation of a mass democratic organization in the bantustan that he headed. Inkatha originated from this agreement.
>
> Unfortunately, we failed to mobilize our own people to take on the task of resurrecting Inkatha as the kind of organization that we wanted, owing

to the understandable antipathy of many of our comrades towards what they considered as working within the bantustan system. The task of reconstituting Inkatha therefore fell on Gatsha Buthelezi himself, who then built Inkatha as a personal power base far removed from the kind of organization we had visualized, as an instrument for the mobilization of our people in the countryside into an active and conscious force for revolutionary change. In the first instance, Gatsha dressed Inkatha in the clothes of the ANC, exactly because he knew that the masses to whom he was appealing were loyal to the ANC and had for six decades adhered to our movement as their representative and their leader. Later, when he thought he had sufficient of a base, he also used coercive methods against the people to force them to support Inkatha.

During 1979, in one of its sessions, our National Executive Committee considered the very serious question of how to respond to a request by Gatsha Buthelezi for him to lead a delegation of Inkatha to meet the leadership of the ANC. By this time, divergences were becoming evident on such questions as armed struggle and disinvestment. After due consideration, the NEC decided that it was correct to meet the Inkatha delegation, once more to explain the position of our movement, and ensure unity of approach to the main strategic requirements of the struggle. An express and agreed condition for holding the meeting was that it would be secret and its deliberations confidential. However, Gatsha announced that we had met and explained the purpose, the contents and the results of the meeting to suit his own objectives, much to the delight of the commercial press of South Africa and other forces in the world that had, in fact, concluded that Buthelezi was possibly "the Muzorewa" of the people of South Africa.[152]

In the hands of Chief Buthelezi, Inkatha was made into far less of a cultural movement than a political organization to which he has given a paramilitary character. He has claimed it as the "third force" in South African politics, counterposed to the ruling whites and the ANC. However, in its behavior and in its pronouncements, Inkatha has been mainly an anti-ANC instrument bolstering white minority rule.

In 1980 Buthelezi ambitiously announced plans to send Inkatha "diplomatic missions" abroad, to establish "diplomatic relations" especially with Black African countries.[153] One of the few tangible results of this was the opening of an Inkatha office in Bonn in 1982, along with the announcement that Inkatha was to get "substantial assistance" from the West German Konrad Adenauer Foundation for a "political cooperation scheme."[154] Buthelezi has won his welcome and support not in Black Africa but in western countries, received as a leading spokesman for the "African majority" in South Africa by President Reagan of the U.S. and by Prime Minister Margaret Thatcher of Britain.

Pictured and quoted prominently in South African government advertisements placed in the press of all leading western countries, as a strong advocate of western investment in the apartheid economy and as a vigorous opponent of disinvestment, Buthelezi is the leading favorite of western interests. Equally, he has been praised by President Botha, for his attacks on the ANC, on the UDF and on South African trade unions.[155] The Buthelezi-Inkatha opposition to the one-man, one-vote principle advocated by the ANC, on grounds that it would adversely affect white interests, making a federal South Africa advisable, has been viewed approvingly by the white rulers.[156] In pursuit of the federal concept, Buthelezi has promoted the idea of a separate governmental structure for Natal (in which KwaZulu territories are located) in which whites and blacks would share administration while staying apart.

As the anti-apartheid struggle has mounted in the 1980s, in the townships, in the growth of Black trade unions, in the rise of the UDF, in the increasing armed struggle of Umkhonto we Sizwe, and in the enormous growth in prestige and acceptance of the ANC, Buthelezi and his Inkatha have come out more and more in active opposition to these main forces for change in South Africa.

Buthelezi himself has denounced armed struggle, calling for "evolutionary change,"[157] has assailed the stayaway actions called for by the UDF, accusing the UDF of "exploiting and misdirecting the anger of the people,"[158] has opposed Black miners' strikes, and has condemned what he calls the "Black vs. Black" campaign by the ANC against collaborators with apartheid.[159] The Buthelezi assault on the anti-apartheid movement, however, has not been confined to verbal opposition. More dangerous has been the increasin use of Inkatha for armed attacks on UDF meetings, on demonstrat rs at the funerals of people killed by the South African police, and on individual UDF and trade union leaders. Buthelezi called on Inkatha in June 1985 to set up "citizens units" for combat purposes, to deal with UDF supporters.[160]

It is significant that the earliest and strongest opposition to Inkatha and Buthelezi has come from the Zulus themselves. Early in 1980 the magazine of the student body at the University of Zululand, *Senzani,* published a stinging attack on Inkatha for sending "a large number of thugs armed with dangerous weapons" to a university graduation ceremony to try to turn it into "an Inkatha rally" in support of Chief Buthelezi, who happened to be chancellor of the university. Said the editorial: "Some people join Inkatha in order to secure their positions either as teachers in KwaZulu schools or as KwaZulu civil servants, businessmen or pupils in schools headed by Inkatha fanatics. However, some join Inkatha under the wrong impression that it is a liberation movement, that it is a movement involved with political realities. This group often discovers that the organization is busy protecting and securing the interests of a single man. Inkatha must know that it is politically irrelevant to the real objectives of the black people of this country."[161]

The increasing anti-Inkatha sentiment in the University of Zululand was answered by Buthelezi in October 1983 by a savage armed Inkatha attack on the students in which five were killed and hundreds injured.[162] This failed to halt student opposition. Finally, in 1984, Buthelezi ordered the complete closing of the university, blaming it on "chaos created by UDF elements."[163] When Buthelezi went to the University of Cape Town to deliver a lecture in that year, he was shouted down by hundreds of students, both Black and white, with cries of "Gatsha is a terrorist!" "Gatsha is a killer!" and "Ngoye's blood in on your hands!" (Ngoye was a UDF leader killed by Inkatha).[164]

As the anti-apartheid revolt intensified in the townships in 1985, Buthelezi stepped up his attacks on the liberation movement, openly denouncing the ANC. Following a viciously slanderous Buthelezi speech against the ANC and the UDF in August of that year, and a subsequent open threat against the lives of UDF leaders and members by a local leader of Inkatha named Sabela in Durban, the ANC, which had sought to refrain from conflict with Buthelezi, finally issued a strong statement against the danger:

> Over the past few years mobs inspired by Chief Buthelezi have been responsible for a pattern of vicious beatings, armed attacks and even murders in the Natal region. During the school boycott of 1981-82, the leadership of Inkatha, under the guidance of Buthelezi, took it upon itself to break up and suppress the boycott in the townships of Natal, ostensibly acting in the defense of the honor of the Zulu Royal House. An Inkatha-organized gang attacked students at Ongoye university College during 1983 and inflicted serious injuries leading to the death of some of their victims. More recently, organized groups of ruffians brandishing spears and other lethal weapons have attacked political rallies, meetings and even funerals where our people have gathered to pay homage to those who have fallen in the course of the struggle. All these outrages have occurred with the overt or covert blessing and support of the leadership of Inkatha. It is also a matter of record that the racist regime's police force has either actively assisted in such attacks or passively connived at their perpetration.
>
> At a time when the vast majority of our people, through the length and breadth of our country, are locked in mortal combat against the oppressive machinery of apartheid colonialism, it is nothing less than the most

abject treachery for any black person, let alone one who claims to be a leader, to enroll as an auxiliary of the racist police force. By choosing to join the racists in the persecution of and repression of members of the democratic movement, the leadership of Inkatha has placed itself in the camp of the enemy. The ANC draws the attention of the democratic movement, other sections of the oppressed, including the rank and file of Inkatha, and the international community, to the dangerous role that has been asssumed by Buthelezi and the leaders of Inkatha.

The African National Congress condemns in the strongest possible terms the criminal conduct of Sabela and his subordinates. Their conduct shall not be easily forgotten nor shall they be easily pardoned . . . We place the blame for these dastardly deeds squarely at the door of Chief Mangosuthu Gatsha Buthelezi and the leading group of Inkatha. We shall hold them individually and collectively, responsible for any injuries inflicted on the persons or property of the patriots whom Sabela has chosen to threaten. For our part, the ANC shall continue, as always, to direct its blows against the principal enemy of the people—the Botha-Malan regime.[165]

In March 1986 the Inkatha "labor section" announced the intention to launch on May Day of that year a new "United Workers Union of South Africa." The head of the Inkatha "labor section" said that the new "trade union" would support the "free enterprise system," oppose socialism, oppose disinvestment by foreign companies, and work for the resolution of political issues "through negotiation rather than violence." This move, which bore the imprint of the apartheid regime itself, was immediately seen by the Congress of South African Trade Unions (COSATU) as aimed at damaging the unity of workers it had built, saying that it was "a divisive act, designed to weaken and divide the trade union movement at a time when the unity of our people is crucial." In factories in Natal the Buthelezi "union" was only able to be set up with the active assistance of employers and rapidly acquired the reputation of a "sweetheart union."[166] With this move Chief Gatsha Buthelezi was reaching new depths of treachery in his war against the liberation movement in South Africa.

"Make Apartheid South Africa Ungovernable!"

In the latter half of 1984 a steadily rising wave of anti-apartheid struggle began in South Africa that showed every sign of mounting unremittingly toward an all-out offensive against the racist regime. It became evident in August 1984 in the effective boycott by the Colored and Indian communities of elections to the segregated three-tier parliament of Botha, and it burst forth even more dramatically in the November two-day stayaway in the Vaal Triangle industrial region.

The strategic aim had been put forward early in 1984 by Oliver Tambo, in an address entitled "Liberation Is in Sight." He said:

> We must begin to use our accumulated strength to destroy the organs of government of the apartheid regime. We have to undermine and weaken its control over us, exactly by frustrating its attempts to control us . . . rendering the enemy's instruments of authority unworkable . . . creating conditions in which the country becomes increasingly ungovernable.[167]

This theme was repeated during the highly impressive November stayaway, which shook the apartheid regime, by the chairman of the Transvaal Stayaway Committee, Thami Mali, who declared:

> No amount of intimidation can stop us on our way to liberation . . . our duty as the oppressed people is to step up our resistance and create an ungovernable situation.[168]

As this trend took shape, the South African Communist Party held its Sixth Congress, in January 1985. The delegates, who came particularly from within South Africa as well as from among the cadres in exile, were imbued with great enthusiasm and reflected the mood of revolt among the people, of which the Congress took note. Said a Congress report: "The participants noted that the Party had continued to grow in strength, especially inside our country, drawing into its ranks outstanding working class and youth activists in particular. Enemy efforts to destroy it, which now span a period of 35 years, have failed."[169] A statement on the Sixth Congress by the central committee of the SACP said:

> The revolutionary situation in our country is maturing. The nation-wide crisis is deepening, affecting both the oppressed and the exploited as well as the oppressors and exploiters. Increasingly the ruling class acts in a way which shows that it cannot rule in the old way. At the same time, growing numbers among the exploited classes and the oppressed realize that revolution is necessary and are prepared to die for it.

The statement emphasized:

> The single most important feature of this crisis is the inability of the racists to stop the growth and advance of the broad movement of national liberation. The ideological, political and repressive measures that the apartheid regime has used during the 37 years of its existence, to try to defeat and suppress the liberation struggle, have all failed . . .

... the better to be able to use their united strength, the people are organizing themselves into democratic organizations, including trade unions, community, youth and women's organizations. The coming together of hundreds of these organizations in a united front and in united action, constitutes one of the most important advances that the democratic movement has made, and is an expression of the objective requirement of the national democratic revolution to unite all classes, strata and national groups that are interested in the victory of this revolution . . .

The aim of the SACP and of the revolutionary alliance headed by the ANC, the objective pursued by the workers and the oppressed masses of the country, is to topple the apartheid regime and take power into their own hands.

In the coming period, these need to advance further towards the situation when we shall take revolutionary mass action strong enough to dislodge the racist regime.[170]

Initially, the main target of the upsurge led by the ANC, the SACP and other allied organizations was the system of township local councils, made up of collaborating Black individuals, and the local police forces they employed. Boycotting of all services and administrative functions allocated to the local councils by the central apartheid regime was undertaken in the people's offensive. It was soon complemented by direct actions to force the collaborating councillors out of the townships entirely. An ANC call to step up this process was made on January 8, 1985. It was responded to so widely and effectively that a second call was issued soon afterward, in April 1985:

Only three months have passed since that call [January 8] was made and already the surge of people's resistance and active defiance have reached new heights. The face of our country is changing before our very eyes . . .

In the black ghettoes of the urban areas the legitimacy of authority of all types is not just under attack, it has been largely destroyed. Most of those who served white rule in so-called urban councils have suffered the wrath of the people. But many have respected the demands of the people by resigning . . .

The people, by their actions, are teaching black police and soldiers that there is no place in our communities for those who wear the uniform of apartheid and who carry out orders to kill, maim and torture their brothers and sisters . . . [171]

Between September 1, 1984, and June 1, 1985, a total of 240 black community councillors and local authority councillors had been compelled to resign. Over 100 black councillors had been physically attacked for not heeding the people's demand, 66 had had their homes burned by angry crowds, many had had their businesses destroyed. At least 360 black policemen had had their homes gutted by fire or other means by July 1985. The local authority system was in a condition of collapse.[172]

From the latter half of 1984 the Botha regime sought to contend with the growing crisis of the control system by putting increasing numbers of the South African Defense Force and of the central white police force into the townships to impose authority with the gun and the sjambok (whip). The indiscriminate shooting of African people, from small children to the elderly, with the aim of terrorizing and subduing the townships, resulted in the killing of 440 people and the wounding of 1500 others in the September 1984-June 1985 period.[173] One of the worst of the episodes was the slaughter of 19 people and the wounding of scores of others as they marched peacefully to a funeral in Langa township near Uitenhage in the Eastern Cape on March 21, 1985: it was the 25th anniversary day of the 1960 Sharpeville massacre.[174]

The use of terror, however, had an effect completely opposite to that of the Sharpeville massacre and the intimidating bannings and repressions of the 1960s. In the townships, now, uncowed Black youth in particular confronted the armored cars (Casspirs) of the troops and police, first with stones, then with petrol bombs, then with the occasional gunshot. Cases occurred of Casspirs being blown up by concealed landmines as they entered townships gradually being turned into "no-go" areas. Authority in the townships began to be assumed by the inhabitants themselves.

In the April 1985 ANC call to the nation it had been proclaimed:

> We call on our communities in the black ghettoes to replace the collapsing government stooge councils with people's committees in every block, which could become the embryo of people's power.
>
> We call on our people and, more especially, our fighting youth in every black community, school and university to find ways of organizing themselves into small mobile units which will protect the people against anti-social elements and act in an organized way in both white and black areas against the enemy and its agents. Every black area must become a "no-go" area for any isolated individuals or pockets of the enemy's police or armed personnel. The people must find ways to obtain arms by whatever means from the enemy and from any other source. Appropriate forms of combat tactics must be developed for situations in which the enemy is on the rampage against the people. The proliferation of such units and their functioning in accordance with all the rules of underground secrecy will add inestimable power and strength to the armed wing of our liberation movement—Umkhonto we Sizwe.[177]

Blacks serving in any capacity in the apartheid machinery were urged to resign or "be shunned and made to feel the anger of the masses in both town and countryside." Blacks in the army and police were called upon to "turn their guns against their masters," whites were urged to refuse to serve in the armed forces of the apartheid state and to move away from support of apartheid; to side with whites participating in the liberation struggle. The call had an eve of revolution ring.[176]

It was vividly clear that the struggles occurring in the townships and the direction they were taking were increasingly a response to these calls of the ANC and of the triple alliance that it leads. An element of spontaneity may have been present, but the developing upheaval was more pertinently the product of years of anti-apartheid propaganda and agitation by the ANC, the SACP and SACTU, and of inspirational blows to the supposedly impregnable apartheid state by Umkhonto we Sizwe.

In the midst of the rising popular struggles and of the enhanced prestige of the liberation movement, the decision was made to hold the Second National Consultative Conference of the ANC. The first, meeting in Morogoro, Tanzania in 1969, had set forth the strategy and tactics of the national liberation struggle, which had been adhered to and had brought millions of people into involvement in that struggle. It was now felt to time to prepare for the stage of achieving the overthrow of the racist regime and the winning of power by the multiracial masses.

The ANC's Second National Consultative Conference was convened in Kabwe, Zambia on June 16-23, 1985, a choice of site in a "front-line" state that was in itself a defiance of interventionist threats from the apartheid regime. Present were 250 delegates from both the internal and external ANC organizations.[177] President Oliver Tambo, delivering the main political report, opened the conference with these stirring words:

> This day, the opening of the National Consultative Conference of the ANC, is a great and moving moment in the history of our struggle for national liberation. The days we will spend here will live forever in the records of that struggle as marking a turning point in the history of all the people of South Africa.
>
> Our Conference itself will be remembered by our people as a council-of-war that planned the seizure of power by these masses, the penultimate convention that gave the order for us to take our country through the terrible but cleansing fires of revolutionary war to a condition of peace, democracy and the fulfillment of our people who have already suffered far too much and far too long.[178]

Reaffirming that "the Freedom Charter remains the only basis for the genuine liberation of all the people of South Africa," the ANC conference resolutions declared that it "calls on the people of South Africa to intensify the offensive to overthrow the apartheid regime which is the ncessary condition for the implementation of the provisions of the Charter and the birth of a united, democratic and non-racial South Africa."[179] Adopted were decisions for: the strengthening of the ANC underground, the intensifying of the armed struggle, and the further mobilization of the people into decisive action and to strengthen the legal mass democratic movement.[180]

One of the features of the conference was the decision to open up ANC membership at all levels to all revolutionaries without regard to color. This gave formal recognition to an important reality of the national liberation struggle, that it involved people from all of South Africa's racial groups, underscoring the non-racial character of the liberation movement. Full organizational rights were thus extended to Colored, Indian and white ANC members. Elected to the ANC executive committee was its first white member, Joe Slovo, who was a political bureau member and chairman of the SACP; two Indian members, Mac Maharaj and Aziz Pahad, and two Colored members, Reg September and James Stuart.

The full composition of the 32-member executive committee elected by the Second Consultative Conference was: Oliver Tambo, president; Alfred Nzo, secretary general; Thomas Nkobi, treasurer general; Thabo Mbeki, publicity secretary; Chris Hani, Umkhonto we Sizwe political commissar; Moses Mabhida; Dan Tloome, deputy secretary general and treasurer general; Johnny Makatini, international department head; Henry Makgothi, education director; Simon Makana, former administrative secretary; Gertrude Shope, women's section head; Joe Modise, Umkhonto we Sizwe commander; Mzwai Piliso; Robert Conco; Jacob Zuma; Florence Mophosho; Sizakele Sigxashe; Pallo Jordan, research department head; Frances Meli, external information head; Anthony Mengalo; Joe Slovo; Mac Maharaj; Aziz Pahad; Reg September; James Stuart; Cassius Make, Umkhonto we Sizwe commander; Ruth Mompati.[181]

During and after the Zambia conference, the ANC's calls to the people were increasingly for a revolutionary offensive.

"Resistance should not be confined to urban areas alone but should be spread to rural areas as well. South Africa's forces of repression should not be enabled to cope with the current uprising by concentrating on one area. Let the attacks against the enemy be spread to all corners of our country so that his forces should be weakened and scattered all over."[182] In essence, this meant expanding the struggle to the bantustans as well as the white rural areas. (Such a call, incidentally, may be contrasted with the dictum of Mao Tse-tung that was accepted uncritically by many on the left at one time—"Surround the cities from the countryside." In South Africa the revolutionary struggle, including the armed struggle, began in the urban areas and spread from there to the countryside, to the bantustans in particular, at a later date.)

Another call went out to Black police and soldiers "to earn your place in the free South Africa that is coming by organizing to turn your guns on your masters."[183] At the same time, however, it was proclaimed:

> The fascist police and army, as well as their puppets and traitors—who are black only by face and yet fascists at heart—shall not be spared by the well-trained and armed cadres of Umkhonto we Sizwe. They are today now the only remaining pillars of the crumbling and doomed regime of terror. They are the enemies of our people both black and white, and no mercy should be shown to them. We make no apologies about having to attack and eliminate those, for they form the most crucial structure of the dictatorial colonial apartheid regime. It is they who are deployed in our townships from the Transvaal right up to the Cape and have now claimed the lives of more than 400 of our people—our unarmed civilians in the townships.[184]

An ominous prospect for the racist exploiting white business interests emerged in a call made in July 1985:

> Let us intensify our strike action by intensifying our campaign inside the factories. We must sabotage the machines either by removing some vital parts or by introducing some foreign and dangerous elements into them. Those working in offices must destroy or confuse important documents. Wherever you are, in whatever department you work, make sure that production is disrupted regularly. Let there be no order and efficiency. Let us ensure that most of the commodities coming out of the assembly lines are useless.[185]

If such actions were not immediately and widely taken up, it was no doubt due to the fact that the time for them had not yet really come, but the perspective for such a step in the struggle had been set out, to be implemented when conditions had further matured, while for white businessmen the specter of a rebelling Black work force and its sabotaging potential was alarmingly projected.

The intensification of the anti-apartheid struggle that was signalled by the ANC's Consultative Conference and its subsequent calls alarmed the Botha government in particular. On July 20, 1985, it declared a state of emergency in 36 magisterial districts (later extended to 38).[186] These did not include the Transkei, where it was said that there had been "severe rioting" for a period of over one year, and where 26 magisterial districts had been under a state of emergency ever since Transkei's "independence" in 1976 when rebellion had occurred against that apartheid step. In South Africa as a whole, in other words, 64 districts were experiencing emergency repression. Three major metropolitan areas—Johannesburg, Cape Town and Port Elizabeth—were included, besides the mining towns of the East Rand. All told, 9.2 million people were affected by the emergency.

A key feature of the decree was the barring of all journalists, television crews and other media representatives from the emergency areas, on the excuse that people were "rioting" in order to get themselves photographed and mentioned in the press, in other words that anti-apartheid struggles were publicity stunts that would end when no cameras were turned their way. Under the state of emergency, however, with no photographers or reporters to record what was happening, thousands of people were arrested and detained, including national, provincial and local United Democratic Front leaders and militant members, trade union leaders and activists, and many of those in the forefront of township struggles. The Congress of South African Students (COSAS) was banned in August 1985, and 74 organizations termed "political" in 30 districts were banned from holding any meetings up to June 30, 1986.[187]

According to carefully compiled figures of the Detainees' Parents Support Committee, the number of people detained from July 20 to December 5, 1985 was 10,731. Of these, 7,183 were detained under the emergency measures, and 1,759 were "security detentions" under regular security laws. In the same period, 399 people were put on trial for alleged political offenses, including 31 charged with treason.[188]

From news filtering out of the townships, the real reason for the banning of press and television presence was to free the police and army from inhibitions in brutal suppression of Black and Colored resistance or actions to eliminate the structure of apartheid authority. The Detainees' Parents Support Committee reported that 965 people had been killed by police and army troops between September 1984 and December 10, 1985.[189] The slaughter went on at an increasing rate from that time. By the end of March 1986, according to the independent South African Institute of Race Relations, over 1,400 people had been slain; the number of wounded was beyond estimate.[190]

The remarkable aspect of these savage measures to try to restore apartheid control—increasingly troops in armored vehicles roved the townships shooting indiscriminately at the inhabitants, especially the youth of any age who were the most defiant and combative—was their failure to intimidate the overwhelming majority of Blacks. A readiness to die for the anti-apartheid struggle had become a prevailing attitude, a strong evidence of a developing revolutionary situation. Furthermore, those who confronted and fought the police and army were no longer armed merely with stones: there was a growing number of incidents in which the apartheid forces were met with gunfire and grenades. To a considerable extent, these were probably the actions of Umkhonto we Sizwe units. The government listed 136 MK attacks in 1985, a 38% inrease over the previous year.[191] However, as the ANC had urged, ordinary Black people were acquiring arms in every possible way and were beginning to set up embryonic revolutionary fighting groups, acting in concert with or under direction of MK cadres (who have been trained as potential officers and not merely soldiers in the struggle).

From the latter 1970s the press in South Africa had been reporting incidents of individual Blacks being killed by persons unknown in the townships. These were steps in a drive by the revolutionary underground to purge the townships of informers. At one time the apartheid regime had boasted of its network of informers on which it relied to maintain suppressive control. Now the informer network was being eliminated. In the beginning Umkhonto we Sizwe units were obviously responsible for the purge, but as the township revolt mounted the people themselves dealt out revolutionary justice on the spot to detected agents of the enemy amongst them.

Along with removal of informers, attacks on Black policemen occurred constantly. The government's Minister of Law and Order, Louis Le Grange, reported to the apartheid parliament that 29 police had been killed and 82 seriously injured in 1985.[192] In November 1985 he had reported that 500 homes of policemen had been burned down, and they had to be evacuated from the townships.[193] From September 1984 to November 2, 1985 a total of 525 shops and factories, 180 development corporation buildings, 200 development corporation vehicles and 75 bottle stores (the latter a target of Black youths endeavoring to clean out degenerating influences in the community) had been destroyed in "rioting."[194]

In the single week of November 19-24, 1985 "unrest" was reported in at least 43 township areas across South Africa, including Soweto, Queenstown, Mamelodi, Tumahole, KwaNobuhle, Soshanguve, Motleno,

Leandra, Steenberg, Philippi, Namonde, Stutterheim, Wynberg in the Cape, Nyanga, Hanover, Petrusville, Bekkersdal, Mohlaking, Zolari, Bongulethu, KwaMugamo, Athlone, Zwelenthemba, Old Crossroads, Bridgetown, KwaZakhele, GaRankuwa, Newtown, New Brighton, Khayeletsha, Bergville in the Boland, Urulazi, Pabalelo, Atteridgeville, Kubusie, Paarl East, Langa near Cape Town, Ndumangini, Langa and Cambridge in the Border area. Police fired into unarmed assemblages in Queenstown, killing 14 people, and in Mamelodi, killing 13. All told, 51 people were shot dead in that one week, and at least 54 wounded; 300 were arrested and detained. Five known grenade attacks occurred in retaliation, causing the wounding of three policemen.[195]

Many of the demonstrations were spearheaded by Black youth, who engaged during 1985 in a year-long boycott of the apartheid schools system, demanding equality in education, the removal of police and troops from classrooms, and the right to elect their own students' representative councils. The issue of prolonging the schools boycott, however, was eventually debated in the Black communities as a whole, with some arguing that it was counter-productive to interrupt education indefinitely while some radical youth raised the slogan "Revolution first, education later." A National Education Crisis Committee was eventually set up, with parents and teachers represented with the youth. In March 1986 it held a 1,500-delegate conference in Durban which decided to end the boycott but not as a retreat: the NECC announced that the people in the townships would take over the schools and run them themselves, as a system of "people's education." Said an NECC organizer, Lechesa Tsenoli: "We are going to run the schools, we are going to organize the syllabuses. It is no longer a question of petitioning the government. We are going to become actively involved in formulating an alternative education."[196]

The confidence displayed in such a decision reflected a growing authority and capability of the people's committees that had sprung up in the townships. While the patrolling armored vehicles of the government's army and police could exhibit authority there in the daylight hours, they usually withdrew cautiously after dark, which meant that the people's committees ruled the townships at night, tackling community problems, dispensing justice and maintaining order.

Most outstanding of all among the features of the anti-apartheid revolt in South Africa in the 1980s, however, was the rapid ascendency of the African National Congress as the recognized leader of the national liberation movement. This was a progressing development that took place internationally as well as within South Africa itself. By the middle of 1982 the ANC had 33 offices or missions in key countries of the world, including 13 in western countries, 12 in African states and 9 in socialist countries.[197] The socialist countries, particularly the Soviet Union and the German Democratic Republic, were giving extensive many-sided assistance, while the African countries, especially the "frontline states," provided numerous facilities for administrative offices, schools and refugee camps. In western countries the ANC enjoyed close association with strong and broad anti-apartheid movements. The Organization of African Unity had long recognized the ANC as a legitimate representative of the South African people, and in September 1985 the 78-member Lome Convention group of states—African, Caribbean and Pacific—formally extended recognition.[198] At the United Nations, among the Non-Aligned states, and in every international forum having to do with liberation, peace and social progress, the ANC had recognition, participation and support.

The principal exception to this massive backing was the U.S. Reagan administration, which depicted the ANC as a "terrorist" organization. In March 1982 it set up hearings by a Senate Sub-Committee on Security and Terrorism, headed by Senator Jeremiah Denton, which conducted a smear of the ANC. It produced "witnesses" arranged for by the South African government, a string of prostituted ANC defectors and government agents, including a Miss Nakonono Kave, who turned out to be a niece of Sebe brothers who ran the Ciskei bantustan with brutal boss rule.

Kave claimed that the ANC was a mere front for the Soviet Union and the SACP, that she had been tortured and sexually abused during a stay in the Soviet Union, and that the ANC committed depraved acts including infecting South African water supplies with cholera germs in capsules. Such "testimony" discredited the hearings rather than the ANC. Chester Crocker participated in the hearings with "testimony" of an unsubstantiated nature claiming that the ANC received 90% of its military aid and 60% of all aid from the Soviet Union. (Alfred Nzo, ANC secretary general, answered Crocker in a typically forthright statement, asserting "Neither the ANC nor the Soviet Union makes any secret about the selfless support that the Soviet Union, the Socialist Community and the progressive forces the world over are granting to the people fighting against oppression, exploitation and human degradation.")[199]

Within South Africa, in the townships across the entire country, support for the ANC was openly proclaimed by the populace and by the people's committees that sprang up in place of the destroyed collaborationist councils.

At the funerals of victims of police and army terror, attended by mourners numbering in some instances up to 60,000, the coffins were draped in the green, black and gold flags of the ANC.

Demonstrations were dotted with the banners and placards of the ANC, and ANC songs were taken up everywhere ("Tambo is in the bush," "We shall follow our Slovo, even if we are detained, even if we are hung," and the widely popular "AK-47 Song" of the MK).[200]

The enormous popularity of Nelson Mandela, the imprisoned leader of the ANC, was displayed in numerous ways—in opinion polls, in resolutions of organizations, at demonstsrations, emblazoned on T-shirts. A "Free Mandela" petition, circulated by the special campaign organization for Mandela's freedom and by the UDF, aimed at and obtained a million signatures. Even in Zulu areas policed by Chief Buthelezi's Inkatha, Nelson Mandela topped the popularity polls. The fastest-growing South African trade union, the National Union of Mineworkers, with 250,000 paid-up members in March 1986, elected Nelson Mandela as its first honorary life president.[201]

A funeral-protest meeting held on March 8, 1986 in the stadium in Alexandra township near Johannesburg typified the growing mood and sentiment of the African people. It was held for the burial of 17 of the estimated 46 residents of the township shot dead by police during a six-day period of mass demands for an end to the emergency, the removal of occupying troops and the release of detainees. More than 60,000 people were massed in the stadium.

Winnie Mandela, wife of the jailed ANC leader, read out a message from the ANC office in Lusaka, Zambia, and there were messages read from SWAPO, the UDF, COSATU and a host of other organizations. A published account of the meeting portrayed its temper:

The stadium—in the middle of the township—saw intense emotion as the 17 coffins of the victims—the youngest of whom was 12 years old—were laid to rest. Draped in the ANC's black, green and gold colors and guarded by khaki-uniformed youths, the coffins were carried into the stadium in a procession led by South African Council of Churches general secretary Dr. BeyersNaude, Johannesburg Catholic Bishop Rev. Reginald Orsmond and Transvaal UDF president Rev. Frank Chikane. Huge banners—among them a Soviet flag [actually the flag of the South African Communist Party–WP] with the hammer and sickle emblem, and others from the ANC—were held aloft by the mourning township residents. The Soviet [SACP] flag called on the workers of the world to unite, while others called for the unconditional release of jailed ANC leader Nelson Mandela and other political prisoners—and an end to oppression. A Freedom Charter banner simply said: "The People shall govern." Banners from the Release Mandela Campaign, National Union of South African Students, Azanian Peoples' Organization, UDF, Johannesburg Democratic Action Committee and the Alexandra Students' Congress were also displayed.

Activists with clenched fists shouted "Viva Mandela, Viva Kathrada, Viva Tambo," and freedom songs in praise of the ANC military wing, Umkhonto we Sizwe and its leadership, shook the packed stadium during the four-hour funeral proceedings.[202]

Basing itself on the heightening and unflinching readiness of the people to struggle, the ANC at the beginning of the new year proclaimed that 1986 would be "The year of Umkhonto we Sizwe—the People's Army." It raised the slogan "Every patriot a combatant— every combatant a patriot." Said the Umkhonto we Sizwe commander, Joe Modise, in a broadcast beamed into South Africa from the ANC's Radio Freedom in Dar es Salaam:

> The armed units of Umkhonto we Sizwe are operating side by side with the people. They are part of the people. Umkhonto we Sizwe is an instrument of the people. It is our people's army. They cannot operate alone. Neither can the people operate without them. It is true that they are the advance detachment among our people's forces. It is equally true that without the people Umkhonto we Sizwe cannot succeed. Umkhonto we Sizwe has rooted itself among the masses with the aim of raising the struggle to a higher level in this year of the army.[203]

Joe Modise also dealt with the call made by the ANC during 1985 to prepare for the carrying of the struggle into the white areas:

> Our people have now demanded from us, because of the brutal repression inside the country, that we pay more attention to the destruction of enemy personnel, and from now onwards, we are going to concentrate a great deal on the destruction of enemy personnel. There are those who regard soft targets as civilian targets. It has never been the policy of the ANC to destroy civilians. But this question of civilians in South Africa needs to be considered very, very carefully. We are finding it very difficult in the South African context to differentiate between civilian targets and enemy personnel because the South African regime has mobilized the white community and organized them into para-military units and they are given combat training. In the rural areas, the white community is organized into commandos. These are support units of the South African Defense Force. In the urban areas, they are organized into the South African Citizen Force, and women in the various cities are organized into clubs, where they are trained to use firearms. This whole exercise is aimed at suppressing the aspirations of the African people.[204]

The political commissar of Umkhonto we Sizwe, Chris Hani, a member of the ANC's executive committee, subsequently elaborated further on this question. In order to make crystal clear the principled position of the ANC on the expanding of the armed liberation struggle:

> We are saying, comrades—and we are correct in saying so—that our country is in a state of civil war. It is true that so far the brunt of suffering has been borne by our people. Our people are attending funerals, our people are mourning for their dead, but comrades, Umkhonto we Sizwe, insti ucted by the leadership of the ANC, is gearing itself to step up activity in white areas so that the entire country should be ungovernable. I want to elaborate on this questions of extending the armed struggle to the white areas.
>
> We don't want to be misunderstood. Unlike Botha, Le Grange, Malan and Chris Heunis, who go out of their way to butcher children, defenseless and unarmed children, women, old people, black civilians, Umkhonto we Sizwe is a revolutionary army and is not about to embark on mayhem against white civilians, against children, but we are going to step up our attacks against enemy personnel. We are referring to the members of the police force, to the members of the SADF, to those in the administration terrorizing and harassing our people, to those farmers and other civilians who are part of the defense force of this country, the military, paramilitary and reserves. The theater of these actions is going to be in the white residential areas, and it is inevitable that white civilians will die.
>
> We are going to step up attacks against those factories, transnational corporations and monopolies, which exploit and maltreat the South African working class and in the process it is more than probable that white civilians will lose their lives. They should be warned, comrades, because they support that regime, they vote for that government, they condone and justify the murders committed in the name of preserving white domination.
>
> But despite that extreme provocation, we are going to deal with instruments of our oppression. But the white population must know that the theater of our operations is no longer going to be confined to Soweto, to Alexandra, to Mamelodi, Gugulethu, KwaMashu, to Mondtsane, Kwa-Zakhele, and New Brighton, but we shall move and act in Hillbrow, Sandton, Brixton, Langlaagte, Waterberg, Clifton, Sea Point and other suburbs in our country. We shall act throughout the country. We are determined to do that. Our people are already acting everywhere in our country and want to increase the insecurity of the regime because we are serious about crushing that regime.[205]*

---

*As the mass struggles against the apartheid authority developed in the townships from 1984 onward, a discussion of armed struggle policies began in ANC and SACP journals. These were centered on a review of classical guerrilla warfare concepts that originally governed Umkhonto we Sizwe operations, and a projection of insurrectionary warfare, which was viewed as more fitting of the kind of mass revolutionary action that was emerging in the country.

POSTSCRIPT

In September 1985 an event of considerable importance in the long struggle against apartheid took place in the Zambian capital, Lusaka. A delegation of some of the leading monopoly businessmen in the apartheid state journeyed from South Africa to meet with leaders of the African National Congress. The approach, the first of its kind that had ever been made, signified a recognition by key sectors of the South African ruling groups that the ANC had to be dealt with and that the time had arrived for the dealing to begin.

Heading the delegation of businessmen was the new chairman of the Anglo-American Corporation, Gavin Relly, who had replaced the retired Harry Oppenheimer in that post. (Oppenheimer approved the meeting with the ANC and had expressed the desire to have such a meeting himself.) Accompanying Relly were: Dr. Zach de Beer, executive director of Anglo-American and chairman of LTA Construction; Tony Bloom, head of the big Premier conglomerate; Peter Sorour, executive head of the South Africa Foundation; Hugh Murray, publisher of *Leadership SA;* and Harald Pakendorf, editor of *Die Vaderland,* the most prestigious Afrikaaner paper. Involved in the arrangements for the meeting were also Barlow Rand's Mike Rosholt, the Sanlam chairman Fred du Plessis, and Chris Ball of Barclays Bank.[1] On the ANC side were Oliver Tambo, Chris Hani, Thabo Mbeki, Pallo Jordan, Mac Maharaj and James Stuart.[2]

No joint or separate statements emerged from this meeting, but Oliver Tambo subsequently commented upon it. He expressed the opinion that the South African businessmen had become concerned about the crisis of apartheid as it affected them, and that "there is room for their participation" in destroying the racist system if they were so minded. However, the ANC leaders were fully aware of the motivations of the businessmen. Said Oliver Tambo:

They assess the apartheid system in terms of the profits or losses it yields. It has always been clear that for them the apartheid system will be useful as long as it delivers the goods . . . If they reach the conclusion that, indeed, the apartheid system is going to destroy their interests, destroy their business, the whole economy, at that point they will want to remove the apartheid system, and will even join forces that are set to destroy the system provided they are sure that the system will not be replaced with something worse for their economy, for their pockets, for their profits. But to the extent that our struggle has demonstrated that there is no future for them or for the economy—to that extent they will begin to move against the regime. Because, within limits, they are still part of it, it means that they can be an additional lever, a position which favors our struggle. And that is how we see their role.

Therefore, if it serves the purpose of weakening the ability of the regime to resist, if it helps to destroy the system, then we welcome that . . . It is the armed component of our struggle which causes the greatest threat for the apartheid system and its economy, and under conditions of our struggle there is instability. They would rather, therefore, that the change were smooth, so that they have time to be adjusting to the change, by way of reforms, which means that there would be no rapid transformation, and that we would be talking and arguing about things while they are making their profits, for 10 years, 20 years, for 30 years, while they are making their profits . . . It is the armed component which has made them want to come to the ANC . . . to see whether there is prospect of this being suspended.

We naturally told them we could not abandon armed struggle. Armed struggle—it was a product, a direct product, of the apartheid system. And this affects the extent to which they can really come to our sides.

What replaces the apartheid system? What would be their position in the new system? Well, they cannot look forward to the kind of system that the ANC has in mind under the Freedom Charter, but at least they understood the reasons why the Freedom Charter had those provisions or why our people thought of putting those provisions in the Freedom Charter. They also want to reform the apartheid system in such a way that the end result is a system which secures their business but is minus racial discrimination. And that is what they are looking for—a system which falls short of the stipulations of the Freedom Charter but moves away from a system which thrives on violence and produces counter-violence. Well, we do not think that such a system is different. We certainly do not think that the regime and its supporters are really thinking of an alternative to the apartheid system. They are thinking of something which may be slightly different. It might even be called something else, not apartheid, but would in practice be apartheid. We must protect our struggle against forces which sound correct, but whose objective is entirely to destroy the cause, the objective, of our revolutionary struggle.[3]

Barely three months after the Lusaka meeting the ANC gave an answer to attempts to deflect it from revolutionary armed struggle: it proclaimed 1986 as "The year of Umkhonto we Sizwe—the people's army."

The initial face-to-face encounter between imperialist-linked business interests in South Africa that have profited enormously from apartheid but which see that the days of racist rule are numbered, and those who are heading the revolutionary struggle that will clearly end apartheid had been a signifiant indicator of the key issue in South Africa as the struggle matures. The monopoly interests in South Africa, both the local white ruling group and of imperialist sources, are hoping that if their apartheid bastion collapses, they can still hold on to the system of exploitation in other forms. They are looking to a post-apartheid capitalism, in which they would still remain in essential dominant control of the country's economy. This is the essential purpose of the "reform" that they project.

As the anti-apartheid struggle matures, therefore, it must inevitably become increasingly more than a battle against racist oppression alone, more than a liberation in the purely national sense, although that must come first and be thoroughly accomplished: it must by force of circumstances be an uninterrupted process toward social emancipation as well.

Having failed to keep the nonwhite masses in suppression in the system of "pure apartheid," the apartheid rulers and their imperialist partners can be expected to fall back on an arsenal of maneuvers and intrigues to prevent a future for South Africa under the Freedom Charter. They can be expected to intensify their splitting tactics, to try to divide the masses with spurious movements, to attempt to split the ANC from its SACP ally, to magnify tribal factors. In its latter stages, the national liberation struggle in South Africa is likely to become more intensely ideological for the liberation movement, both to defeat the imperialist-apartheid intrigues and to shape the society and the forces within it that will follow the end of apartheid. The international anti-apartheid movement needs to understand and to support the developing phases of that struggle.

The great anti-apartheid liberation struggle in South Africa is an integral part of the overall historical trends of social progress on the African continent. As an apartheid state, South Africa has been in the large sense an imperialist instrument for holding back and trying to reverse those trends, and in particular for trying to reverse the trend toward a socialist orientation, as developed out of the anti-colonial revolutions in Angola, Mozambique and Zimbabwe, on South Africa's borders.

In its main aspects, the South African revolution is the close companion of those struggles. Its victory will not only release these neighboring frontline states from imperialist intervention and sabotage but must inevitably merge with and help accelerate the socialist transformation of all Africa.

History will prove that by allying itself with apartheid, and aiding and abetting it, imperialism has created gravediggers for itself in Africa as a whole.

APPENDIX

(On June 25-26, 1955 a Congress of the People was held in the township of Kliptown, near Johannesburg, South Africa. It was convened by the African National Congress, together with the South African Indian Congress, the South African Colored People's Organization and the Congress of Democrats (the latter an organization of anti-apartheid white South Africans). The Congress was attended by 2,888 delegates who approved unanimously a Freedom Charter that has since been the main policy document of the liberation movement in South Africa.)

THE FREEDOM CHARTER

We, the people of South Africa, declare or all our country and the world to know:

— that South Africa belongs to all who live in it, black and white, and that no government can justly claim authority unless it is based on the will of all the people;
— that our people have been robbed of their birthright to land, liberty and peace by a form of government founded on injustice and inequality;
— that our country will never be prosperous or free until all our people live in brotherhood, enjoying equal rights and opportunities;
— that only a democratic state, based on the will of all the people, can secure to all their birthright without distinction of color, race, sex or belief;

And therefore, we the people of South Africa, black and white together—equals, countrymen and brothers—adopt this Freedom Charter. And we pledge ourselves to strive together, sparing neither strength nor courage, until the democratic changes set out here have been won.

The people shall govern!

Every man and woman shall have the right to vote for and to stand as a candidate for all bodies which make laws;

All people shall be entitled to take part in the administration of the country;

The rights of the people shall be the same, regardless of race, color or sex;

All bodies of minority rule, advisory boards, councils and authorities shall be replaced by democratic organs of self-government.

All national groups shall have equal rights!

There shall be equal status in the bodies of state, in the courts and in the schools for all national groups and races;

All people shall have equal right to use their own languages, and to develop their own folk culture and customs;

All national groups shall be protected by law against insults to their race and national pride;

The preaching and practice of national, race or color discrrimination and contempt shall be a punishable crime;

All apartheid laws and practices shall be set aside.

The people shall share in the country's wealth!

The national wealth of our country, the heritage of all South Africans, shall be restored to the people:

The mineral wealth beneath the soil, the banks and monopoly industry shall be transferred to the ownership of the people as a whole; All other industry and trade shall be controlled to assist the well-being of the people; All people shall have equal rights to trade where they choose, to manufacture and to enter all trades, crafts and professions.

The land shall be shared among those who work it!

Restrictions of land ownership on a racial basis shall be ended, and all the land redivided amongst those who work it, to banish famine and land hunger; The state shall help the peasants with implements, seed, tractors and dams to save the soil and assist the tillers; Freedom of movement shall be guaranteed to all who work on the land; All shall have the right to occupy land wherever they choose; People shall not be robbed of their cattle, and forced labor and farm prisons shall be abolished.

All shall be equal before the law!

No one shall be imprisoned, deported or restricted without a fair trial; No one shall be condemned by the order of any government official; The courts shall be representative of all the people; Imprisonment shall be only for serious crimes against the people, and shall aim at re-education, not vengeance; The police force and army shall be open to all on an equal basis and shall be the helpers and protectors of the people; All laws which discriminate on grounds of race, color or belief shall be repealed.

All shall enjoy equal human rights!

The law shall guarantee to all their rights to speak, to organize, to meet together, to punish, to preach, to worship and to educate their children; The privacy of the house from police raids shall be protected by law; All shall be free to travel without restriction from countryside to town, from province to province and from South Africa abroad; Pass laws, permits, and all other laws restricting these freedoms, shall be abolished.

There shall be work and security!

All who work shall be free to form unions, to elect their officers and to make wage agreements with their employers; The state shall recognize the right and duty of all to work, and to draw full unemployment benefits; Men and women of all races shall receive equal pay for equal work; There shall be a forty-hour working week, a national minimum wage, paid annual leave, and sick leave for all workers, and maternity leave on full pay for all working mothers; Miners, domestic workers, farm workers, and civil servants shall have the same rights as all others who work; Child labor, compound labor, the tot system and contract labor shall be abolished.

The doors of learning and culture shall be opened!

The government shall discover, develop and encourage national talent for the enhancement of our cultural life; All the cultural treasures of mankind shall be open to all, by free exchange of books, ideas and contact with other lands; The aim of education shall be to teach the youth to love their people and their culture, to honor human brotherhood, liberty and peace; Education shall be free, compulsory, universal and equal for all children; Higher education and technical training shall be opened to all by means of state allowances and scholarships awarded on the basis of merit; Adult illiteracy shall be ended by a mass state education plan; Teachers shall have all the rights of other citizens; The color bar in cultural life, in sport and in eduation shall be abolished.

There shall be houses, security and comfort!

All people shall have the right to live where they choose, to be decently housed, and to bring up their families in comfort, and security; Unused housing space to be made available to the people; Rent and prices shall be lowered, food plentiful and no one shall go hungry; A preventive health scheme shall be run by the state; Free medical care and hospitalization shall be provided for all, with special care for mothers and young children; Slums shall be demolished, and new suburbs built where all have transport, roads, lighting, playing fields, créches and social centers; The aged, the orphans, the disabled and the sick shall be cared for by the state; Rest, leisure and recreation shall be the right of all; Fenced locations and ghettoes shall be abolished, and laws which break up families shall be repealed; South Africa shall be a fully independent state, which respects the rights and sovereignty of nations:

There shall be peace and friendship!

South Africa shall strive to maintain world peace and the settlement of all international disputes by negotiation—not war; Peace and friendship amongst all our people shall be secured by upholding the equal rights, opportunities and status of all; The people of the protectorates—Basutoland, Bechuanaland and Swaziland—shall be free to decide for themselves their own future; The rights of all the peoples of Africa to independence and self-government shall be recognized, and shall be the basis of close cooperation; Let all who love their people and their country now say, as we say here:

"These freedoms we will fight for, side by side, throughout our lives, until we have won our liberty."

NOTES

The references in this book to material from periodicals in South
Africa are mainly obtained from the admirable *News Briefing,* published weekly in London by the African National Congress.

I

1. *Sechaba* (organ of the African National Congress), First Quarter, 1976
2. Quoted in *The Rise of the South African Riech,* by Brian Bunting,
   Penguin Books, 1964, p. 20
3. Ibid., p. 175
4. Ibid., p. 175
5. Ibid., p. 129
6. *Financial Mail* (SA), April 30, 1982
7. *Times* (UK), March 29, 1974
8. *Rand Daily Mail* (SA), October 16, 1979
9. *International Affairs* (SU), September 1979; *Guardian* (UK), September
   13, 1980
10. *Rand Daily Mail* (SA), May 28, 1982; *Sunday Tribune* (SA), May 30,
    1982
11. *International Affairs* (SU) and *Guardian* (UK), see n. 9
12. *Sowetan* (SA), March 24, 1983
13. *Observer* (UK), June 9, 1985
14. *Financial Mail* (SA), January 18, 1980
15. *Johannesburg Star* (SA), August 7, 1980
16. *Cape Times* (SA), May 25, 1981
17. *Rand Daily Mail* (SA), December 6, 1980
18. *The Star,* (SA), December 11, 1982
19. *Natal Mercury* (SA), January 25, 1980
20. *Rise of the South African Reich,* p. 260
21. *Sechaba,* July 1973
22. *The African Communist,* 3rd Quarter, 1984

II

1. *The African Communist,* 4th Quarter, 1984
2. *The Citizen* (SA), May 26, 1979
3. *Observer* (UK), May 25, 1980; *Guardian*(UK), June 5, 1980; *Post* (SA),
   August 8, 1980
4. *Times* (SA), April 11, 1982
5. *In Search of Enemies,* by John Stockwell, New York, 1978, pp. 51, 180
6. *Sechaba,* 2nd Quarter, 1978
7. *Asia and Africa Today* (SU), No. 2, 1980
8. *Social Sciences* (SU), No. 2, 1977, p. 95
9. *Race to Power: The Struggle for Southern Africa.* Africa Research
   Group, Cambridge, Massachusetts, 1971, p. 60
10. *Social Sciences,* op. cit., p. 98
11. *In Search of Enemies,* pp. 182, 185

12. Newsweek,May 17, 1976
13. Cape Times (SA), October 6, 1980
14. *Sechaba,* see n. 6
15. Ibid.; *International Affairs*(SU), No. 3, 1983
16. *8 Days,* February 28, 1981
17. *Times* (UK), September 4, 1985
18. *Rand Daily Mail* (SA), March 14, 1979
19. *The Argus* (SA), June 25, 1980
20. *Guardian* (UK), September 2, 1985
21. *The African Communist,* 3rd Quarter 1981; 1st Quarter 1982
22. *The Star* (SA), May 24, 1983; *Times* (UK), May 25, 1983
23. *Guardian* (UK), September 15, 1981
24. *Guardian* (UK), March 13, 1983
25. *Sunday Express* (SA), June 1, 1980; *Observer* (UK), September 28, 1980
26. *Eastern Province Herald* (SA), March 10, 1981; *Windhoek Observer* (Namibia), March 7, 1981
27. *Guardian,* (UK), January 29, 1981
28. *The Star* (SA), February 2, 1981
29. *The Star* (SA), March 3, 1982
30. *New Times* (SU), No. 2, 1983
31. *Sunday Post* (SA), February 24, 1980
32. *New Times,* see n. 30
33. *New Statesman* (UK), October 19, 1984
34. Ibid.
35. *The African Communist,* 2nd Quarter, 1985

III

1. *International Affairs* (SU), No. 4, 1974
2. *Asia and Africa Today* (SU), No. 6, 1976
3. *International Affairs* (SU), No. 12, 1974
4. *International Affairs*(SU), No. 6, 1981; *The African Communist,* 4th Quarter, 1984
5. *The African Communist,* Ibid.
6. *International Affairs* (SU), No. 10, 1980
7. New Times (SU), No. 7, 1982; No. 14, 1983
8. *New Times* (SU), No. 14, 1983
9. "Ideological Expansion of the West in Africa," by Y. Tarabin *Mirovaya Ekonomika i Mazhdunarodye Otnosheniya,* No. 3, 1972 (SU)
10. *The African Communist,* 4th Quarter, 1984; *Sovietskaya Rossia* (SU) October 16, 1984
11. *International Affairs* (SU), No. 10, 1980
12. *Party Life* (India), July 22, 1981
13. *Rand Daily Mail* (SA), November 15, 1984; *The African Communist,* 2nd Quarter, 1985
14. *Evening Post* (SA), May 15, 1981
15. *International Affairs* (SU), No. 4, 1978
16. *New Times* (SU), No. 41, 1983
17. *The Star* (SA), June 24, 1980
18. *International Herald Tribune* (US), April 11, 1982
19. *Sunday Times* (SA), June 13, 1982
20. *Rand Daily Mail* (SA), December 29, 1979

21. *Daily News* (SA), September 26, 1980
22. *The Star* (SA), November 17, 1981
23. *New Times* (SU), No. 21, 1984
24. *Rand Daily Mail* (SA), October 22, 1981; *New Times,* ibid
25. *New Age* (India), September 20, 1981
26. *The Star* (SA), June 17, 1980; *The Times* (UK), May 14, 1981
27. *Sechaba,* May 1973; *Rand Daily Mail* (SA), January 27, 1981
28. *Sunday Times* (SA), November 9, 1980
29. *Sunday Times* (SA), September 9, 1980
30. *The Citizen* (SA), November 5, 1982; *Times of India,* November 10, 1982
31. *New Times,* No. 41, 1983
32. *The Citizen* (SA), June 13, 1980
33. *Rand Daily Mail* (SA), November 6, 1980
34. *Daily Telegraph* (UK), March 16, 1981
35. *The Times* (UK), May 16, 1981; *Daily News* (SA), May 11, 1982
36. *Daily News* see n. 21
37. *Evening Post* (SA), April 30, 1981
38. *Rand Daily Mail* (SA), April 2, 1981
39. *The Citizen* (SA), October 15, 1980
40. *Rand Daily Mail* (SA), April 20, 1981
41. *Sunday Times* (SA), April 19, 1981
42. *Rand Daily Mail* (SA), July 9, 1981
43. *Sunday Times* (SA), November 19, 1980
44. *Sunday Express* (SA), May 24, 1981
45. African National Congress Press Statement, June 4, 1981 (*Weekly News Briefing,* No. 23, 1981, London)
46. *Financial Times* (UK), September 3, 1981; *The Star* (SA), April 7, 1981
47. *Rand Daily Mail* (SA), December 22, 1981; *Financial Times* (UK), March 1, 1982; *Rand Daily Mail* (SA), October 23, 1982; *Financial Mail* (SA), December 17, 1982
48. *Rand Daily Mail* (SA), October 15, 1982
49. *Rand Daily Mail-Business Day* (SA), October 6, 1883
50. *Daily News* (SA), January 13, 1981; *Sunday Express* (SA), October 10, 1982
51. *International Affairs* (SU), No. 3, 1984; *Financial Mail* (SA), December 17, 1982; *Rand Daily Mail* (SA), January 20, 1983
52. *The Star* (SA), March 11, 1982
53. *In Search of Enemies,* by John Stockwell, New York, 1978, p. 187
54. *Rand Daily Mail* (SA), June 3 and June 9, 1981; *Asia and Africa Today* (SU), No. 4, 1983
55. *Rand Daily Mail* (SA), May 5, 1982; *The Star* (SA), June 2 and June 23, 1982
56. *The African Communist,* 4th Quarter, 1984
57. *Financial Mail* (SA), October 1, 1982
58. *Asia and Africa Today* (SU), No. 4, 1983
59. *Sunday Times* (UK), September 22, 1985; *New Statesman* (UK), October 19, 1984
60. *New Statesman,* ibid.
61. *Observer* (UK), January 22, 1984
62. African National Congress Press Statement, June 4, 1981, see n. 45

IV
1. See *Namibia: The Facts*. International Defense and Aid Fund booklet, London, 1980
2. *New Perspectives*. World Peace Council, No. 2, 1983
3. *Observer* (UK), November 3, 1985
4. *Namibia: The Facts*, p. 25
5. *New Times* (SU), No. 41, 1983
6. Ibid.; *Asia and Africa Today* (SU), No. 1, 1984
7. *New Statesman* (UK), October 6, 1984
8. *Namibia: The Facts*, pp. 53-54
9. *Sunday Post* (SA), July 6, 1980
10. *Cape Times* (SA), Januafy 15, 1981
11. *Cape Times* (SA), November 24, 1981
12. *Daily News* (SA), July 8, 1980
13. *Financial Mail* (SA), September 19, 1980
14. *Namibia: The Facts*, p. 50
15. *White Paper on Acts of Aggression by the Racist South African Regime Against the People's Republic of Angola, 1975-1982* People's Republic of Angola, 1982, pp. 13-32
16. *Rand Daily Mail* (SA), September 13, 1980
17. *Daily News* (SA), July 8, 1980
18. *Times* (UK), April 16, 1981
19. *African Communist*, No. 4, 1984, p. 24
20. *Rand Daily Mail* (SA), July 29, 1981; *The Star* (SA), July 31, 1981
21. *Times* (UK), July 23, 1981
22. *The Star* (SA), August 21, 1980
23. *African Communist*, No. 4, 1984, p. 14
24. *Financial Times* (UK), May 30, 1981; *African Communist*, No. 4, 1984, p. 24
25. *Party Life* (India), July 22, 1981
26. *Morning Star,* (UK) September 27, 1982
27. *Guardian* (UK), January 13, 1983
28. *The Star* (SA), March 20, 1984
29. *Rand Daily Mail* (SA), January 27, 1982; *Times* (UK), February 18, 1984
30. *Guardian* (UK), March 14, 1984
31. Ibid., July 3, 1984
32. Ibid., October 2, 1985; *Financial Times* (UK), October 2, 1985
33. *Sunday Times* (UK), September 22, 1985; *Observer* (UK), September 22, 1985
34. *The Star* (SA), October 1, 1982
35. *Rand Daily Mail* (SA), August 25, 1984
36. *Sunday Express* (SA), September 12, 1982
37. *The Sowetan* (SA), February 17, 1982
38. *New Perspectives*, World Peace Council, No. 2, 1983
39. *Cape Times* (SA), October 1, 1983; *Rand Daily Mail* (SA), February 11, 1984
40. *Rand Daily Mail* (SA), February 2, 1984
41. *Observer* (UK), September 9, 1984.
42. *Guardian* (UK), May 14, 1984

V

1. *Rand Daily Mail* (SA), April 19, 1984
2. Ibid., March 12, 1983
3. *The Sowetan* (SA), April 12, 1984
4. *The Star* (SA), May 5, 1982
5. *Rand Daily Mail* (SA), May 29, 1982
6. *Pretoria News* (SA), September 14, 1983
7. *Observer* (UK), August 12, 1984
8. *Sunday Tribune* (SA), February 22, 1981
9. Ibid., January 9, 1983
10. *Sechaba* (ANC), April 1980
11. *Rand Daily Mail* (SA), May 18, 1982
12. Statement by the South African Communist Party, September 1983
13. *Cape Times* (SA), November 17, 1982; SACP Statement
14. *Rand Daily Mail* (SA), June 10, 1983
15. SACP Statement, n. 12
16. *The Star* (SA), July 7, 1983
17. Ibid., March 19, 1982
18. *Rand Daily Mail* (SA), April 23, 1985
19. Ibid., December 6, 1980
20. *Sunday Times* (SA), January 30, 1983
21. *Cape Times* (SA), November 17, 1982
22. *The Star* (SA), October 10, 1980; African Communist, No. 1, 1981
23. *Rand Daily Mail* (SA), June 18, 1982
24. *Financial Mail* (SA), September 14, 1984
25. *African Communist*, No. 4, 1979
26. *The Times* (UK), December 12, 1980
27. *The Star* (SA), July 16, 1980
28. *Guardian* (UK), February 3, 1981
29. *Rand Daily Mail* (SA), June 28, 1984
30. Ibid., October 22, 1981
31. Ibid., December 14, 1982
32. *Sunday Times* (SA), November 30, 1980
33. *Financial Mail* (SA), June 27, 1980
34. Ibid.
35. *Sunday Tribune* (SA), February 22, 1981; SACP Statement, n. 12
36. *Financial Mail* (SA), June 27, 1980
37. SACP Statement, n. 12
38. *Year of Fire, Year of Ash*, by Baruch Hirson. Zed Press, London, 1979, p. 122
39. Ibid., pp. 131-132
40. Ibid., pp. 133-143
41. Ibid., p 142
42. *New Perspectives* (World Peace Council), No. 6, 1979
43. *Sunday Express* (SA), September 16, 1979
44. *African Communist*, No. 4, 1979
45. *Rand Daily Mail* (SA), October 25, 1980
46. *African Communist*, No. 4, 1979
47. *African Communist*, No. 1, 1980
48. *The Argus* (SA), June 11, 1980
49. *Sunday Express* (SA), May 27, 1979

50. *Beeld* (SA), March 8, 1982; *African Communist*, No. 2, 1984
51. *Sunday Times* (SA), November 6, 1983
52. *Rand Daily Mail* (SA), October 3, 1983
53. *Sunday Times,* n. 51
54. Ibid.
55. *Rand Daily Mail* (SA), December 3, 1983
56. Ibid., November 4, 1983
57. *Sunday Times*, n. 51
58. *Sechaba* (ANC), April 1980
59. *Rand Daily Mail* (SA), September 12, 1983
60. *African Communist*, No. 1, 1980
61. "The African Petty Bourgeosie: A Case Study of NAFCOC 1964-84," by Z. Pallo Jordan. African National Congress Research Paper, Lusaka, Zambia, 1984
62. *Sunday Times* (SA), May 11, 1980
63. *Rand Daily Mail* (SA), October 8, 1980
64. "The African Petty Bourgeosie"
65. *The Star* (SA), June 24, 1983
66. SACP Statement, n. 12
67. *Cape Times* (SA), March 15, 1983
68. *Sechaba*, n. 58
69. *New Times* (SU), No. 8, 1984
70. *Rand Daily Mail* (SA), October 23, 1984
71. *The Star* (SA), March 23, 1984
72. *Sechaba*, n. 58
73. *Financial Mail* (SA), January 15, 1982
74. *The Star* (SA), July 16, 1981
75. Ibid., September 16, 1980
76. *Rand Daily Mail* (SA),September 19, 1981
77. *Financial Mail* (SA), April 30, 1982
78. *Rand Daily Mail* (SA), September 14, 1981
79. *Sunday Tribune* (SA), January 9, 1983
80. *Guardian* (UK), May 21, 1983
81. *The Star* (SA), August 15, 1984
82. *Newsweek* (US), September 29, 1980
83. *Rand Daily Mail* (SA), December 20, 1983
84. Ibid., June 18, 1983
85. *Sunday Tribune* (SA), October 7, 1984
86. *Rand Daily Mail* (SA), March 24, 1982
87. Ibid.
88. Ibid., September 15, 1983
89. *The Times* (UK), June 8, 1984
90. *Rand Daily Mail* (SA), December 23, 1983; *Daily News* (SA), January 19, 1984
91. *New Times* (SU), No. 8, 1984
92. *Morning Star* (UK), July 17, 1983
93. *Sunday Times* (SA), October 14, 1984; *Rand Daily Mail* (SA), November 20, 1984
94. *The Star* (SA), March 15, 1982
95. *Rand Daily Mail* (SA),September 29, 1981
96. *Sunday Times* (SA), July 10, 1983

97. *Rand Daily Mail* (SA), November 2, 1983
98. *Sunday Tribune* (SA), July 22, 1984
99. *Financial Mail* (SA), February 17, 1984
100. *Sunday Express* (SA), August 12, 1984; *Financial Mail* , ibid.
101. *The Star* (SA), January 25, 1985
102. *Daily News* (SA), April 29, 1983
103. *Rand Daily Mail* (SA), April 18, 1985
104. Ibid., September 18, 1981
105. *The Star* (SA), January 28, 1981
106. *The Times* (UK), February 13, 1981
107. *Financial Mail* (SA), May 18, 1984
108. *Guardian* (UK), February 2, 1981
109. *Sunday Post* (SA), August 31, 1980
110. Ibid.
111. *Financial Times* (UK), December 2, 1985
112. *Sunday Post* (SA), n. 109
113. *Sunday Post* (SA), September 7, 1980
114. *Financial Times* (UK), December 2, 1985
115. *Cape Times* (SA), October 17, 1980
116. *Financial Mail* (SA), September 18, 1981
117. *Rand Daily Mail* (SA), January 11, 1982
118. *Daily News* (SA), April 27, 1982
119. *The Times* (UK), October 22, 1982
120. *Daily News* (SA), November 10, 1980
121. *Sunday Times* (SA), November 9, 1980
122. *Financial Times* (UK) August 20, 1983
123. *Financial Times* (UK), January 27, 1983; *Financial Mail* (SA), January 21, 1985; *The Economist* (UK), September 21, 1985
124. *The Citizen* (SA), March 27, 1985; *Rand Daily Mail* (SA), March 25 and April 10, 1985; *Daily Telegraph* (UK), March 30, 1985
125. *Rand Daily Mail* (Business Day) (SA), October 6, 1983
126. *Daily Telegraph* (UK), April 15, 1985
127. *Guardian* (UK), November 28, 1985
128. *Sunday Times* (SA), October 14, 1984
129. *Rand Daily Mail* (SA), October 16, 1984; *Sunday Times* (SA), April 3, 1985; *Cape Times* (SA), January 22, 1985
130. *Financial Times* (UK), May 9, 1985
131. Ibid., November 18, 1985

VI

1. *Fifty Fighting Years* , by A. Lerumo. Inkululeko Publications, London, 1971, pp. 6-18; *The Origin of the Family, Private Property and the State*, by Frederich Engels (Selected Works, Vol. II, p. 254); *Weekly News Briefings* , ANC, London, for the year 1979
2. *Fifty Fighting Years*, op. cit., p. 29
3. Ibid., p. 29
4. *The African Communist*, 1st Quarter, 1972
5. *The African Communist*, 1st Quarter, 1977
6. *The African Communist*, 1st Quarter, 1972
7. *The African Communist*, 1st Quarter, 1977
8. *Fifty Fighting Years*, op. cit., p. 52.

9. Ibid., p. 63
10. *The African Communist*, 1st Quarter, 1972
11. Ibid.
2. *Fifty Fighting Years*, op. cit., p. 82, 84-86
13. *The African Communist*, 4th Quarter, 1975
14. Evidence and testimony in 1963 treason trial
15. *Fifty Fighting Years*, op. cit., p. 94
16. Ibid., p. 97
17. *The African Communist*, 4th Quarter, 1975
18. *Forward to Freedom, Sechaba* supplement, 1969
19. *Fifty Fighting Years*, op. cit., p. 103; *Guerrilla Warfare* , ANC publication, 1969, p. 39
20. *The African Communist*, 3rd Quarter, 1980
21. *Weekly News Briefing*, ANC, London, October 20, 1981
22. *The World That Was Ours*, by Hilda Bernstein. Heinemann, London, 1967, p. 174
23. *Guerrilla Warfare*, op. cit., p. 33, 57-67
24. Ibid., p. 3-4
25. *The Southern African Revolution.* Special *Sechaha* edition (undated)
26. *African Communists Speak.* Documents of the South African Communist Party. Nauka, Moscow, 1970, p. 146
27. "Forward to People's Power and the Challenge Ahead," booklet, Inkululeko Publications, London, 1979
28. *Forward to Freedom*, op. cit., p. 8-9
29. "Prospects for Armed Struggle in South Africa," speech by Joe Slovo, Oxford, England, March 9, 1968
30. BBC Monitoring Report from Johannesburg, April 8, 1985. (In ANC *Weekly News Briefing*, No. 15, 1985)
31. *Rand Daily Mail* (SA), February 7, 1985
32. "Strategy and Tactics of the South African Revolution," *Forward to Freedom*, op. cit.
33. "The Road to South African Freedom," *African Communists Speak,* op. cit., p. 138
34. *The African Communist*, 4th Quarter, 1981
35. *Year of Fire, Year of Ash*, by Baruch Hirson. Zed, London, 1979, p. 98
36. Ibid., p. 103
37. Ibid., p. 104
38. Ibid., pp. 177-178
39. Ibid., pp. 212, 237-240
40. Ibid., p. 253
41. *The African Communist*, 1st Quarter, 1977
42. *Financial Times* (UK), January 31, 1981
   Rand Daily Mail, (SA), December 21, 1982
   The Times (UK), April 5, 1980
   nday Post (SA), January 20, 1980; April 6, 1980
   ncial Mail (SA), September 24, 1982
   y News (SA), August 18, 1982

48. *The African Communist*, 3rd Quarter, 1983
49. Ibid.; *The Star* (SA), May 27, 1981
50. *Rand Daily Mail* (SA), August 1, 1980
51. *The Star* (SA), November 14, 1980
52. Ibid.
53. *Cape Times* (SA), November 26, 1983; *Guardian* (UK), December 5, 1983.
54. *Rand Daily Mail* (SA), November 2, 1984
55. *Sunday Post* (SA), July 6, 1980
56. *The Star* (SA), September 6, 1984
57. Ibid., January 10, 1985
58. *Ukusa* (SA), December 8-14, 1981
59. *Rand Daily Mail* (SA), September 27, 1984
60. *The Star* (SA), November 20, 1984
61. *Cape Times* (SA), August 12, 1985
62. Ibid.
63. *The Star* (SA), July 12, 1985
64. *City Press* (SA), August 4, 1985
65. *Sunday Times* (SA), August 11, 1985
66. *Business Day* (SA), July 23, 1985
67. *Sunday Times* (SA), April 28, 1985
68. *Business Day* (SA), May 29, 1985
69. *The Star* (SA), February 12, 1985
70. *Sunday Times* (SA), August 25, 1985
71. *City Press* (SA), June 16, 1985
72. Ibid., August 11, 1985
73. *The African Communist*, 3rd Quarter, 1984
74. Ibid.
75. *Rand Daily Mail* (SA), January 24, 1983
76. *Sunday Express* (SA), May 29, 1983
77. Ibid.
78. *The Argus* (SA), August 19, 1983
79. Ibid.
80. *Financial Mail* (SA), September 7, 1984
81. *The Argus* (SA), December 19, 1983
82. Ibid.
83. *The Sowetan* (SA), April 9, 1985
84. Ibid., August 22, 1983
85. *The Star* (SA), April 3, 1985
86. Ibid., August 3, 1985
87. *Financial Times* (UK), April 20, 1985
88. *The Star* (SA), January 22, 1986
89. *The Argus* (SA), January 23, 1985; *Guardian* (UK), June 13, 1985
90. *The African Communist*, 4th Quarter, 1968
91. *The African Communist*, 3rd Quarter, 1980
92. Ibid.; *The African Communist*, 3rd Quarter, 1984
93. *The African Communist*, 2nd Quarter, 1985
94. *The African Communist*, 4th Quarter, 1984; 1st Quarter, 1985
95. Ibid.
96. *New Statesman* (UK), November 16, 1984
97. *The African Communist*, 3rd Quarter, 1980

98. *The African Communist*, 3rd Quarter, 1984
99. Ibid.
100. *Rand Daily Mail* (SA), October 31, 1980
101. *The Star* (SA), October 20, 1981
102. *The African Communist*, 4th Quarter, 1981
103. *The Star* (SA), October 20, 1981
104. Ibid.
105. Ibid.
106. *The Star* (SA), June 26, 1985
107. *Daily News* (SA), February 5, 1982; *Rand Daily Mail* (SA), February 8, 1982
108. *The Sowetan* (SA), February 15, 1982
109. *The African Communist*, 4th Quarter, 1983
110. *The African Communist*, 3rd Quarter, 1984
111. *Financial Mail* (SA), September 24, 1982
112. Ibid., November 9, 1984
113. *The Star* (SA), November 20, 1984
114. *The Argus* (SA), October 21, 1983
115. *The Sowetan* (SA), December 20, 1984
116. Ibid.
117. Ibid., January 15, 1985
118. *Rand Daily Mail* (SA), August 8 & 10, 1981; *The Star* (SA), August 10, 1981
119. *The Sowetan* (SA), April 27 & 30, 1982
120. *Cape Times* (SA), July 6, 1982; *Rand Daily Mail* (SA), July 22, 1982
121. *Cape Times* (SA), April 11, 1983; *Rand Daily Mail* (SA), April 18, 1983
122. *Financial Mail* (SA), August 9, 1985
123. *Cape Times* (SA), December 2, 1985; *Business Day* (SA), December 3, 1985
124. *ANC, SACTU, COSATU Communique*, ANC release, March 7, 1986
125. *Financial Times* (UK), April 15, 1986
126. *Sechaba*, November 1981; *The African Communist*, 4th Quarter, 1981
127. *Sechaba*, op. cit.
128. *Sunday Express* (SA), August 26, 1979
129. *The Star* (SA), February 23, 1982
130. *The Sowetan* (SA), April 16, 1982
131. Ibid., October 22, 1981
132. *Rand Daily Mail* (SA), February 4, 1982
133. *Sunday Times* (SA), February 21, 1982
134. *Year of Fire, Year of Ash* op. cit., pp. 77-78
135. Ibid., p. 85
136. *The African Communist*, 1st Quarter, 1977
137. Ibid.
138. *The African Communist*, 1st Quarter, 1974
139. *The African Communist*, 1st Quarter, 1977.
140. *Sechaba*, October 1985
141. *Sechaba*, November 1985
142. *The Star* (SA), October 14, 1980; *Financial Times* (UK), January 31, 1981
143. *The Star* (SA), May 13, 1985
144. *The African Communist*, 3rd Quarter, 1984
145. Ibid.

146. *Rand Daily Mail* (SA), June 13, 1983
147. *Sunday Tribune* (SA), May 5, 1985
148. *The Star* (SA), January 9 & 14, 1985
149. Ibid.
150. *The Argus* (SA), May 6, 1985
151. *Weekly Mail* (SA), April 10, 1986
152. *Sechaba*, December 1985
153. *Sunday Express* (SA), July 27, 1980
154. *Rand Daily Mail* (SA), March 31, 1982
155. *Guardian* (UK), December 3, 1984
156. *Rand Daily Mail* (SA), April 26, 1985
157. *Daily News* (SA), February 11, 1983
158. Ibid., November 23, 1984
159. *The Citizen* (SA), August 8, 1985
160. *City Press* (SA), June 30, 1985
161. *Cape Times* (SA), August 14, 1980
162. *Daily News* (SA), October 31, 1983
163. *Rand Daily Mail* (SA), October 22, 1984
164. *Sunday Tribune* (SA), August 26, 1984
165. Press statement by ANC, signed by Alfred Nzo, Augut 30, 1985
166. *Financial Mail* (SA), April 4, 1986; BBC Monitoring Report, (SAPA), March 22, 1986
167. *The African Communist*, 2nd Quarter, 1984
168. *The African Communist*, 2nd Quarter, 1985
169. Ibid.
170. Ibid.
171. "The Future is Within Our Grasp," ANC Statement, April 1985
172. *Daily News* (SA), June 14, 1985; *Cape Times* (SA), June 20, 1985; *The Citizen* (SA), July 16, 1985
173. *Cape Times* (SA), June 20, 1985
174. *The Star* (SA), March 22, 1985
175. "The Future is Within Our Grasp," op. cit.
176. Ibid.
177. *City Press* (SA), June 30, 1985
178. *Sechaba*, October 1985
179. Statement by ANC Information Department, Lusaka, June 25, 1985
180. *Umsebenzi*(Voice of the South African Communist Party), No. 2, 1985
181. *City Press* (SA), June 30, 1985
182. ANC's Radio Freedom broadcast, May 25, 1985 (BBC Monitoring Report)
183. *Financial Times* (UK), June 28, 1985
184. Ibid.
185. ANC's Radio Freedom, Addis Ababa, July 15, 1985 (BBC Monitoring Report)
186. *The Star* (SA), October 29, 1985; *Observer* (UK), November 3, 1985
187. *City Press* (SA),September 1, 1985; *The Star* (SA), January 9, 1986
188. *Weekly Mail* (SA), December 19, 1985
189. Ibid.
190. *Financial Times* (UK), March 29, 1986
191. *Daily Dispatch* (SA), February 19, 1986
192. Ibid., March 5, 1986

193. *Weekly Mail* (SA), November 28, 1985
194. BBC Monitoring Report (SAPA), November 2, 1985
195. *Business Day* (SA), November 26, 1985
196. *The Star* (SA), March 30, 1986; *Times* (UK), March 31, 1986
197. *Cape Times* (SA), May 13, 1982
198. *The Star* (SA), September 26, 1985
199. *The Sowetan* (SA), March 29, 1982 and April 13, 1982; *Rand Daily Mail* (SA), March 27, 1982 and April 13, 1982; *The Star* (SA), April 1, 1982; ANC Statement, April 1982
200. *The Star* (SA), November 3, 1983
201. *City Press* (SA), February 23, 1986
202. *City Press* (SA), March 9, 1986
203. BBC Monitoring Report, January 21, 1986
204. Ibid.
205. ANC's Radio Freedom, Lusaka, March 1, 1986 (BBC Monitoring Report)

Postscript
1. *Business Day* (SA), September 3, 1985; *Sunday Times* (SA), September 15, 1985
2. Ibid.
3. ANC's Radio Freedom, Addis Ababa, October 18, 1985 (BBC Monitoring Report)

INDEX